Cultures of Letters

Richard H. Brodhead

Cultures of Letters

*Scenes of Reading and Writing
in Nineteenth-Century America*

THE UNIVERSITY OF CHICAGO PRESS

Chicago and London

Richard H. Brodhead is the Bird White Housum
Professor of English, former chair of the
Department of English at Yale University, and dean of Yale College.

Published with the assistance of the Frederich W. Hilles
Publications Fund of Yale University.

The University of Chicago Press, Chicago 60637
The University of Chicago Press, Ltd., London
© 1993 by The University of Chicago
All rights reserved. Published 1993
Printed in the United States of America

02 01 00 99 98 97 96 95 94 93 1 2 3 4 5
ISBN: 0-226-07525-7 (cloth)

Library of Congress Cataloging-in-Publication Data

Brodhead, Richard H., 1947–
  Cultures of letters : scenes of reading and writing in nineteenth-century
America / Richard H. Brodhead.
      p.   cm.
  Includes bibliographical references and index.
  1. American literature—19th century—History and criticism.   2. Literature
and society—United States—History—19th century.   3. Authors and
readers—United States—History—19th century.   4. Books and reading—
United States—History—19th century.   5. United States—Civilization—19th
century.   6. Authorship—History—19th century.   I. Title.
PS201.B68   1993
810.9′003—dc20   92-30967
                                                                        CIP

  ⊗ The paper used in this publication meets the
minimum requirements of the American National Standard
for Information Sciences—Permanence of Paper for
Printed Library Materials, ANSI Z39.48-1984.

For Daniel Brodhead

CONTENTS

ACKNOWLEDGMENTS

This is a book about communities and the way they shape the writing created within them. In completing it I am strongly aware of the community that has supported my own writing efforts. The community formed around the study of American literature and culture at Yale has given me companionship, challenge, and continual stimulation during the writing of this book. My students have helped me work through the ideas presented here, and my primary debt is to them. Among colleagues, I would acknowledge the immense benefit I have derived from sharing intellectual space with Jean-Christophe Agnew, Hazel Carby, Nancy Cott, John Demos, Michael Denning, Robert Stepto, Alan Trachtenberg, and Candace Waid; and I would particularly thank Bryan Wolf, Jonathan Freedman, Lynn Wardley, and Patricia Meyer Spacks for their careful readings of my work in progress. Waichee Dimock, Paul Lauter, Susan Williams, and Laura Wexler have also read chapters of this book, and I have benefitted from their thoughtful criticism. As readers for the University of Chicago Press, Michael Davitt Bell and Myra Jehlen came as close as could easily be imagined to incarnating the Ideal Reader. They have my special gratitude.

Two chapters of this book have appeared in print in slightly different forms, chapter one in *Representations*, no. 21 (Winter 1988): 67–96, and chapter two in *American Literary History* 1 (Summer 1989): 273–94. They are reprinted here with the permission of the publishers.

On the Idea of Cultures of Letters

Let me begin with three scenes from American literary history.

In the late 1880s Theodore Dreiser moved from the Indiana towns of his youth to Chicago, the great urban magnet of the late nineteenth-century Midwest. As his memoirs record, he held there a succession of jobs on the margins of the Chicago service economy—dishwasher in a Greek diner, payment collector for a company selling furniture on time—until the city itself created a new and stronger vocational desire. "It finally came to me, dimly, like a bean that strains at its enveloping shell, that I would like to write of these things," Dreiser says of Chicago's daily sights. But though he "seethed to express himself," this desire remained almost wholly "nebulous"[1]—unactable because too vaguely imagined—until he acquired a more specified concept of writing as worldly work, also taken in from his surroundings: the idea of the writer as reporter, learned from Chicago's daily newspapers. Answering a Help Wanted ad from the *Chicago Herald* in the winter of 1891, the twenty-year-old Dreiser thought he was entering the place where the will to expression could be fulfilled, but instead he found a different scene. The *Herald* job turned out to be as a screener of applicants for a cynically managed holiday giveaway program in which the poor were lured by the prospect of magical

1

material delights, then put off with shoddy merchandise, while the paper used the fraudulently represented program to advertise its bounty and boost its circulation.

Dreiser eventually got beyond this false antechamber to the newspaper world, working his way through a succession of reporter jobs in the early 1890s, then writing for cheap, mass-circulated magazines in New York. But all of these scenes of his writer's work had something in common with his first place of literary employment. They all made writing inseparable from a larger action of advertising, the media's creation of consumer desire that helps boost the publisher's profit. The newspapers that circulated Dreiser's reporting were kept cheap by revenue from the multitudinous advertisements they also ran. *Ainslee's,* one of Dreiser's regular magazine outlets in the late 1890s, directed his features toward an audience it then advertised as a potential market in this way:

> An Argument for Advertisers
>
> The Reading Public which is at once economical and intelligent, buys a magazine that costs little, not for its cheapness, but for its literary and artistic value. This same public constitutes the surest patronage of the best advertisers, i.e., those who advertise solid worth at fair prices. *Ainslee's Magazine* is supported by such an economical and intelligent public.[2]

My second vignette involves another Chicago literary debut in the 1890s, but this time the story is very different. Herbert S. Stone, born the same year as Dreiser, came out of a Chicago milieu the ill-connected Dreiser could only gape up at. The son of Melville E. Stone, founder-editor of Chicago's most prestigious paper the *Daily News* (and patron of Dreiser's first writer-ideal, Eugene Field), Herbert Stone was educated by tutors at various European watering holes before going to Harvard, the high-aesthetic Harvard where the teachings of Charles Eliot Norton—"a kind of mental aristocracy, a fastidiousness, an assumption that beauty and delicacy were things it was not effeminate to love, a vigorous and unyielding independence of judgment"—as Stone recalls, "formed a kind of background to which the new student learned to fit his life."[3] While still a Harvard undergraduate, Herbert Stone founded a publishing house based in his hometown with his college classmate Ingalls Kimball, another scion of the owner-managerial class. This firm aimed to cultivate a fine-art or high-art zone of the American literary market. Stone and Kimball's books, like the magazine it created, the once-celebrated *Chap-Book*, were materially distinguished from other 1890s publications by the quality of their paper and their substantial investment in design: Stone and Kimball commissioned Aubrey Beardsley to illustrate the large-paper edition of the *Works of Edgar Allan Poe*, one of their first house projects. They were distinguished too by the kind of work they elected to publish *in* such form. An import house with a specialty trade in what it called "the cleverest of the young men,"[4] Stone and Kimball brought the United States what knowledge it had of fin de siècle European writing. Before its dissolution at the end of the 1890s, this Chicago-based firm became the place of the American publication of Verlaine, Mallarmé, Yeats, Shaw, and Maeterlinck, as well as of such cognate American works as Henry James's *What Maisie Knew* and Kate Chopin's *The Awakening*.

A third literary debut can be found in early 1890s Chicago, and this story is different again. Ten years Dreiser's and Herbert Stone's senior, Szczesny Zahajkiewicz had been a teacher, poet, playwright, and general cultural activist in Lvov, Poland, where he taught at the Piramowicz School of Intellect. Emigrating to Chicago in 1889, he joined a large Polish immigrant community that provided new settings for his cultural activities. Hired as a teacher at the St. Stanislaus Parish high school, he organized a high-level amateur dramatic society that played in the school auditorium, one of whose performances has been extensively recorded. In August 1892, Zahajkiewicz lured Helena Modjeska, the Polish-born actress who had since become an international celebrity for her work in high tragedy, to star in his amateur production of *Jadwiza, Queen of Poland* (*Jadwiga, Krolowa Lechitow*). A Polish newspaper reports the event as follows:

St. Stanislas Auditorium was in a state of siege last night. Over six thousand people came to see Modjeska. All aisles were packed, with crowds standing inside the auditorium as well as in the street, watching the performance through the windows. When the perfor- mance ended, no one left. Endless applause greeted the star, and, eventually, the author. He came upon the stage with the script in his hand. With great effort he quieted the audience, and finally said: "After such a magnificent performance no one else should ever per- form the heroine of this play. In a tribute to Madame Modjeska, I tear up my manuscript." And he actually tore it up into shreds and tossed the pieces from left to right over the audience. The standing public in the front rows momentarily disappeared, fishing out from the floor the manuscript pieces to save them as souvenirs of the most bewitching night they ever witnessed.[5]

My intention in citing these cases is not to begin a literary his- tory of Chicago, which even if confined to the 1890s would have to include many other chapters than the ones I have mentioned. Instead I invoke them to make a more general point about Ameri- can literature and the way its history can be known. The literary products of each of the scenes I have sketched could find a place in a familiar account of American literature, or at least in a very catholic version of such an account. Dreiser's work would appear in the time-honored category of American literary naturalism. Stone and Kimball could be incorporated into the prehistory of American modernism, since they published writings of decisive im- portance to the modernist generation and pioneered the charac- teristic modernist vehicle, the "little magazine." Zahajkiewicz (if remembered) could be sorted without further reflection into the container for American ethnic writing. But the scenes presented here should remind us that the works we separate out in this fash- ion often shared social space, having been created and consumed in the same historical world. And they will make clear that the differences among such works do not flow from their exemplifi- cation of abstract categorical groupings, however we might insert them in such groupings later on, but require a different under- standing of their source.

What even so brief an account will have suggested is that these three bodies of Chicago writing arose in differently organized (if adjacent) literary-social worlds, in differently structured cultural settings composed around writing and regulating its social life—in different cultures of letters, to give this phenomenon a shorthand name. In each of these scenes, writing has no general existence, no existence merely as "writing." Each has its own quite distinct means of literary production, and so gives writing a different mode of social reality. Writing as Dreiser first admires it means something published in the newspaper, the genre of the cheap, the factual (and commercial), the readily consumable and disposable, and the up-to-the-minute. Stone and Kimball's way of publishing links writing instead to the world of highly crafted and enduring objects: the firm's first book was *First Editions of American Authors*, a guide for collectors and connoisseurs. *Jadwiza, Queen of Poland* was published, in a certain sense, but it was not printed. Here the work is rendered public not in writing but through live performance, the production entailing a highly specific network of community groups and community spaces: the theater company, the parochial school and the adjacent church, the parish as "public," and so on.

In the literary situations I have sketched, writing has no life separate from the particularized mechanisms that bring it to public life. But these instruments do not work on their own. Each of these schemes of literary production is bound up with a distinct social audience: *in* its production each addresses and helps call together some particular social grouping, a portion of the whole potential public identified by its readerly interests but by other unifying social interests as well. Zahajkiewicz's play is of course wholly specific in the audience it implies. The language it is written in marks it as being for Polish speakers only, and the context of its performance aims it yet more precisely at Polish immigrants newly arrived in Chicago as part of the eastern and southern European migration of the 1880s, a group that was busy reconstituting its "foreign" culture in the American world. Stone and Kimball's publications do not put up the same barriers against outsiders that Polish-language theater does, and in a sense they were available to anyone who could pay the purchase price of a book. But they too project a very clear message of who, socially, they understand themselves to be "for." "Paris has long witnessed the triumph of the apparently unread. Apparently only, for the illuminate [*illuminati*] read,"[6] an early issue of *The Chap-Book* announces, overtly identifying itself with a nonmass or nonpopular audience of cultural cognoscenti. Even in the absence of such declarations, Stone and Kimball's publications—by their relatively high cost, their nonutilitarian investment in aesthetic refinement, their emphatic and even polemical cosmopolitanism, and the high level of literary education they assume—draw a clear portrait of their most "natural" readers. They were geared toward members of the upper or leisure class artistically acculturated through college educations and touristic initiations—the class that provided the social backing for a distinctive high-cultural order in late nineteenth-century America and that used its "cultured" tastes to express its social superiority to an influx of social others.[7] Dreiser's newspapers and magazines won a much larger and more heterogeneous audience than the publics Zahajkiewicz or Stone and Kimball courted, but they too spoke to a relatively distinct social interest. The center of gravity of the audience for Dreiser's first publishing organs was in a non-elite class that was as marked a social feature of the late nineteenth century as eastern European immigrants or the culture-worshipping upper orders: the large population newly drawn into the urbanized and mass-market-based "modern" order of the late-century decades, a group whose deepest needs—namely, to learn how things work in the still-strange city-world and how to participate in the still-unfamiliar consumer order—these ad-heavy, nonfiction-centered publications helped to meet.[8]

Each of my scenes of writing ties literary production to a group with a distinct social character and historical situation. But it needs to be insisted that these differently constituted social publics did not just provide different audiences for writing. They provided audiences for different kinds of writing: each supplied a public for the particular selection or version of writing that spoke to its cultural identity and social needs. The ardent viewers packed into the

St. Stanislaus school auditorium did not come to see a play only. They came through the performance of a play to have their group identity renewed—to hear their own language, to revive their own heroic national mythology, to see one of themselves become a figure of transcendent accomplishment in the New World. This audience provided an attentive public for literature, then, but for literature defined in a highly specific way: a way that conjoined the literary with particular ethnic linguistic traditions, with the politics of Polish national liberationism, and with the cultural work of immigrant ethnic self-affirmation. Stone and Kimball's menu of publications are "literary" in a more familiar sense of the term. The announced intention of *The Chap-Book* was "to be a distinctly literary periodical,"[9] and the work this firm published includes a large portion of the late nineteenth-century writing since designated as literature. But here too we could note that this system published literature not in some absolute sense but in a particular understanding of the term: a sense that strongly dissevers writing from the ethnically local and overtly political and conjoins it instead with careful craftedness, cosmopolitan internationalism, and the exercise of educated tastes. This implicit definition of the literary, we could add, reflected another group's different group values: specialized education as a ground of social preeminence (Stone's "mental aristocracy"), highly trained aesthetic competence (Stone's "fastidiousness"), and so on. Dreiser's early periodicals were subliterary by *The Chap-Book*'s lights, but they printed and circulated their own different version the literary, modelled on their different audience's different needs. The writing they featured is linked neither to ethnic traditionalism nor to aesthetic refinement but to urban reportage, emphatic contemporaneity, the rendering accessible of the otherwise-obscure history of today, and the transmission of commercial messages. This specification of writing, like the others I have detailed, not only characterized the work these organs printed but oriented the practice of those who wrote in their orbit. When Zahajkiewicz wrote his Polish nationalist plays, he was writing inside the understanding of the literary that pertained in one cultural milieu. When Dreiser writes a prose relatively empty of stylistic refinement but overwhelmingly charged with the love of facts, hyperattentiveness to the immediate social present, and an obsessional will to retrace the circuits of consumeristic desire, he is enacting the different sense of writing learned in a different literary-cultural scene.

The larger point my examples have meant to carry is the simple but perhaps not wholly obvious one that writing is always an acculturated activity. Writing is not, Michael Warner aptly says, "a medium itself unmediated,"[10] an internally self-defined practice of unchanging potentials that manifests itself as it will in changing historical settings. Writing always takes place within some completely concrete cultural situation, a situation that surrounds it with some particular landscape of institutional structures, affiliates it with some particular group from among the array of contemporary groupings, and installs it some group-based world of understandings, practices, and values. But this setting provides writing with more than a backdrop. A work of writing comes to its particular form of existence in interaction with the network of relations that surround it: in any actual instance, writing orients itself in or against some understanding of what writing is, does, and is good for that is culturally composed and derived.

This book is written in the belief that writing has been envisioned and practiced in many different ways in America—ways neither wholly self-invented nor merely dictated from without but realized from among the possibilities set in different cultural situations. My largest contention is that the history of American literature needs to be understood not as the history of literary works only but also as the history of literature's working conditions—the history of the diverse and changing worlds that have been constructed around writing in American social life. More precisely, since works and the way they *work* their situations are integral to the story, this book argues that American literary history should be rethought as the history of the relation between literary writing and the changing meanings and places made for such work in American social history—a history not of texts or contexts alone but of the multiform transactions that have taken place between them. The chapters that follow propose a set of inquiries into writing worlds socially assembled in the United States during the nineteenth century. My particular objects of focus are first the domestic culture of letters brought together in the 1830s and 1840s, then the fracturing of the cultural field that brought a distinctly demarcated high-literary culture into existence in the 1860s and after (though other cultures of letters—the literary world organized in black schools in the South after Reconstruction, for instance—are considered along the way). At the same time, these chapters also consider a wide variety of nineteenth-century texts, studying how their meanings change when they are read in light of the cultural-historical grounds for their creation.

This may be enough to say about the book's subject. But I should probably add that these studies are also written in a certain spirit. The history I have called for—a history of the interactions between American writing and the changing conditions of its social life—is not a subject that lies plain to our viewing, waiting only to be looked into to be properly understood. Rather, the relationships that make up this history, as I understand them, are all problematic in some fundamental way: matters possibly not susceptible to definitive explanation or analysis, and certainly not at the current state of our knowledge. For this reason the studies that follow present themselves not so much as fully achieved chapters in some brave New History of American Literature but rather as explorations, essays in the original sense of trials or attempts: experimental efforts, working with the materials of given historical instances, to see how more general problems in the cultural history of literature could be worked through. The chapters here feature various sides of the question of literature's cultural mediations. Some focus on historical circumstances of literary production; some focus on the relation of literary writing to emerging social audiences; some investigate the other concerns and agendas with which the category of literature has been bundled together in different cultural settings; some focus on the figure of the author, and the different ways authorship has been made imaginable in different literary-social situations. But whichever aspect of the problem is temporarily featured, each chapter proposes itself first of all as an inquiry, an attempt to ask how a question of this sort can be posed and thought through.

Finally, this book has another set of questions on its mind as well. As will be sufficiently obvious, my investigations are driven not just by historical curiosity but by a set of concerns that have become prominent in contemporary literary study: the issue of literature as social agent or doer of cultural work; the issue of canonicity and of literary discrimination; the issue of women's writing and its possibly different traditions; the issue of minority access to literary power. These questions are continually addressed in the pages that follow, but they are not (for the most part) addressed abstractly. Rather, my effort has been to reroute theoretical discussions into particular historical instances, to the end of letting history qualify theory. The following chapters use the specificity of the local case at hand not just to exemplify but to test and criticize currently familiar critical propositions, to show how differently such matters play themselves out in history than they do in the realm of abstract critical reflection.

Moved into the arena of critical controversy, for instance, my initial examples would supply just such a testing ground for one contemporary crux: the issue of difference. Recent criticism has equipped us with the notion that certain groups of people have their own separate relations to writing, so that there are such distinct things as "women's writing," "African-American writing," and so on. Another body of criticism teaches us to the contrary that all differentiation in the literary sphere is invidious and factitious, a discrimination retrospectively enforced by the culturally empowered. To move these debates into the historical case I began with would be to see the inadequacy of both lines of reasoning, and also a way to get beyond them. Eighteen nineties Chicago naturalism, 1890s Chicago ethnic writing, and the work marked "literary" in 1890s Chicago have had different values assigned to them in subsequent decades, but the difference between them is not a matter only of latter-day and external evaluation. These bodies of writing are different as writing because they differentiate themselves from one another in the act of their composition—and they do so because the writers who produced them internalized and worked from different understandings of writing itself. But the different literary programs the authors engaged do not derive from their membership in some generalized social category of humanity. Rather, these understandings of writing—the fine-art conception, the reportorial-commercial conception, the ethnic-political conception—were molded through a social organization of the literary field specific to that time and place; and writers enlisted themselves in one or another of these literary divisions through the way they sought to take up a position in that particular literary-social world. Zahajkiewicz became an ethnic playwright by taking up that newly available social role, not by "being" an "immigrant" or "ethnic American." Another immigrant of the exact same vintage, the Lithuanian-born Bernard Berenson, became a chief exemplar of Stone and Kimball-like high-cultural cosmopolitanism and connoisseurship by taking another culturally structured career route; Dreiser, born of immigrant parents, chose a different place of writerly self-realization, and so a different scheme of writerly practice. Literary difference, this instance proposes, is neither a pseudoreality nor an automatic consequence of social identity but something effected through the mediations of literary-cultural situations. This suggestion can stand as a preliminary sample of the revisionisms that the study of literary cultures can help to produce.

Is "historically" the only way literature can be studied? My reply would be certainly not. Once works have come into existence, readers are free to place them in different frames and put them to different uses: if it were not so, no work could survive its initial moment. A cultural study of the sort attempted here features one of writing's many relations; for this aspect to monopolize consideration—for a newfangled "far" reading to replace the once-mandatory "close" reading—would not represent an escape from limitations of knowledge, only a restructuring of their bounds. The most compelling reason for studying the social relations of literary forms is that this dimension has been so long and so systematically ignored. Once this territory has been scouted as thoroughly as some others, visiting it will become comparatively less rewarding.

But during the time that it is still to a certain extent a terra incognita, it is an interesting place to work: a place where new
things can be learned and old understandings reconceived. Interesting—intensely so—the current study has been to its author. It
is now time to see if the reader will find it so as well.

Sparing the Rod
Discipline and Fiction in
Antebellum America

Why does discipline become
a key Trope at This Time?

I

CORPORAL PUNISHMENT has been one of the most peren-
nially vexed of questions in American cultural history. Discipline
performed on the body became an issue in America as early as the
eighteenth century with the importation of Lockean educational
thought. Since then, attitudes toward this practice have remained
both passionate and sharply divergent, and the issue of the corporal continues to be reignited through the frictions of local cultural
conflict. (The Supreme Court was adjudicating one such conflict
when it ruled in 1977 in *Ingraham v. Wright* that corporal correction as practiced in Florida schools is not cruel and unusual punishment.)[1] But if it is by no means confined to one period, it is still
fair to say that the issue of the corporal has its historical center of
gravity in America in the antebellum decades. In the 1830s, then
even more prominently in the 1840s and early 1850s, the picturing of scenes of physical correction emerges as a major form of
imaginative activity in America, and arguing the merits of such
discipline becomes a major item on the American public agenda.
Noting this fact, we might ask: What is at issue when corporal
punishment is most intensely at issue in American cultural history? What is being thought when the lash becomes a figure of
thought in the antebellum years?

The antislavery movement is one obvious headquarters for the antebellum imagination of the lash. Frederick Douglass's searing accounts of whippings witnessed and endured in his *Narrative* (1845); the other slave narratives of the 1840s and 1850s that, like Douglass's, make whipping not just a memorably experienced scene but specifically the scene of initiation into slavery; Theodore Dwight Weld's compendium of "documentary" horror stories, *American Slavery as It Is* (1839), in which whipping scenes are multiplied with truly Boschian iteration: such examples can remind us how compulsively the scene of corporal correction is repeated in American antislavery writing, and how central it is made to the image of slavery that writing constructs.[2] We could analyze the particular contours that these picturings give to their subject— noting how they foreground the embodiedness of whipping, the bodily enacted and bodily received nature of its disciplinary transaction; the perfect asymmetry of power expressed in the whipping scenario; the indignity that whipping inflicts on the slave through its dramatization of his or her powerlessness; or the erotics of authoritarianism that whipping both excites and discharges. But such a nuancing would scarcely be necessary to say what the imagination of whipping *means* here. For as such works determine it, whipping *means* slavery. It emblematizes both one actual practice and the whole structure of relations that identify Southern slavery as a system.

One answer to the question of what is at issue in corporal punishment in the antebellum decades is that slavery is at issue in it; and considerable evidence suggests that the more general imaging of such punishment at this time has slavery as its ultimate referent, whatever the immediate occasion. Before 1850 the United States Navy was committed to a corporal scheme of discipline featuring the cat-o'-nine-tails, the colt, and public flogging. In the early nineteenth century there was a certain amount of discussion about this disciplinary system, but the question of flogging seems to have been phrased in a sector-specific way: if, it was reasoned, an abhorrence of flogging made many Americans avoid naval enlistment, then the United States Navy would be manned largely by non-Americans in time of war; but if this was so, was flogging compatible with the needs of national security? Naval flogging es-

calated into a subject of full-fledged public controversy, and so began making its own contributions to public imagining of the lash,
only in the 1840s. This happened when the growing antislavery
conflict annexed the previously separate subject of naval discipline
and made it a skirmishing ground for its own contending forces.[3]

Congressional debate over the abolition of naval flogging came
to a head during the extension-of-slavery crisis of 1850. In the
congressional vote, Northerners were virtually unanimously for,
and Southerners unanimously against, this disciplinary reform.
Such facts make clear that it was really slavery (certainly much
more than the navy itself) that was at issue when corporal punishment was contested in the naval context; and this in turn lends
support to the more general view that slavery was the buried referent, and control of slavery the hidden agenda, behind all antebellum agitation over the lash. But this reading, however well
founded locally, has serious limitations. For when we look out beyond the cultural settings that the slavery issue had infiltrated with
its debate, we find the same kind of representational activity going
on without slavery's provocation. The whipping scenes that mark
an antislavery text like Douglass's *Narrative* or a merchant marine
reformist text like Richard Henry Dana's *Two Years Before the Mast*
(1840) could find close equivalents in Elizabeth Palmer Peabody's
Record of a School (1835), with its astonishing account of Bronson
Alcott making his pupils whip *him* for their disciplinary infrac-
tions. (When "at first they did it very lightly," Alcott asked of his
weeping pupils "if they thought that they deserved no more punishment than that? And so they were obliged to give it hard.")[4] I
will be presenting considerable further evidence that whipping
scenes (if not always so perversely organized) are endemic to antebellum educational writing; but these imagings (unlike those in
naval writing) seldom draw parallels with the whipping of slaves.
(Although there is eventually a considerable interchange between
antislavery personnel and school reformers, it is a striking fact that
such figures' care for bodily correction as an educational issue often precedes, not follows, their antislavery commitment.) Not to
proliferate examples: the antislavery movement made the lash
stand for Southern slavery in a powerful way; but who can be

confident that that resonance is at work in the domestic education text Bernard Wishy has uncovered, in which a mother who knows that she ought to discipline her child and the child who knows he ought to *be* disciplined spend two days together contemplating, in uncertainty and dread, the lash they cannot resolve to use?[5]

Such evidence sharply challenges the interpretation we began by considering. It suggests at the least that corporal discipline arises as an issue in many different antebellum settings, not from its Southern use alone. More radically it suggests that in the antebellum decades, a will to think about whipping exists prior to and somewhat independent of the social settings in which whipping was practiced, and that so far from responding to a horrid custom prevailing here and there in the world, this thought partly seizes *on* those settings—schoolroom, naval vessel, even plantation—to help dramatize a scene it already wants to see. The fact that the imagination of whipping so exceeds its ostensible "sources" must occasion a shift in our direction of inquiry. It makes clear that we need to ask not so much what the antebellum imagination of corporal correction refers *to* but rather: What is the structure of thought such scenarios proceed *from* and function *in?* What mental need is being met, what cultural work is being done, through the insistent thinking of this "unthinkable" scene?

Phrased in this way, the issue of the corporal becomes the kind of question that Michel Foucault has taught us a powerful new way to answer. Placed in the somber light of Foucault's magisterial *Discipline and Punish*, American uses of lash, cat, and rod reappear as local instances of that older mode of discipline Foucault describes in which the wrongs of the transgressor (and the power of authority to correct such wrongs) are visited on his body in a publicly visible form. Conversely, the compulsive antebellum rehearsals of the evils of such instruments reappear as American incarnations of that "cry from the heart" that, Foucault argues, began stigmatizing physical punishment in early modernity as an outrage to "humanity," while also thereby helping to replace the old disciplinary mode with new technologies—less visible but more pervasive, less "cruel" but more deeply controlling—of modern social regulation.[6]

from shame
to quiet culture
external → internal

The reading that offers these new identifications to the parties to the antebellum corporal debate strikes me as an inescapable aid to the understanding of this subject. Posing it in a Foucauldian framework makes sense of extremely obvious but hitherto obscure *Question* features of this episode, not least: Why was corporal punishment, among all the other possible evils of the systems they opposed, the evil that fixated antebellum reformers? Situating it in this frame also generate a suggestive account of what the other, opposed cultural development was that American anticorporal thinking was covertly furthering. But great cultural changes never work themselves out except through the interplay of forces specific to actual social sites, and a Foucauldian reading cannot tell the whole history of nineteenth-century American anticorporalism without considerable adjustment for historical specificity. If certain nineteenth-century American institutions resembled the ancien régime in making the body the site of correction, their institutional differences from the ancien régime (as from one another) are still evident enough; and of course they resisted reformation not only with their corporal disciplinary strategy but with their whole particularity as cultural forms. Similarly if some body of nineteenth-century American thought performed the double office of stigmatizing one regulatory practice and so ushering in another, it was not as an ungrounded force toward *surveiller* that it operated. This pattern of thought shaped itself within the mentality of a historically specific cultural group; it shaped itself not around a noncorporal disciplinary model in general but that group's particular version of such a model; and its public assertion promoted not that model alone but all the other interests and practices that identified that group as well. *middle class*

The history of the particular antebellum American mind-set partly defined by its need to picture scenes of bodily correction is what I propose to reconstruct in this chapter. I read this scenario as forming part of the thinking of the American middle class as that class redefines itself in the antebellum decades. More particularly I will try to show its centrality to the theory of socialization that is this middle class's greatest creation, absorption, and self-identifying badge: a theory that might be labelled disciplinary in-

timacy, or simply discipline through love. But the interest of the
thought so based is that it does not sponsor correctional reform
alone. As I describe it, the cultural assertion embodied in disciplinary intimacy generates on one front an animus against corporal
punishment; on another front a normative model of character formation; on another, a particular configuration of training institutions designed to support that character-building plan; and on yet
another, a new place for literary reading in cultural life. This chapter begins with bodily correction, moves on to the history of home
and school, and ends up in the field of literature, but it does so in
hopes of having shown why these developments are not unrelated: for how these developments were given together is the story
the history of disciplinary intimacy has to tell.

II   Book on child

The theory I have called disciplinary intimacy—to recompose it
first *as* a theory—is not at all difficult to reconstruct.[7] It is articulated with massive repetition all across the literature of the child,
one of the most distinctive textual productions of the American
1830s and 1840s. Books on the child in the home, especially the
newly popular domestic manuals; books on the child in school;
and, as in the case of Horace Bushnell's *Christian Nurture* (1847),
books on the child in the church were largely absorbed in the task
of elaborating and offering instruction in this disciplinary model,
whose distinctive features might be outlined here.

   The first and invariable mark of this program is that it mandates
an extreme personalization of disciplinary authority. In a familiar
older scheme of things, authority is centered in a person (a king, a
father) understood to stand for a transpersonal Right whose authority is represented *in* but by no means confined *to* his person.
In Foucault's reign of *surveiller* (as in the panoptic prison he makes
paradigmatic of modern discipline) the person in authority becomes invisible; indeed authority leaves an actual person to inhere
in a disciplinary *function* that can be performed by anonymous interchangeable personnel.[8] Against both of these formulations, the
program I am describing doubly insists that disciplinary authority

reside in persons *and* that persons *in* authority make their authority, as it were, dissolve into their merely personal presences. Bushnell argues accordingly that the child can only eventually know
the right after he has first known it in an unabstracted, wholly
personalized form: "The child is under parental authority too for
the very purpose, it would seem, of having the otherwise abstract
principle of all duty impersonated in his parents, and thus brought
home to his practical embrace."[9] The centrality this program as-
signs to the personalization of authority is evident in its down-
grading of any presentation of authority as abstract imperative. It
is evident even more tellingly in the instruction these texts regularly give authority figures on how to humanize themselves to
their disciplinary charges. Bushnell's chapter "Family Government" gives lessons in how to replace "the violent emphasis, the
hard, stormy voice" of one parental presentation with "a kind
of silent, natural-looking [though obviously carefully calculated]
power." Catherine Beecher's *Treatise on Domestic Economy* (1841)
gives guidance on how to come down toward one's charges, how
to mitigate authority's distance from the spontaneity of the child:
"Those, who will join with children, and help them along in their
sports, will learn, by this mode, to understand the feelings and
interests of childhood; while, at the same time, they secure a degree of confidence and affection, which cannot be gained so easily,
in any other way."[10]

    A first feature of this collectively composed disciplinary model
is that it requires authority to put on a human face. A second feature is a purposeful sentimentalization of the disciplinary relation:
a strategic relocation of authority relations in the realm of emotion,
and a conscious intensification of the emotional bond between the
authority-figure and its charge. For Bushnell the well-nurtured
child is not surrounded with rules but bathed in "genial warmth
and love": the authority around him or her expresses its power
not as authority but as affection, through an intensification of af-
fectional warmth.[11] As these writings envision it, this ideally intensified *love*-power has the effect of holding—indeed of virtually
enclosing—the disciplinary subject in a field of projected feeling:
Bushnell's child is "enveloped" in his or her parents' spirit; the

ideal mother figure in Mary Peabody Mann's *Moral Culture of Infancy* (1841) "encompasse[s]" her children "with her tenderness."[12] As it enfolds the child in its love, this mode of authority knowingly aims to awaken a reciprocal strength of love, and to fix that love back on itself. Lyman Cobb utters a commonplace when he instructs the would-be "parent or teacher" that he should "*first of all, secure the* LOVE *and* AFFECTION *of his children or pupils.*"[13]

Within this account, enmeshing the child in strong bonds of love is the way authority introduces its charge to its imperatives and norms. From the child's perspective, what the parent-figure believes in comes across indistinguishably from his love, so that the child imbibes what the parent stands for in a moral sense along with the parent's physical intimacy and affection. The child's first love *for* the parent becomes, accordingly, an inchoate form of allegiance to what the parent represents—a fact this scheme of rearing then exploits. In later development the child's continuing desire for its parents' warmth and favor—the disposition that this whole plan of nurture aims to intensify and to transform from a primal instinct into the ground of the child's emerging selfhood—establishes an agency, within the child's nature, that enforces the feeling of obligation to parentally embodied values. Lydia Sigourney's *Letters to Mothers* (1839) captures to perfection this plan's scheme of nurture and this nurture's intended goal: its strategic intensification of normal family romances; its aim, through this cultivation of closeness, to *center* the child emotionally on the loving parent; then, climactically, its plan to use this centering to implant the parent known *outwardly* only as love as an *inwardly* regulating moral consciousness:

> [The mother] should keep her hold on his affections, and encourage him to confide to her, without reserve, his intentions and his hopes, his errors and his enjoyments. Thus maintaining her preeminence in the sanctuary of his mind, her image will be as a tutelary seraph, not seeming to bear rule, yet spreading perpetually the wings of purity and peace over its beloved shrine, and keeping guard for God.[14]

When it reaches this point, discipline through love reveals itself as a strategy not, finally, for the humanization of authority but rather for a superior introjection of authority with humanization's aid. Sigourney's disciplinarian seems "not to bear rule" in the child's world in order the more surely to establish her rule in her child's mind; Bushnell's child is bathed in affection not only to shelter or support him but so that his parents may "work a character" the more deeply "in him."[15] (What are such letters to parents if not blueprints for the construction of superego, using others' subjectivities as one's building sites and others' needs for love as one's tools?) In its heightened emphasis on introjection, the discipline of love reveals itself as a mechanism, in turn, not for the mitigation of authority but really for the extension of its regulating hold. When loved parents are properly enshrined in the sanctuary of mind, no space is out of their sight; so an 1830s *Mother's Magazine* poet rather menacingly writes: "Every day and every hour the mother is with her child." Omnipresent, such tutelary seraphs become, in theory at least, unlimitedly controlling: "A child or pupil, who obeys his parent or teacher from LOVE purely, can be relied on when *absent,* as well as when *present,*" according to Lyman Cobb.[16]

Given its exact inversion of the understanding that sponsors corporal discipline—its view of authentic power as expressing itself in tenderness, not rigor; as operating "by methods that are silent and imperceptible,"[17] not visible and tangible; as working through intersubjectivity, not the stark polarization of authority and its subject; as aiming toward inward colonization, not outward coercion—it is not surprising that discipline through love should enlist this rival as its defining opposite. Invidious comparison with a bodily scheme of correction is a virtually mandatory move in this scheme's self-articulation: so Bushnell rises up in wrath against those who "talk much of the rod as the orthodox symbol of parental duty," then "storm about their house with heathenish ferocity, [and] lecture, and threaten, and castigate, and bruise, and call this family government."[18] Cobb's book, entitled *The Evil Tendencies of Corporal Punishment as a Means of Moral Discipline in Families and Schools Examined and Discussed* (1847), advances its disciplinary in-

timacy orthodoxies through an endlessly sustained refutation of
every possible argument for physical correction. Cobb's party's
righteous conviction is that it can spare the rod because it has created a nearer and surer enforcer. In its correction system, "self-
reproach," or the subject's self-consciousness itself (appropriately
molded by others), becomes "the whip that scourges his faults."[19]

So far I have spoken of disciplinary intimacy as if it were wholly
a system of thought. But it will already be clear that this theoretical
model travels together with particular social structures. The fact
that it is propagated so largely in home-management manuals
of the 1830s and 1840s bespeaks this idea's connection, in a
dominant way, with nineteenth-century middle-class domesticity.
Books like Sigourney's *Letters to Mothers,* or Catharine Sedgwick's
Home (1835), or Lydia Maria Child's *The Mother's Book* (1831),
quite overtly posit as their audience a family closed off from extended relations; a family prosperous, but not luxuriously wealthy;
a family where home life is relieved from the heavy labor of primary economic production; a family in which the mother, now
the chief presence in the home, is able to devote her whole attention to raising her children. They address, in short, exactly the
family formation that historians have shown to be emerging as a
new middle-class paradigm in the decades around 1830.[20] These
manuals instruct families in how to "make" a home in this new
sense. But what they most instructively show is the intimate alli-
ance, the relation, really, of mutual entailment, between this disciplinary theory and this newly consolidating social form.

By addressing it early on and in exquisite detail, such books
establish that this scheme is the disciplinary practice of the new
model family, is indeed the first art such a family must learn. But
within these manuals this scheme also functions not just to identify the family's actual practice but in a powerful way to *necessitate*
its family *form.* The primary assumptions of discipline through
love—its assumptions of extreme physical and emotional closeness between parent and child, and of the parent's availability to
make the child the center of his or her attention—codify, as if in
the realm that objective moral truth, the new middle-class social
fact of a parent disoccupied from other labors. In its assumption of

the traditionally feminine *affection* as the mode of authority appropriate for nurture, the scheme of discipline through love codifies
no less clearly the fact of the mother's ascendancy to new primacy
as child raiser, as the father begins to go out of the home to work.
And the whole thrust of disciplinary theory in the manuals is
at once to *reflect* that the family now *is*, and to *require* that the
family now *be*, organized on these terms. By making a warm af-
fective environment the prerequisite for the growth of moral selfhood in children, this scheme mandates, as the condition for
proper character construction, the priority of the mother in nurture. And by making the undivided attention of the mother the
prerequisite for proper nurture, in similar fashion, this scheme
mandates that the mother be unoccupied except with child rearing. How can the mother "secure *time*" to perform her "highest
duties" of "form[ing] deep and lasting impressions" on the "immortal beings" in her "charge"? Mrs. Sigourney asks. She replies
that "the remedy is, for the mother to provide herself with competent assistance, in the sphere of manual labour, that she may be
enabled to become the constant directress of her children, and
have leisure to be happy in their company."[21] So it is that child
nurture, the devoted labor of the leisured mother, confirms her
moral right and duty to *be* unemployed—and to put someone else
to work as a domestic in the service of her domestic idyll.
The other institution this belief system helped to construct
in the antebellum decades is the remodeled school that arose
with the new middle-class home as its tutelary adjunct.[22] The public school movement, active throughout the North from the late
1830s on, had its greatest champion in Horace Mann. From his
newly created post as secretary to the Massachusetts State Board
of Education, Mann led the fight for those revisions that mark the
reformed school's institutional newness: the breaking of schools
into progressive classes or grades; the qualification of teachers in
state normal schools; most crucially the rendering of school atten-
dance universally compulsory—in other words the rendering of
the school as *the* place, not one place among many, for the child's
elementary instruction. (Truancy was made a criminal offense,
and the first truant officer hired, in Boston in 1850.)[23] An equally

essential part of Mann's work was to build a case for such a school
that would win it social assent. In his annual reports, Mann
mounted powerful arguments for the reformed public school as
training ground for republican citizenship. He characterized it as
the place where a potential rabble could be taught respect for
property rights. But in a no less central move he also represented
the reformed school as disciplinary intimacy's second home. In his
reports we can watch Mann building this structure of thought,
plank by plank, into his idea of a school. The school as he proposes
it is a place of personified authority: the properly trained teacher
he offers to produce "moves before the eyes of his pupils as a personification of dignity and learning and benevolence." The school
sentimentalizes the disciplinary relation: the well-trained teacher
knows that his "first great duty" is to awaken "sentiments in the
breasts of his pupils," to activate their "social and filial affections."
In consequence, the reformed school lifts discipline off of the body:
one of Mann's most constant contentions is that in a school so
taught, pupils will feel inwardly motivated to learn, so that the use
of the rod will wither away.[24]   Mann

Mann's success in framing the school reform debate in the idiom
of disciplinary intimacy is attested to by the fact that the single
great controversy his reforms touched off was fought out entirely
within this set of terms. In 1844, thirty-one Boston schoolmasters,
members of the older educational establishment Mann was trying
to dislodge, issued an impassioned retort to his seventh annual
report. Threatened by all of Mann's reforms, the ground they chose
for their defense was that of disciplinary philosophy. Reactivating
the beliefs of an older social order (their rhetoric consciously ties
them to a patriarchal family form and an unliberalized Protestantism under heavy assault by the 1840s),[25] the schoolmasters argue
that right discipline consists *not* in winning cheerful compliance
(through personal charm but in winning recognition of authority
as impersonally valid. From this point of view they proclaim that
the "kind treatment and agreeable manners" of Mann's humanized school represent a perversion of the school's disciplinary
function, and that the traditionary practice of bodily correction—

"present[ing] to their senses, in tangible shape, the actual rod"—is a fully *proper* means of moral instruction.[26]

The Boston schoolmasters' "Remarks on the Seventh Annual Report of the Hon. Horace Mann" reminds us that there were two sides to the question of bodily correction in the North in the 1840s. But it also shows that Mann had succeeded in framing the school question as a question of corporal versus "kindly" discipline. And it was the nature *of* that frame to be able to turn procorporal opposition, when Mann succeeded in producing it, into a major polemical resource. Mann is never more rhetorically powerful than in his righteously indignant "Reply to the 'Remarks' of Thirty-One Schoolmasters" (1844), where he turns his assailants into sadistic authoritarians exulting in the "Power, Violence, Terror, and Suffering" of "cowhide and birch." And he is nowhere more persuasive of the necessity of the reformed school's supplementation (even supplanting) of home instruction than he is when he makes such abuse the ill-bred child's domestic lot, and the school a second mother offering humane refuge at her soft breast:

> Was it not, and is it not, one of the grand objects in the institution and support of Common Schools, to bring those children who are cursed by vicious parentage, who were not only "conceived and brought forth," but have been nurtured in "sin;" who have never known the voice of love and kindness; who have daily fallen beneath the iron blows of those parental hands that should have been outstretched for their protection;—was it not, and is it not, I say, one of the grand objects of our schools to bring this class of children under humanizing and redeeming influences; to show them that there is something besides wrath and stripes and suffering, in God's world; to lift these outcasts and forlorn beings from their degradation, by gentle hands, and to fold them to warm and cherishing bosoms?[27]

These polemics are in a sense just one more enactment of that antebellum thought propelled by the denigration of the corporal; but they are peculiarly revealing of how that thought does its work

in the world. Mann's words show how this structure of thought
helps its adherents mark their difference from other social groups.
As he uses it, corporal correction becomes the sign—and sign of
insufficiency—first of the older patriarchal New England culture
of the Boston schoolmasters, then of the Irish immigrant culture
(Mann all but names it) growing around him as he speaks; on
another occasion it could as effectively identify the inferiority
of some other rival formation: say, the culture of the Southern
planter class. At the same time that it gives a new middle-class
culture the means to think its cultural superiority, Mann's example
shows, the concepts of disciplinary intimacy also help it build the
practical means for extending its sway. What we see Mann modelling is an institution with the power to break in upon the quite
different acculturation systems of other American cultures and de-
liver their children to training on a now-"universal" plan: the public school recast, at this moment, in the middle class's disciplinary
image.[28]

It needs to be insisted that the middle-class social model, like
the disciplinary plan that gave it its sense of mission, was far from
being socially established in the antebellum decades. Even where
it was accepted as an ideal, we always find intriguing disparities
between this scheme and the organizations of actual lives in this
period. And of course, outside its pale, its plan of enclosed domesticity and discipline through maternal affection was only one
among the many social schemes, traditional and novel, that structured the life of this time. (Mormon patriarchal polygyny and
Oneida communitarianism—which insisted that children not be
raised in domestic privacy, and not subjected in a specializing way
to their biological parents' love—are two more creations of the
American 1840s.) But if this model was not established then, the
antebellum decades were the time when the newly defined middle
class began its push to establish its model as a social norm; and it
is as an agent in this assertion that the theory of discipline through
love (together with its anticorporal insistences) had its force. This
theory supplied an emerging group with a plan of individual nurture and social structure that it could believe in and use to justify
its ways; more, it helped shape and empower the actual institu-

tions through which that group could impress its ways on others. At a time when it was in no sense socially normal, the new middle-class world undertook to propagate itself as American "normality"; and it is as a constituent in this new creation of the normative that the complex I have traced had its full historical life.

III Literature

I have been careful so far to keep literature separate from the disciplinary history I have been composing. But if we were now to reintroduce the literary into this history, its separateness would come to appear largely fictitious. Posed within the history I have been telling, many well-known literary works could be reseen at once as workings-out, in the literary sphere, of disciplinary problems more generally cultural in their framing. Similarly, many modes of antebellum writing that appear unconnected when focussed on a literary ground could be grasped as related when focused on this wider cultural ground instead.

One body of writing that hooks up at once with this matrix of disciplinary thought is the antebellum fiction of total institutions. The great whipping scene in Dana's *Two Years Before the Mast,* mentioned earlier as a protest against the rigors of discipline in the merchant marine, might be more largely understood now as a case of that mental rehearsal of the evils of bodily correction that we have found crucial to the articulation of a softer, more internalized disciplinary system. (In this context we will not be surprised to learn that before he became the seaman's friend, Dana was party to a protest against excessive corporal discipline in school.)[29] Herman Melville's *White-Jacket* (1850)—by the end of which the navy virtually becomes an institution for flogging, and flogging an excuse for reformatory indignation—is another work clearly in Dana's vein. But could we not say that Nathaniel Hawthorne's *The Scarlet Letter* (1850) too belongs, if in a more displaced way, to the same category of imagining? *The Scarlet Letter* is known as the great novel of seventeenth-century Puritanism. But from the point of view outlined here the striking fact about *The Scarlet Letter* is that it is almost exclusively the Puritan disciplinary system—its prison

house, stocks, scaffold, and penal letters, not its practice of piety
or its habit of trade—that Hawthorne concerns himself with. From
the historical perspective I have assembled, it will be clear at once
that what this seventeenth-century system embodies is exactly that
other kind of discipline that the mid-*nineteenth* century feels compelled to look in the face: one involving severe depersonalization,
shameful publicity, and above all, correction performed through
the external, visible marking of the body.[30]

Another kind of writing that might be said to belong to this
matrix of disciplinary imaginings is American gothic fiction. The
gothic, we know, is the genre of fantastical defamiliarization; but
it would not take much labor of imagination to see that American
gothic works of the 1840s and 1850s defamiliarize with the specific goal of clarifying the inner world valued and normalized by
the disciplinary strategies of this time. The character of Arthur
Dimmesdale, Hawthorne's great secret sinner, is a representation of
nothing if not inwardness as these strategies recommend its manufacture. Unexposed before and unjudged by visible, external authority, Dimmesdale (like Sigourney's well-reared child) is thereby
compelled to feel himself judged all the more from within the sanctuary of his mind. (In Dimmesdale's relation to Roger Chillingworth—unbeknownst to Dimmesdale "not a spectator only, but a
chief actor, in the poor minister's interior world"[31]—Hawthorne
explores in particular how subjectivity, as this system devises
it, becomes condemned to experience as inexplicably proceeding
from *within* the self a moral censure produced *as* inwardness by
an invisibly disciplinary other.) As much as the propaganda of this
time would boast, Dimmesdale shows how correction becomes an
infinite process by being wholly interiorized. Unstaged without,
the scene of his condemnation therefore becomes compulsively
and continuously restaged within. Indeed it is enacted with such
cumulative psychic force that Dimmesdale regenerates, but as ex-
pressions of inward impulses, external discipline's traditional corrective tools: the tangible lash that the lash of conscience leads him
to revive the practice of, and the letter branded out onto his body
by the heat of inward guilt.

Read in this light, Hawthorne's whole project in *The Scarlet Let-*

ter could be thought of as an attempt to weigh the methods and powers of a newer against an older disciplinary order, by juxtaposing a world of corporal correction (embodied in the Puritans' punishment of Hester) and a world of correction by interiority (embodied in Chillingworth and Dimmesdale). Taking the measure of this new order might be said to be the task of Edgar Allan Poe's altogether weirder gothic as well. One of the two or three human fates known to Poe is that of the man who, having committed the perfect crime, is nevertheless overwhelmed by the urge to denounce himself to the authorities who fail to indict him. ("'Villains!' I shrieked, 'dissemble no more!'" the narrator of "The Tell-Tale Heart" [1843] cries to the police, "'I admit the deed!—tear up the planks!'"[32] But the police of the state of Poe have heard it all before: in "The Imp of the Perverse," "The Black Cat" [1845], and elsewhere.) It is more than unreasonable that the successful criminal should want to turn himself in: it is, to these speakers, literally uncanny. But what they experience as uncanny is really the form of selfhood that disciplinary intimacy wants to make standard issue. As with Cobb's trustworthy child, there are no authority-figures in sight around these tellers. Nevertheless in this situation of what Foucault calls "enigmatic leniency" an inward police of irresistible power can be counted on to bring the culprit to the bar.[33] And since it is not allowed to see how this force has been produced inside itself or in service of what external authority this force operates, the self can only know this impulse as overwhelmingly powerful yet incomprehensible in origin—"a *mobile* without a motive, a motive not *motiviert*"[34]—and as inscrutably *of* itself yet alien to it too. (What is "William Wilson" but a gothicization of this maxim of disciplinary intimacy, from Sedgwick's *Home:* "The only effectual and lasting government,—the only one that touches the springs of action, and controls them, is *self*-government"; or this maxim, from Peabody's *Kindergarten Guide:* "The best way to cultivate a sense of the presence of God is to draw the attention to the conscience, which is very active in children, and which seems to them . . . another than themselves, and yet themselves"?)[35]

The romantic fantasies of Hawthorne and Poe are often said to embody a realism of the buried psyche. What I am suggesting is that they be considered as the chartings not of some universal "mind" but specifically of a version of "mind" that was promoted and made intellectually salient by contemporaneous cultural developments. But I leave this idea only hinted in order to turn attention to a third body of writing that I want to treat at some length. America's first best-seller novels are exact contemporaries of the works I have been discussing. The moment of *White-Jacket* and *The Scarlet Letter* is also the time of emergence of a kind of book that attained a circulation ten or even twenty times that of previous American fiction. And if other writings show a connection with the disciplinary thought of this time, the mass-circulation fiction of the 1850s has this thought written all over it.

Susan Warner's *The Wide, Wide World* (1850), which went on to become one of the four or five most widely read American novels of the whole nineteenth century, is often cited as the first of the new best-sellers. And it is Warner's book that offers the most impressive recognition of discipline through love as a culture-specific historical formation. *The Wide, Wide World* is a historical novel in a systematically restricted sense of the word. Throughout this book Warner poses the extradomestic world outside of her sphere, in a place unavailable to her literary knowing. Its initial harmony devastated by a lawsuit, neither the book's characters nor the book itself can get access to the transprivate world in which they could know what the suit's occasion was. Through the same strict observation of the limits of her sphere, Warner makes *history* in the usual sense unavailable to her knowing: what is going on in the world outside of certain family spaces is, in this book, a sealed book. But if she fails to locate her characters' private lives in relation to any sort of generalized process of collective change, part of Warner's power as a writer is that she implicitly grasps the households she represents as historically different formations of the domestic sphere. Aunt Fortune, to whose grumpy care Warner's child heroine Ellen Montgomery is shipped off after the book's opening crisis, plays the role in *The Wide, Wide World* of a fairy tale's cruel stepmother. But Warner registers her milieu quite concretely—not in local color or idiosyncratic detail only, but in such a way as to grasp its surface features' relation to its sociohistorical form. While this point is never commented on overtly, every feature of Aunt Fortune's household exemplifies the logic of the old-style household economy: Fortune is always busy, because this home is a place of work; her house is smelly and noisy, because this house is still a scene of production; her coverlets are of linsey-woolsey, because the necessities of life are still homemade in her world; she scorns Ellen's desire to go to school, because in her world knowledge means knowing how to do practically productive tasks; entertainment at her house takes the form of an apple-paring and pork-packing bee, because in her world entertainment is not disconnected from the household's economic productivity, and so on through a legion of comparable details. The other households in the book differ from Aunt Fortune's on every count. But they differ not just because they are the homes of other people, but because they embody different social formations of the home's place and work: the more genteel (and less productive) formation of a historically later phase, in the case of Alice and John Humphreys; the altogether leisured, pleasure-oriented formation of a Europeanized gentry class, in the case of the aristocratic Lindsays.

While this point too is never registered in any abstract form, Warner's picturing strikingly represents the discipline of love as inhering in a differentiated way in one of these social formations. In contrast to Aunt Fortune's, the household associated with Ellen's mother and Ellen's exemplary friend Alice is characterized by a raised threshold of decency and comfort. (Its furniture is tastefully ornamental, not only functional; Ellen's traumatic experiences at Aunt Fortune's suggest that she is used to indoor plumbing.) In it women are conspicuously exempted from productive functions. (Alice does the more delicate baking, but has a maid to do heavy housework; Ellen's mother, with the wearying exception of one shopping trip, does nothing at all.) Its forms of entertainment are mentally uplifting, and also unproductive and privatized. (Where Aunt Fortune has a bee, these women read.) And this household is also and indistinguishably two more things: it is affectionate, so much so that the cultivation of close relations might be said to *be its* productive activity; and it is pious, specifi-

cally in a way that makes its female heads feel called to the work
of improving others' spiritual characters. (When Ellen first meets
Alice, Alice at once picks up the task of revivalistically reforming Ellen's temper that her mother had left incomplete.) This
reformatory lovingness is profoundly different from any disciplinary method seen elsewhere in the book. Aunt Fortune, untender
and impious, is too busy to *care* about Ellen in Alice's and Mrs.
Montgomery's way, let alone to care about her moral nurture;
her discipline is confined to occasional bouts of highly arbitrary
authoritarianism, backed up (in one instance) by blows.[36] The
Lindsays, more genial but quite secular, try to make Ellen sleep
late, drink wine, cut back on religious reading, and be more fun at
parties: theirs is another discipline entirely, training for life in the
very different gentry world. Moralizing lovingness is confined to
scenes that have all the marks of the new middle-class feminine
domesticity. Warner knows *that* discipline as *that* social formation's
pastime and work; she knows *that* discipline as forming the *self*
that world aims to reproduce.

    Part of the distinction of *The Wide, Wide World* is that it specifies
the cultural location of this *scheme* of acculturation so precisely.
Another of its distinctions is that it plots the actual psychological
transactions this scheme entails with unmatched precision and
care. The novel begins, thus, by showing what it would mean, in
human terms, to be encompassed with tenderness as this plan requires. Ellen Montgomery lives with her mother at the novel's
opening, but this phrase does not begin to describe the form of
their attachment. It would be more accurate to say that she lives *in*
her mother, in the *Umwelt* her mother projects. Her mother is always with her, her mother is the whole world available to her
(when her mother sleeps Ellen looks out the window, but the
world outside the window is inaccessible to her; hired food pre-
parers and even Ellen's father sometimes intrude on this domesticity, but when they withdraw "the mother and daughter were
left, as they always loved to be, alone" [1:43]). Enclosed within
her mother's emotional presence, Ellen has been bred to a recip-
rocating strength of love that makes her feel each event first in
terms of how it will bear on her mother's frame of mind. And this

other-centeredness or (as we say) *considerateness* is what makes her responsive to the authority of her mother's codes. As she surrounds her child with her highly wrought emotionality, Mrs. Montgomery also fills the world so centered with moral prescription. She has a rule for everything, a rule in each case absolutely and equally obligatory: "Draw nigh to God" is her religious requirement for her daughter, but her rules of etiquette, even of fashion—one must never ask the names of strangers; girls' cloaks must be of medium-grade merino wool, and not green (1:26, 65, 56–57)—are put forward as binding in no less a degree. And as the beginning of the novel demonstrates (a little pathetically), Ellen's love for this authority-figure—her continual impulse to think of her mother before she thinks of herself, and the absolute imperative by which she feels compelled to maintain her mother's favorable emotional atmosphere—makes Ellen, in and of herself, want to do and be what her mother would require of her. While her mother pretends to nap in the first chapter, Ellen makes the tea and toast, and she not only makes them but makes them *just so*, with a ritualistic precision of observance. She performs this labor and follows this tight prescription because the tea is for her mother, and she is driven by "the zeal that love gives" (1:14). Crushed to hear that her mother (quite incomprehensibly) must abandon her and move with her father to Europe now that the lawsuit is lost, Ellen is required to suppress her grief in consideration of her mother's fragile state—"try to compose yourself. I am afraid you will make me worse," the tyranically delicate Mrs. Montgomery says. This injunction is hard for the aggrieved Ellen to obey, but the stronger emotion of "love to her mother" has "power enough" to make her "exert all her self-command" (1:13).

What the opening of *The Wide, Wide World* really dramatizes is the primitive implantation of moral motivation, as discipline by intimacy specifies that practice. Made into a compulsive love-seeker, Ellen shows how the child so determined becomes driven, by her heightened need to win and keep parental favor, not just to accept but really to *seek out* the authority of the parent's moral imperatives. What the rest of the novel then dramatizes is the ongoing career of authority-seeking that this primal scene initiates.

Two facts constitute Ellen's initial world: the fact that the world is centered in the mother, and that the mother is going to be lost. The news that inaugurates this narrative, the news that the lawsuit is lost and Ellen must be abandoned, carries a powerful sense of womens' victimization by the nondomestic, masculine economic world they are now dependent on but shut out from knowledge of. (When the separation scene finally arrives, Ellen is viscerally wrenched from her mother by the disruptive stranger who is her father.) But in another sense the separation crisis that inaugurates this novel simply recognizes that oneness with the mother is what one cannot *not* lose—a fact that the child's new centrality to the mother's life in middle-class domesticity makes in new measure traumatic.

What the plot of this novel shows is how an acculturation system like Ellen's makes this newly intensified grief of separation a psychic resource for the disciplining of the subject. In *The Wide, Wide World,* to love one's mother is to wish to do things her way, but to love her and lose her is to have this wish heightened into full-fledged moral imperative. Loving and losing her mother commits Ellen to a career of seeking for substitutes for this lost beloved. But since the mark of others' substitutability for the mother is that they simultaneously give warm baths of affection and impose strict codes of obligation, this way of repairing an emotional breach drives Ellen deeper and deeper into the territory of psychological regulation. (The final beloved regulator, John Humphreys, does not even tell Ellen his final requirement of her, "but whatever it were, she was very sure she would do it!" [2:333].) Coached by such surrogates, Ellen's achievement as the novel plots it is to move toward ever more perfect internalizations of parental authority— an achievement whose psychic payoff, as the book shows it, is to restore oneness with the mother now lost.[37] Conscience, at last grown strong enough to make her obey even the most outrageous of Aunt Fortune's commands, lets Ellen hear an inner voice that she knows as coming from "her mother's lips" (1:317). When she then undergoes the conversion her mother had covenanted her to, Ellen at once accepts the authority of her mother's religious system and recovers, through participation in that system, felt contact with the mother herself: after her conversion "there seemed to be a link of communion between her mother and her that was wanting before. The promise, written and believed in by the one, realized and rejoiced in by the other, was a dear something in common, though one had in the mean while removed to heaven, and the other was still a lingerer on the earth" (2:72).

Jane Tompkins, the strongest recent champion of Warner's novel, writes in a fine phrase that "a text depends upon its audience's beliefs not just in a gross general way, but intricately and precisely."[38] This is exactly the relation *The Wide, Wide World* has to the living-scenario adumbrated in the philsosophy of disciplinary intimacy: proof that the world this novel knows and speaks is by no means only the (in her formulation apparently universal) mid-nineteenth-century American evangelicalism that Tompkins has nominated as its cultural context, but the quite particular middle-class world (evangelical Protestantism was one of its constituents) that coalesced around this socializing strategy in the antebellum years. The suspicion that *The Wide, Wide World*'s intricate reflection of this culture's patterning of experience was a source of this book's *popularity* is supported by another case. The ultimate mass-circulation novel of the 1850s, the book that far exceeded the circulation records set by Warner's novel a year before, is *Uncle Tom's Cabin* (1852). And *Uncle Tom's Cabin* is the book that deploys the disciplinary conceptions I have been discussing with greatest profundity and force.

Uncle Tom's Cabin is the great literary version of the antebellum meditation on corporal correction. Stowe claimed that her novel originated in a vision she suffered of a gentle slave being flogged to death.[39] And throughout her novel the act of whipping, never far offstage, reverberates with peculiar power. Little Eva dies of sensitivity to the horror of slavery; and the particular horror said to "sink into [Eva's] heart"[40] is the death through overdiscipline of Prue, the mother who had been made destitute of offspring by slavery's exploitations and who has been so harshly corrected for her grief that "her back's a far sight now,—she can't never get a dress together over it" (321). Simon Legree, locus of the evil of slavery in its most monstrous form, is made monstrous particularly

through his identification with physical correction: Legree's human mark is his strong (and obscenely physical) fist, the fist that
he boasts "has got as hard as iron *knocking down niggers*" (483).
And Tom's battle against the earthly power embodied in Legree is
imagined as a battle, specifically, over corporal punishment: Tom
triumphantly dies for his refusal to obey Legree's command that
Tom assume the office of the whip, flogging the slaves Legree finds
weak and underproductive.

As she raises corporal punishment to this pitch of moral inten-
sity, Stowe also strongly conjoins this correction system with that
other system which peculiarly courts the corporal as its defining
opposite. One of this novel's notable narrative features is its redun-
dant use of inset tales to underline points made in the main plot.
(Stowe's narrative motto is the Victorian schoolmaster's: "twenty
repetitions for the bright child.") In the Kentucky chapters of her
book, Stowe's insets are all tales of the breaking of families. But in
a notable departure the exemplary insets of the long middle sec-
tion set in New Orleans become increasingly composed of tales of
discipline in slavery. The pattern of these episodes is to have slavery demonstrate the irreparable failings of its disciplinary system,
only to have these apparently insuperable difficulties transcended
by conversion to the discipline of middle-class domesticity. Augustine St. Clare tells Miss Ophelia the story of Scipio, "a regular
African lion" (345) of such force and pride that he could not
be broken to the slave's subjection. Certified as incorrigible by
St. Clare's brother Alfred, the harsh physical disciplinarian who is
their father's son, Scipio is handed over to St. Clare. St. Clare then
attempts another method: he *mothers* the slave Alfred whips: "I
took him to my own room, had a good bed made for him, dressed
his wounds, and tended him myself." And when he has nursed
Scipio in this tender way, "in one fortnight I had him tamed
down as submissive and tractible as heart could desire" (346). In
another chapter, Alfred St. Clare's son Henrique whips his boy-
slave Dodo for a slight provocation, "forc[ing] him on to his knees,
and beat[ing] him til he was out of breath" (388). St. Clare and
Alfred, looking on, are quick to read the general evil this episode
reveals. They discuss how, through its transferring of burdens to

others, the slave system rears its own children in systematic self-indulgence; then how the proximity of this lax discipline to the harsh discipline used for slaves leads the master class to exercise its self-indulgence through petulant use of the whip.[41] But this systemic failing of slavery—this time the failure it entails in the disciplining of the masters—again prepares for an exhibition of another way. Whipping is "the only way to manage" slaves, Henrique assures Eva (389). But Eva, intuiting that Dodo's problem is that he "had been only a few months away from his mother," extends him "a kind word, kindly spoken" (390); and she thereby wins command of Dodo as Henrique cannot.

The great instance of this pattern, and altogether one of Stowe's great narrative inventions, is the drama centrally placed in *Uncle Tom's Cabin* involving the training of Topsy. Topsy is Stowe's version of the wild child, a monster on whose nature nurture will never stick. She is also, readers forget but Stowe always remembers, a battered child: St. Clare purchases her from "a couple of drunken creatures that keep a low restaurant" because he is "tired of hearing her screaming, and them beating and swearing at her" (354). St. Clare gives Topsy to his moralistic and efficiency-minded aunt Miss Ophelia as an object lesson in disciplinary science. Stowe, like Warner in this respect, knows Miss Ophelia's disciplinary format as having a specific cultural origin and history. Hers are the "set and definite" educational ideas "that prevailed in New England a century ago, and which are still preserved in some very retired and unsophisticated parts, where there are no railroads" (they were also preserved, as Horace Mann learned, in the unmodernized Boston schools): "to teach [children] to mind when they are spoken to; to teach them the catechism, sewing, and reading; and to whip them if they told lies" (357). Ophelia brings energy and conviction to her mission of carrying "real" education into the benighted South, but her old-fashioned Northern discipline effects no change in Topsy. In the realm of domestic arts she can teach Topsy to do anything, but she cannot make her keep doing things the right way of her own accord. In the moral realm she can exact compliance, but she cannot make Topsy understand or feel the principle that ought to have commanded compliance:

Topsy will confess to her thieveries whenever ordered, whether she has done them or not (361). Tired of unmade beds, petty larcenies, untrue confessions, and unchecked spirits, Ophelia quickly reaches her last resource: "I don't see how I'm going to manage that child, without whipping her," she tells St. Clare (362). But he reminds her that this apparent last resort has already been tried and failed: "I've seen this child whipped with a poker, knocked down with the shovel or tongs, whichever came handiest, &c.; and, seeing that she is used to that style of operation, I think your whippings will have to be pretty energetic, to make much impression" (363).

The moment when the issue of Topsy reaches this impasse is a moment of great power in *Uncle Tom's Cabin*. This power derives from the fact that Stowe here presses through any kind of prefabricated critique of slavery to grasp deep problems of discipline itself. Topsy is a slave child, and her wildness, like Henrique's sadism, exhibits the limits of Southern slavery as a system in which to rear children. But Topsy is here made to embody not just the slave child but really *the* child, as the paradigmatic case of the disciplinary object, and so too the problem discipline faces in the child or in any of its objects: the problem of unmotivatedness, of another's lack of inward disposition toward what one knows as the right way. Ophelia is an old-style Northern educator going to work on a Southern charge, but the image of Ophelia teaching her perfectly unmotivated pupil bares, in similar way, the underlying logic of any disciplinary transaction. It reveals discipline as someone's attempt to make someone else do what he does not want to do, someone's attempt to make someone else obey an authority he only imperfectly recognizes. And her recourse in distress, the whip, appears not as a Southern or a now-old-fashioned Northern practice alone but as the means of compliance any and every disciplinary system must fall back on to the extent that it cannot make its authority felt inside of the subject: the authority of force, of moral superiority expressed on a less powerful other as superiority of physical power alone.

At this juncture, when the slave and child has revealed herself as incorrigible, and when the teacher or parent-surrogate is on the verge (in the name of her moral mission) of reinventing slavery itself, or at least slavery's rule by the lash; at this juncture, when the ultimate question of disciplinary ethics—"What is to be done with a human being that can be governed only with the lash?" (363)—has been brought up from the depths, but found unanswerable by any lights yet available; this is the place where Stowe mounts her grand exhibition of the magic of discipline through love, presented as that which transcends the difficulties that both Southern and premodern Northern disciplines find terminal. Little Eva is a child, but she bears a mother's name. Confronted with Ophelia's incurable case, Eva rediagnoses Topsy as suffering from a deficiency not primarily of regulatory faculty but first of all of love. Topsy, product of a speculator who has female slaves impregnated so that he can sell their issue, has had a biological mother, but is unmothered in a social and psychological sense. She has never known herself as the object of someone's maternal affection, she has never known herself as someone's child (hence her theory of her nonhuman origin: "I spect I grow'd" [356]); and in the orthodox philosphy of domesticity that prevails in *Uncle Tom's Cabin,* her lack of the experience of having her life from a loving other is what renders her without the facilities for taking social authority up inside herself. Diagnosing Topsy's maternity deficiency, Eva offers her the flow of affection and the primitive tactile *sign* of affection withheld from Topsy in her faultily constructed origin: "'O, Topsy, poor child, I love you,' said Eva with a sudden burst of feeling, and laying her little thin, white hand on Topsy's shoulder; 'I love you, because you haven't had any father, or mother, or friends;—because you've been a poor, abused child!'" Good mother-surrogate that she is, Eva not only casts her love around Topsy but infuses that love with moral expectation. "I love you, and I want you to be good," she continues; "I wish you would try to be good, for my sake" (409). And by orienting Topsy toward her, by supplying Topsy with a previously missing origin in her affection, Eva instantly succeeds in getting Topsy to internalize such expectations as an inwardly felt obligation. Touched by Eva's love and so penetrated by Eva's moral vision, Topsy at once begins "trying to be a good girl" (415). When Ophelia, humanized out of her moral abstraction by the grief of Eva's death, in turn learns both to love Topsy and (in love) to touch her, she too "from that hour . . . acquired an influence over the mind of the destitute child that she never lost" (432).

In this central scene of *Uncle Tom's Cabin* the plan of discipline through love emerges from the ruins of its cultural rivals as a kind of miraculous transcendence of their apparently inevitable limits. Corporal correction in all of its still-visible forms is summoned to the task of demonstrating the glory and necessity of this softer yet surer correction. A loving discipline again advertises its superiority by dramatizing its ability to render the whip unnecessary to the authorities, and so to rescue children from physical abuse. (Isn't Topsy the classic version of the battered child who energized Mann's and Bushnell's disciplinary discourse?)

But if it shows the justificatory logic of disciplinary intimacy in all its glory, Stowe's work perhaps more than any other also shows the somewhat grimmer implications this system has had built into it all along. No champion of discipline through love makes love a more loving force than Stowe does. And Stowe for one gives real thought to the question of how this magical agent performs its appointed office: in the Topsy story she meditates with considerable subtlety on the way early parental love initiates the child into a world of other-directedness, and in that sense begins the socialization of identity that is this system's real concern. But Stowe's scene of disciplinary magic also makes plain the sheer emotional manipulation this system mandates in practice. Eva's caritas is shot through with hypochondriac self-regard; Eva makes Topsy's obedience nominally a tribute to God and the Good, but really a means to keep the mother figure in a fragilely maintained "good state": "I am very unwell, Topsy, and I think I shan't live a great while; and it really grieves me, to have you be so naughty" (409), is her extension of the phrase "I want you to be good." This line looks back directly to Mrs. Montgomery's disciplinary motto in *The Wide, Wide World:* be good or I'll get sicker and die. From even further back, it recalls the reams of advice that antebellum domestic manuals give parents to discipline their children with such sayings as: "Do you not know that I toil, from day to day, to provide things for you? Is it *kind* in you, then, to do any thing that will make me *feel bad* when I come home?"[42] Taken together such evidence strongly suggests that when the rod gets laid aside in nineteenth-century domesticity, it is because it is no longer needed in the disciplinary arsenal, having been replaced by psychological weapons with new orders of coercive power.

Similarly, of the authors studied here, Stowe has the strongest sense of the subjection that bad discipline involves. The bodily coercion and the resultant impairment of human selfhood that the party of love always sees in corporal discipline are *realized* by Stowe in an unparalleled way. But she also shows how something not wholly unlike slavery gets entailed by the disciplinary process she prescribes. Ophelia causes St. Clare to set Topsy free, but Topsy escapes from St. Clare's lifelong ownership only to fall under Eva and Miss Ophelia's lifelong "influence," where she becomes not herself but the "good" self they have invented for her.[43] This is no freak: rather, it realizes the ultimate implication of disciplinary intimacy itself. When celebrations of this way reach a certain pitch they invariably begin implying that love's beauty, as a disciplinary force, is that it creates a more thorough order of subjugation. In praising maternal love over old-style paternal force, the upstate New York *Mother's Magazine* says: "These silken threads are harder to burst than the iron chains of authority." In his "Reply to the 'Remarks' of Thirty-One Boston Schoolmasters," Horace Mann says of his model disciplinarian Captain Maconochie, governor of the twice-transported criminals of Norfolk Island: "He struck off the iron shackles and fetters of the convicts, and replaced them with the stronger bonds of sympathy and confidence." "The parent or teacher should, *first of all,* secure the LOVE and AFFECTION of his children or pupils," Lyman Cobb writes in *Corporal Punishment in Families and Schools;* then he adds: "He will then have an *unlimited* control over their minds and conduct."[44] Emancipated and morally reclaimed, Topsy shows that the loving discipline of middle-class domesticity gives new modes of freedom to its charges, but not without delimiting their freedom in other ways. She shows how middle-class governance releases its citizens from the harsh external authoritarianisms of previous regimes—an extraordinary achievement, in history as in this book. But she shows that this order effects this release by committing its citizens to a training that makes authority a constituent of identity, and so makes the self the governor of the self.

IV

The novels we have considered tell us that so far from being a world elsewhere, American literature in its antebellum phase was deeply embroiled in cultural projects. They show that literature was another venue in which the problems set by middle-class disciplinary theory were worked through, was even (as in *Uncle Tom's Cabin*) a chief medium through which that theory was vindicated and broadcast. But the sheer massiveness of the evidence assembled here will by now have altered the question we put to it. Given the interinvolvement of fiction and disciplinary theory that we have seen, by now we must want to ask: How does this interinvolvement arise? How does it come that American fiction should have middle-class disciplinary thought (of all developments) as its main cultural connection in this phase of its life? And how does it happen that literature is so pervious to this context at this particular time?

A body of recent criticism that sees the novel becoming a disciplinary institution in the nineteenth century could offer one answer to these questions. Noting the fact that the novel's coming to hegemony as a literary form coincides with the rise of less overt yet more tightly webbed regulatory technologies in the realm of social policing, D. A. Miller and others have suggested that the novel itself, in its classic period, became a link in what Foucault calls the disciplinary archipelago, another agency in the world of proliferating agencies functioning at once to bring the body of ordinary experience to visibility and to think it into a normative order.[45] A reading like Miller's would help us to the thought that postcorporal discipline is the antebellum novel's subject because postcorporal discipline has become that novel's function; but how this functionality arose would still remain unclear. Unless one assumes either a Power of discipline so omnipotent that no cultural

institution could resist enlistment in its service or a novel so pro-
miscuous that it gives itself to whatever force solicits it, then every
disciplinary conjunction that we find in literary history poses a
further historical question: by what process literature has been
gathered into that cultural configuration? This is the question I
would put to the antebellum American case.

If we ask again how the distinctive disciplinary agendas of one
American social formation came so generally to infiltrate antebellum literary writing, part of the answer would be that the producers of that writing came out of that formation in a disproportionate
way. Stowe emerges to authorship quite directly from the milieu
that evolved the assertions of disciplinary intimacy. The sister of
an important domestic pedagogue (Catherine Beecher) and the
wife of an important publicist of school-reform models (Calvin
Stowe reported on the public school movement's admired Prussian
schools six years before Horace and Mary Peabody Mann toured
those schools on their honeymoon), Stowe herself ran a home and
taught a school while writing *Uncle Tom's Cabin*. Catharine Sedgwick—whose bestseller *Home* is both a literary fiction and a book
of domestic instruction, and who was regularly involved with
the Stowes, Beechers, and Manns in school board activities—is
one of many women writers of this time who mounted careers
as popular authors with the domestic-tutelary complex as their
base.[46] And this grounding was not reserved for scribbling women.
Hawthorne, still too often conceived of as a child of the Puritans
or a squinter at Transcendental pieties, had this formation as his
lived social world. Brother-in-law of the Manns and Elizabeth
Peabody, Hawthorne was a conscientious citizen of the new world
of middle-class domesticity—as witnessed by his notebook's absorption with his children's domestic discipline, or his censure of
the Manns for being insufficiently home centered.[47]

These particular careers bespeak the opening of a way into literature from a newly emerging social sector defined by the domestic and teaching practices we have described. This restructuring of
literary access finds its explanation, in turn, in the repositioning of
literature as a cultural category in the antebellum years. The great
fact of antebellum literary history considered as the history of lit-

M-C primarily readers of novels

erature's life in the world is the abrupt and quite extraordinary
enlargement of the American literary market at this time. The figures are well known: the book publishing industry did $2.5 mil-
lion worth of business in the 1820s, but $12.5 million worth in the
1850s; around one hundred novels were published by Americans
in the 1820s, but one thousand were printed in the 1840s; successful novels might sell five or six thousand copies in the 1820s,
but in the 1850s they regularly sold sixty, eighty, or even a hundred thousand copies in a year.[48] While the demographics of readership are notoriously hard to establish, and while novel reading
was surely not delimited to any one American group, the available
evidence suggests that this enlargement of the public for literature
was not undifferentiated but strongly centered in the domestically
defined middle classes. From the vantage of her survey of antebellum book reviews, Nina Baym asks who read novels in the
mid-nineteenth century and replies, "everybody"; but since her
evidence links reading particularly to women and children housed
in domestic privacy, this must mean principally "everybody" as
middle-class life produced that category.[49] It is scarcely an exag-
geration to say that the new periodicals that flourished in America
after 1840—*Godey's Ladies Book, The Home Journal, Arthur's Home
Magazine, Peterson's National Ladies' Magazine*—gained audiences
in proportion as they identified themselves with the home in the
middle-class formation of that term. As the cases of Warner and
Stowe show, mid-century American novels won "mass" markets
precisely to the extent that represented this class's understanding
of the world.

Rather than universally increasing, then, the market history of
the 1840s shows literature augmenting its audience principally
within one audience sector. And what lies behind this development is the newly formed middle class's creation of a newly central
place *for* literature among its organizing habits and concerns. The
1830s domestic manuals show just this development: for a notable
fact about these manuals is that the same books that propagate the
figure of the home as an enclosed zone of domestic leisure, con-
secrated to the creation of character through loving nurture, also
specify *reading* as the home's other principal activity. Sedgwick's

Home puts an exemplary disciplinary incident in its second chapter, so important is the instilling of self-government to the home's *work* as she conceives it. But her first chapter narrates the assembling of the ingredients by which the home is constituted in the first place—and in this account the family's books (made visible in its conspicuous bookcase) are listed with its first priorities. Lydia Maria Child, concerned to tell imperfectly initiated mothers how to create just that domestic atmosphere in which the characters of children will be rightly formed (Child assumes such nurture will be the mother's whole concern), makes it one of her chief instructions that the books of the family be carefully chosen—and so sets reading as the nurture-centered home's chief pastime, gathering point, and instrument of domestic instruction.

The same social developments that promoted the idea of discipline through love as the family's essential work also recreated reading as a family pastime of first resort. The same developments that made the enclosed family the preferred agent and scene of discipline also made a new place for literature—or at least its most publicly accessible form, the novel—as "in some sort a member of the family."[50] And it is this historically particular process of cultural conjunction, I would argue, that lies behind antebellum fiction's disciplinary thematics. Prose fiction was singularly open to middle-class disciplinary imaginings at this time not because "The Disciplinary" was everywhere (paranoid allegorical fantasy!) but because of the way fiction's position as a cultural category was configured at that moment. After a different social formation had institutionalized support for a nonpopular or "serious" literary culture in America a decade or two later, novelists had to engage the quite different matrix of values—not mother love, not anticorporalism, but cosmopolitanism, secular urbanity, the sacralization of high culture, the canonical presentation of artistic value—that this other grounding conjoined with the literary realm.[51] Novelists of an earlier moment are engaged with the notions of disciplinary intimacy because their work's place is established primarily inside the world those notions defined.

If we think of the novel as being taken up inside a certain formation of family life in the early nineteenth century—if we see the

novel being placed as another of those adjacent institutions (like
the public school) that the middle-class family recruited in support
of its home-centered functions—then a last question will present
itself: namely, What was it about the novel of all forms or pastimes
that qualified it to fill this cultural position?[52] And might not the
answer lie in the way novel reading replicates the central experience this social formation is founded on? Nina Baym tells us that
the great word for novels among antebellum readers is "absorbing."[53] A novel, in other words, is something to "get into": like the
parent-child bond of middle-class disciplinary theory, the novel
opens up a world-within-a-world with the power to enclose the
reader within its projected horizons. The nature of this world
in both cases is that it brings desires to intensified expression: it
is deeply involving, "absorbingly interesting." Like the normative
mother, the novel shapes the participations it arouses into a peculiar intimacy: it sponsors an intensely private relation that is still a
relation, a going-out of oneself into intersubjective space (though
in both cases that "mutual" space is really contrived by someone
else). *And like* the mother's, the novel's intimacy is a tool for in-
forming its "partner's" mind: since the power of an "absorbing"
novel is the power to transpose its orderings into its reader's felt
understanding through an invisible persuasion.

Whether such a theory governed—or merely excused—the real
act of novel reading in the nineteenth-century domestic context
we are not likely to be able to learn. But a theory analogizing
reading to the nurture scheme of disciplinary intimacy certainly
marks the novels that antebellum culture made popular. In Stowe's
prototype for entertainment as cultural action, Little Eva does not
merely die but makes a scene of her death. Through this representational labor she opens up a space that both enables and actively
solicits deep emotional participation. Their love for this mother-
surrogate (and the fact that they are going to lose her) is what Eva's
spectacle makes its audience feel; and it is through her maximiza-
tion of these feelings that she implants her monitions in their souls
as inwardly felt commands. *The Wide, Wide World* holds to an older
attitude that sees novel reading as morally perilous, but isn't what
Stowe images the sort of experience this novel actually offers? *The*

Wide, Wide World represents Ellen's progress toward perfect inter-nalization as a psychological manipulation promoted by one his-torically contingent contemporary culture *and* as a progress to holiness and saving grace. In the first of these aspects the book seems to know just how "we feel" as subjects of disciplinary inti-macy, indeed it brings those feelings to a high pitch of outrage and grief. But the interest it thus excites is the means by which the book involves us in its representation of *this same* disciplinary structure as sacredly founded and morally immitigable: it works such beliefs *in* us, in Bushnell's words, through the feeling it calls forth *from* us. Sum

Reconsiderations of antebellum domestic fiction have already closed down into debates about whether such books promote or subvert domestic ideology, subjugate or empower their (presum-edly female) reader.[54] But we do not grasp the nature of their lit-erary action until we see that these opposed functions are not just mixed but functionally cooperative in these books: that they not only free up wayward feeling *and* inscribe authority in the reader but inscribe authority by way of the feeling they invite. This char-acteristic textual action, in turn, is what most profoundly links such books to their culture of origin. As we now know, in the nineteenth century bodily correction was made odious through the articulation of another correctional model that made warmly embracing parental love the preferred instrument for authority's exercise. If the culture that formed around this model also made a place for the novel in its midst, we can surmise in conclusion, it was because the novel offered endlessly to renew its primal trans-action: the transaction by which a near one opens a world of sym-pathy and through that act carries authority deep inside. The novel became "in some sense a member of the family" in America *when* and *as* corporal correction became the family's special aversion. It gained this new home on this specification of its function: that it become another monitory intimate, another agent of discipline through love.

CHAPTER
2

Veiled Ladies
Toward a History of
Antebellum Entertainment

WHEN SHE IS NOT at Blithedale, the Priscilla of Hawthorne's *The Blithedale Romance* has a career. She makes public appearances as the Veiled Lady: clothed in a silvery white veil, which purportedly insulates her from terrestrial reality, she goes onstage as a human conduit to occult knowledge, giving sibylline answers to the questions her audience puts. Hawthorne, we know, felt a final dissatisfaction with this figure of his creation. When *Blithedale* was finished but unnamed, he considered "The Veiled Lady" as a possible title for the book but ruled that "I do not wish to give prominence to that feature of the Romance."[1] But would he or no, prominence is just what *Blithedale* gives the Veiled Lady. The book begins with Miles Coverdale "returning to my bachelor-apartments" from "the wonderful exhibition of the Veiled Lady."[2] Its plot machinations—unusually intricate for a Hawthorne novel— all turn on moves to rescue Priscilla from or to reimprison her in her onstage role. And if any figure in *Blithedale* might be said to be figurally belabored, it is the Veiled Lady, this book's prime site of symbolic overdevelopment. The question I want to put in this chapter is what, historically, is on Hawthorne's mind when he writes *Blithedale* (1851–52), and by extension, what cultural situation would a novelist have had to address at this moment of American literary history. I begin with the Veiled Lady on the assumption that she embodies answers to questions of this sort.

48

What cultural history could Hawthorne's Veiled Lady stand for? She is "a phenomenon in the mesmeric line" (5), and she has as her most obvious referent the "magnetized" subjects used by the importers of mesmeric lore—Charles Polen and his many imitators—to demonstrate theories of animal magnetism to American publics after 1836. (In her clairvoyance the Veiled Lady is meant specifically to demonstrate the supermagnetized state that Mesmer's follower the Marquis de Puysegur termed "extraordinary lucity.")[3] More generally the Veiled Lady images, as a salience of contemporary life, the cultural attraction of what *Blithedale* calls "new science[s]" (5), that congeries of systems—Swedenborgianism, phrenology, utopian socialism, and Grahamite dietary lore are other examples—that developed into something between fad philosophies and surrogate religions in the American 1840s. Grouped as she is with Hollingsworth, Zenobia, and the Blithedalers, Priscilla shows such new sciences as literally living together with many other social movements of comparably recent birth: penal reform, the women's rights movement, communitarianism, and so on. In this sense this exhibit of the "new truths" of mesmerism appears as one manifestation of the variously directed energy of social and intellectual reconstruction that touched almost all aspects of American culture in the 1840s, known by the generic label *reform.*

But history teaches us that the hectic innovations of antebellum reform developed alongside the establishment of new forms of social normality in America, in particular the normalization of the nineteenth-century model of middle-class domestic life; and Hawthorne's Veiled Lady is figuratively implicated in this development quite as much as in the history of reform. Priscilla is a woman, but the Veiled Lady is a presentation or representation of a woman; and the representation that the Veiled Lady embodies intricately reflects the representation of "woman" in the domestic ideology of Hawthorne's time. The Veiled Lady is a lady, but in being *veiled* she is made into a lady who does not appear in public. As such she images woman being publicly created into a creature of private space, a native of that separate nonpublic, nonproductive zone marked off in nineteenth-century ideology as the home or wom-

an's sphere. Bred in a "little room," her existence has been circumscribed in such a way that extradomestic space has become
terrifyingly alien to her: "The sense of vast, undefined space, pressing from the outside against the black panes of our uncurtained
windows, was fearful to the poor girl, heretofore accustomed to
the narrowness of human limits" (36), Hawthorne writes, in a
perfect description of the agoraphobia that Gillian Brown has presented as the psychological equivalent of middle class women's domestic enclosure.[4]

As it erases her as a public figure, the Veiled Lady's veil specifically puts her body out of sight, or paradoxically makes her appear
without a body. In this sense the Veiled Lady might be called a
figure for the disembodiment of women in nineteenth-century domesticity, that is, for the construction of "woman" as something
separate from or opposed to bodily life and force. "Wan, almost
sickly" of complexion, her brown hair falling "not in curls but
with only a slight wave" (27), possessed (in the emphatically un-
disembodied Zenobia's contemptuous term) of "hardly any phy-
sique" (34), Priscilla's carefully noted body type minutely reflects
the one that (as Lois Banner has shown) was normalized as a feminine ideal in America in the antebellum decades, that pallid, fragile, unvoluptuous, unrobust physical type that realized, at the
bodily level, a social model of domestic leisure and feminine un-
productiveness.[5] (In Priscilla's "tremulous nerves"—a sensitivity
so overdeveloped as to render her liable to regular collapses of
spirits and strength—Hawthorne describes the neurasthenia that
is the medical signature of this social type.)

When she is veiled, this woman, already strongly repressed at
the level of physical life, loses her physicality altogether and becomes what woman most essentially is in the nineteenth-century
domestic conception: the embodiment of spiritual forces. Augustine St. Clare's mother in *Uncle Tom's Cabin*—the ideal woman as
dreamt by the cult of domesticity (Little Eva ·is her reincarna-
tion)—is so fully identified with spirit that St. Clare can say of her:
"*She* was *divine!* She was a direct embodiment and personification
of the New Testament."[6] Produced as she is, the Veiled Lady too
can be said to be "in communion with the spiritual world," indeed

to "behold the Absolute!" (201). The "tremulous nerves" that are the sign of her physical devitalization confer on her at least the appearance of spiritual privilege, or in the book's locution, "endow her with Sibylline attributes" (2). Similarly, the veil that bounds her off from public and physical life is (or is at least said to be) what *creates* her as spiritual being: by "insulat[ing] her from the material world," this mark of delimitation "endow[s] her with many of the privileges of a disembodied spirit" (6).

The figure of the Veiled Lady may originate in the history of American cult movements and pseudosciences, I am suggesting, but this figure is not readable wholly in terms of such movements. In the terms of her constitution she precisely reflects another development just as much a part of *Blithedale's* historical moment as mesmeric exhibits or communitarian experiments: the cultural construction of a certain version of "woman," and of the whole set of social arrangements built upon this figure of domestic life. This, much more than mesmerism or even reform, is the real subject of historical meditation in the Veiled Lady portions of *Blithedale.* Yet what is most interesting about the Veiled Lady is that this personification of woman domestically defined is in no sense domestic. Produced as a creature of physical invisibility, the Veiled Lady nevertheless leads a life of pure exhibitionism. Rendered an insular or private spirit, her sphere is nevertheless always the public sphere, and her work is not to make a home but to "come before the public" (1) on the most spectacular of terms. In this respect she challenges us to find a rather different historical meaning for her than any we have established thus far.

The Veiled Lady is most essentially an image of woman as public performer; and if we insisted on reading this image as historically based, she could help us to the realization that the same period already known to us as the decade of reform and of the establishment of a more privatized and leisured model of middle-class domesticity could also be described as the time of the emergence of some women—specifically women in the entertainment sector—to an exaggeratedly public life.[7] Behind the Veiled Lady we could see arrayed the new female celebrities who, first in the 1840s, then more decisively around 1850, began to appear before newly huge audiences and to be *known* to publics much greater yet. Mesmerism did not produce a female celebrity of this order. But as a "name" attraction the Veiled Lady could find her likeness in Fanny Elssler, the Viennese dancer who made a triumphal tour of America in 1841. Or she could find her likeness in Jenny Lind, whose American tour exactly at *Blithedale's* moment of composition—Lind concluded her eighteen months of concerts in May 1852, the month *Blithedale* was completed—consolidated enduring patterns of American mass-cultural stardom: the road tour with entourage, the mobbing of the star's vehicle and the surrounding of her hotel, the conversion of ticket acquisition into a high public drama (tickets to Jenny Lind's concerts were auctioned off at newsworthy prices), the exposure of the well-guarded star in carefully arranged public appearances. (When she came before the public, Lind too was dressed in white.) [8]

The Veiled Lady might also find her likeness in another group of entertainers who emerged into mass visibility at just the same time: the women novelists who attained to a new degree of popularity right at *The Blithedale Romance's* moment. The scale of the American market for literary goods, we know, expanded abruptly at this time. As the previous chapter noted, where a "decided hit" might have sold five or six thousand copies in America heretofore, around 1850, books like Susan Warner's *The Wide, Wide World* and Maria Cummins's *The Lamplighter* (1854) began to sell tens (and in the case of *Uncle Tom's Cabin,* hundreds) of thousands of copies. Born together with this new scale of circulation was a new kind of publicity that broadcasted such authors' wares *as* popular, proclaiming them the object of insatiable and universal demand: the literary publicity campaign that seized on the mass medium of journalism to announce the staggering sales record of a newly published book was pioneered by the printer of *Uncle Tom's Cabin* in *Blithedale's* year, and became industry standard almost at once. [9] As the focus of these developments, the new best-selling writers of the early 1850s found audiences and became names on terms quite similar to Jenny Lind's. Ruth Hall, the successful author-hero of Fanny Fern's book of that name (1855), has a steamship named after her, as a suitable tribute to (and advertisement of) her popular fame. Fern herself had a railroad parlor car named in her honor, among other trumpetings of her name. When *Uncle Tom's Cabin* was published in 1852, Stowe became, exactly, a celebrity. Visiting New York after completing the novel, Stowe got into one of Lind's last concerts—long since sold out—*as* a celebrity, by being recognized as the famous Harriet Beecher Stowe. Her English tour of 1853 recapitulated the Lind tour with a writer in the singer's place. Stowe drew her own dockside crowds, had her own travel plans publicly announced, packed her own halls, appeared before audience after audience as her celebrated self: that is, she found a career, like Lind or like the Veiled Lady, as a famous object of public attention.[10]

Such likenesses suggest that what lies behind *Blithedale* is a development specific to the history of entertainment quite as much as any development in general social life. What the Veiled Lady registers, we might say, is the historical emergence, at midcentury, of a more massively *publicized* order of entertainment in America. She images a remaking of the social organization of entertainment by which artistic performance (broadly understood) came to reach larger and more stabilized mass publics, and by which participation *in* performance came to yield enlarged public visibility, to women above all. Or, to draw the many sides of this figure together, we might say that the Veiled Lady registers the creation of a newly publicized world of popular entertainment taking place simultaneously with the creation of a newly privatized world of woman's domestic life. She embodies the suggestion that the same contemporary cultural processes that worked in one direction to delimit women to dephysicalized and deactivated domestic privacy also helped open up an enlarged publicity that women could inhabit in the entertainment field—a suggestion rich in historical implication.

After all, the steep escalation of literary sales figures around 1850 must be understood to have reflected not only improved production factors like cheaper printing technologies or more active marketing campaigns, but quite as essentially the historical creation of a new social *place* or *need* for literary entertainment to fill. The mass-market novels of the 1850s address middle-class domes-

ticity because it was above all the institution of this social formation that created for literature its new mid-nineteenth-century
place. As the previous chapter showed, the canons of domestic
instruction that defined the home as a private, leisured, non-
materialistic, feminine space in the antebellum decades also and
with almost comparable insistence defined reading as a preferred
domestic activity. In consequence of this linkage, the implementa-
tion of this social model in the decades after 1830 had the second-
ary effect of enlarging the demand for reading for the home—and
so too of creating public roles for literary producers and public
attention for literary works.

The new popular women novelists whom the Veiled Lady images in part are the figures who most fully seized the public life
that domestic privacy helped to construct. As Mary Kelley has
shown, by using their own feminine domestic competence to address the domestic concerns that identified the new mass audience,
these women were able to escape from domestic confinement and
capture a new public role: the role of author. (But as Kelley also
notes, winning a transdomestic social place did not help such authors escape from domestic self-conceptions. Among other mani-
festations of this entrapment, they typically attained to public
identities without feeling entitled to assert themselves as public
creatures: hence their regular use of pseudonyms, the literary
equivalent of that highly public erasure of oneself in public embodied in the Veiled Lady's veil. "I have a perfect horror of appearing in print," Catharine Sedgwick wrote before the publication of
her first novel, echoing the Veiled Lady's terror of the public or
published domain. "We all concur in thinking that a lady should
be veiled in her first appearance before the public,"[11] Sedgwick's
brother Harry wrote at this time, in a sentiment *Blithedale*'s Professor Westervelt would share.) But the historical situation in which
writers like Elizabeth Wetherell, Fanny Fern, and Marion Har-
land—behind the veil, Susan Warner, Sara Willis Eldridge Parton,
and Mary Virginia Terhune—capitalized was, we need to remember, not theirs alone. They were only the most successful exploiters
of a cultural restructuring that affected the whole field of literary
writing, and adjacent entertainment fields as well. Accordingly, if

we find Hawthorne meditating on such public-private figures in the Veiled Lady of *Blithedale,* we need to understand that they embody for him not just new literary competition but the new social conditions of literary production under which he too finds himself working at this time: a situation in which artistic creation has had a potentially massive new public life created for it on the condition that it align itself with a certain structure of private life.

At this point it is important to acknowledge that the historical situation of the literary that *Blithedale* addresses cannot be understood from *Blithedale* alone. Most glaringly, Hawthorne shows no grasp of the enabling side of the publicity that he knows as new at this time. The Veiled Lady is a victim of her display. In celebrity she is only exploited. But her real historical sisters-in-celebrity won wealth, power, prestige, and a measure of independence from their performing careers. The saucy and independent-minded Fanny Fern—to cite the figure most antithetical to the droopy, dependent Priscilla—entered into a prenuptial contract giving her sole control of the property her royalties had amassed: a Priscilla who struck for such a deal would represent a revision indeed.[12] The successful author's gloating over the bank stock she owns at the end of *Ruth Hall* suggests a second possible attainment newly open to the woman-celebrity of this time: not just wealth but the pleasure that wealth brings as a mark of achievement and entitlement. (A Priscilla who took pleasure in performance or its rewards would be someone else.) The Veiled Lady displays no talent; her "performance" is a hoax of someone else's devising. But Lind sang, Elssler danced, E. D. E. N. Southworth and Stowe and Warner wrote, Fanny Fern spoke her piece: the opening that brought them publicity also expanded their field of *expression,* certainly not the least of their gains. Hawthorne is in no position to see this side of the contemporary picture, of which we must learn from other accounts. But partial though it is, *Blithedale* makes its most interesting sense as a reading of the new literary situation of its moment; and *Blithedale* has things to teach about this newly emerging order not easily learned from other sources.

To name a first: *Blithedale* reflects a world in which artistic performers, and preferentially women, have won a new capacity to

amass large audiences for themselves. But it also suggests that the
development that puts performance in this new relation to popularity installs it in other relations at the same time. The Veiled Lady
wins celebrity not by herself but through her bond to Professor
Westervelt. This "attraction" is one half of an entertainment part-
nership, the other member of which is her manager. As such this
figure brings back to our attention the mid-nineteenth-century female celebrity's typical dependence on a male handler to achieve
her public "life." P. T. Barnum was Jenny Lind's Westervelt. Che-
valier Wyckoff, who Barnum beat out for the right to manage
Jenny Lind, was Fanny Elssler's manager, or in Barnum's phrase,
the "speculator" who had Elssler "in charge." Fanny Fern and
E. D. E. N. Southworth found the eventual sustainer of their long-
lived popular success in Robert Bonner, publicist-publisher of the
New York Ledger. [13] At the bittersweet close of *Ruth Hall* the popular author Ruth stands at her husband's grave with her daughter
and the man in her new public/literary life, her publisher-agent
John Walter.

More than a manager, Westervelt is in the full sense of the term
the Veiled Lady's *producer*. Having contracted for the rights to
Priscilla as an entertainment property, he has made her *into* the
Veiled Lady, has created a public identity for her and created public
attraction *to* this identity—and he has done so not disinterestedly
but as a way to increase the take. In this respect *Blithedale* reminds
us that the handlers newly prominent in the popular entertainment of the time are really the sign of such entertainment's entrance into new relations to market forces. The Jenny Lind chapter
in Barnum's autobiography, *Struggles and Triumphs*—which spells
out the terms of the performer-manager contract that *Blithedale*'s
Fauntleroy chapter left vague—is fitly called "The Jenny Lind Enterprise." [14] In herself a woman, in Barnum's hands Jenny Lind
became a business venture, a singer made *into* Jenny Lind the musical wonder by Barnum's incessant promotional activities, to the
end of enriching them both. Similarly, the literary-historical meaning of the new mass-market novels of the 1850s is not just that
they were more popular than earlier books but that they mark a
historical change in the meaning of the word *popular*, a term

that now comes to denote not just "well-liked" or "widely-read" but specifically production *into* a certain market status through the commercial management of a book's public life. The new promotional campaigns mounted by the publishers of such works to an altogether new extent produced public demand for them, demand which was then republicized as a way of creating further demand. Publisher J. P. Jewett's early ad for *Uncle Tom's Cabin*—"TEN THOUSAND COPIES SOLD IN TWO WEEKS!"—or James Cephas Derby's hyping of *Fern Leaves from Fanny's Portfolio* (1853)—"FANNY FERN'S BOOK, 6,000 Copies Ordered in Advance of Publication!"— promoted these books *as popular,* and make their popularity the basis of their market identity.[15] Of course the publicity that made these books known to the public also made them into wares marketed to the public: it is not for nothing that we establish the popularity of such works by enumerating their sales.

In *Blithedale* the Veiled Lady's public life is managed toward commercial ends, but it is the particular nature of this management to be hard to see. A curious but persistent feature of narration in this book is that the many dramatically crucial scenes in which Priscilla's deployment as Veiled Lady is arranged or contested all take place off the narrative record. The Veiled Lady's performance thus opens the novel, except that it is finished just before Coverdale begins his tale. The scene in which Old Moodie then intercedes with Hollingsworth to take Priscilla to Blithedale occurs between chapters, so that we never learn what understanding he reached with Hollingsworth or what relation his act had to her career of display, though there is a later hint that her contract with Westervelt has just run out. The subsequent interview in which Westervelt by some means (blackmail?) talks Zenobia into returning Priscilla to his charge occurs before Coverdale's eyes, but out of his earshot. The scene of the Veiled Lady's recapture—the scene in which Zenobia lowers the veil back over Priscilla—is seen and heard but wholly misunderstood: "we thought it a very bright idea of Zenobia's, to bring her legend to so effective a conclusion" (116), Coverdale says of this reveiling, with even greater than usual obtuseness. A presumably contemporaneous scene in which Hollingsworth agrees to the plan to turn Priscilla over to Westervelt

("he bade me come" [171], Priscilla later states—but in consideration of what? Zenobia's offer of her fortune?) is missing altogether.
Later, Coverdale sees Priscilla through his hotel window in the
city, but he fails to see how she got there or where she is taken off
to next. In "The Village Hall" he sees her exhibited again, but she
is again produced out of nowhere; when Hollingsworth now in-
tervenes to rescue her from onstage life—for reasons we never see
him arrive at—he too takes her we know not where. Finally, when
Hollingsworth rejects Zenobia's schemes for Priscilla's and his life,
our man on the scene arrives a little late, and so succeeds in missing this decisive exchange.

Did ever a book miss so much of the story it purports to tell?
But this insistent narrative *missing*, usually thought merely inept,
is itself deeply interesting in the context I am considering. In its
narrative organization *Blithedale* constructs a zone in which highly
interested arrangements are made and remade around the figure
of a female entertainer, and it renders that zone at once controlling
of the apparent action and yet imperfectly available to knowledge.
In this respect the book might be said to image not just the management of high-visibility performance as commercial attraction
but the simultaneous effacement, in such entertainment, of the
interests and deals through which its public life is contrived. The
new popular entertainment of the mid-nineteenth century works,
in part, through just this cloaking of its business end. Barnum, an
apparent exception to this statement, made secret neither his role
in Jenny Lind's tour nor the terms of their commercial engagement. But even this most exhibitionistic or least *veiled* of publicists
erased a portion of his act. Barnum's publicity for Lind works by
creating the fascinating sense that she both is and is not his creation, that she is both the object of his shameless exploitation and
at the same time a self-directing agent beyond the reach of his
consumeristic wiles. But through its apparent frankness about its
own motives, such publicity conceals the extent to which Barnum
both manufactured the appearance of the "untouched" Jenny and
exploited that appearance as a marketing resource. The divinity
of "the divine Jenny" was essential to her appeal; but Barnum
helped establish her divine appearance, for example by arranging

for her to sing Handel oratorios. When Jenny Lind gave her concert proceeds to public charities, Barnum publicized her charitable-
ness and so made her yet more commercially valuable. In other
words, he arranged a commercial payoff by advertising her separation from commercial ends.

Fanny Fern's *Ruth Hall* provides a much more overt instance of
a popular entertainment that hides the commercial ground of its
generation. *Ruth Hall* tells of a contentedly domestic woman left
destitute by her husband's death and threatened with the loss of
her child until, in her darkest hour, she finds her way to the work
of writing. Against all odds, by dint of unforeseen talent and
strength of maternal will, Ruth establishes herself as a best-selling
author and literary celebrity (Fern prints sample fan mail), and is
at last able to reconstitute her broken family with the proceeds of
her literary success. This book tells one story of the relation of
women to writing; but that story keeps us from suspecting another
story quite different in character—the story of how Fern's own
book came to be written. Susan Geary has established that the
writing of *Ruth Hall* was first proposed not by Fern but by a publisher—Mason Brothers—eager to bring this profitable author into
its fold; that so far from winning its way to popularity by its irresistible strengths, the book was made popular through a highly
premeditated and unprecedentedly intricate advertising campaign;
and that so far from merely earning, after publication, the reward
her book deserved, Fern was moved to write the book by the terms
Mason Brothers offered "up front," not least their pledging, in the
language of their contract, "to use extraordinary exertions to promote the sale thereof, so as, if possible, to make it exceed the sale
of any previous work." [16]

Performance with this backstage: a veiled zone of contrivance
in which potential popular entertainments are dreamed up and
contracted for with an eye to their commercial profit; a zone in
which strategies are contrived to *make* the mass popularity no
longer allowed to just happen; a zone that allows itself to be
known to exist, indeed that shows its commercialism a little as part
of the glamorization of its product; but a zone that shuts the public
out from detailed knowledge of its motives or arts of contriv-

ance—*this* is show business as show business begins to exist in America at *Blithedale*'s historical moment. This recognition would help us to the further perception that the entertainment industry that is one of the most decisive identifying marks of the modern cultural order has its inception in America not in modernity but in the age of the so-called cult of domesticity, taking the literature produced for domestic consumption as one of its first sites of industrial development. But if it helps bring this little-recognized fact into sharpened focus, *Blithedale*'s most interesting historical suggestion is that the same restructuring of entertainment that produced these arrangements in the sphere of cultural production around 1850 produced corresponding novelties in the sphere of consumption: changes figured, I would suggest, in Miles Coverdale.

Coverdale and Priscilla are incongruous as lovers, but they constitute a couple in several related senses. Coverdale is, the book repeatedly suggests, the *man* who corresponds to Priscilla's version of the term *woman*. Imaged as Theodore in Zenobia's tale "The Silvery Veil," his prurient interest in yet insurmountable terror of female sexuality are read as the masculine by-products of the cultural construction that disacknowledges, or requires the veiling of, woman's erotic embodiedness. But in no less important a sense, Coverdale is also the spectator constituted by the Veiled Lady's version of spectacle. Passive in person, Priscilla only acts when she goes onstage, into a separate zone of spectacle marked off from its seated audience. Such a construction of *acting* finds its complement in someone else's passive, nonperforming *watching*, in short, in the Coverdalean habit of mind. The language of *Blithedale* urges us to give the word *observer*, as a term for Coverdale, the intensified sense of he who exists only in and as a watcher. "As if such were the proper barrier to be interposed between a character like hers, and a perceptive faculty like mine" (160), Coverdale huffs when Zenobia lowers the curtain on his peeping, his words baring his assumption that others are full persons and performers, but he a mental faculty only equipped to register their performances. "You are a poet—at least, as poets go, now-a-days—and must be allowed to make an opera-glass of your imagination, when you look at women" (170), Zenobia later mockingly retorts, correctly identifying Coverdale's relation as self or mind to the instrument used by spectators of nineteenth-century mass entertainments to enable them (just) to *see*. [17]

"Men of cold passions have quick eyes," Hawthorne writes in a remarkable notebook entry, by which I take him to mean: people who systematically deaden themselves at the level of primary drives arrange a surrogate life—contrive to be quick, not dead—in their sense of sight.[18] What makes Coverdale powerful as a description of the spectator is not just his self-delimitation to a visual self but the book's sense that eye-life has become his way of *having* life. In a moving passage, Coverdale speaks of "that quality of the intellect and heart, that impelled me (often against my will, and to the detriment of my comfort) to live in other lives" (160), and these words well explain what makes watching a compulsive or compulsory activity for him. Life as Coverdale understands it is not what he has or does but something presumed to be lodged in someone else. Watching that someone, inhabiting it through spectatorial self-projection and consuming it through visual appropriation, becomes accordingly a means to "live" *into his* life some part of that vitality that always first appears as "other life."

What the entertainments of the mid-nineteenth century did to the mass publics that consumed them, like all questions about the real history of literary reception, is something we cannot know without considerable aid from speculation. But there is good evidence to support *Blithedale*'s surmise that the formation of entertainment new in America at its time sponsored a Coverdalean mode of participation. All of the spectacles we have considered strongly reinforce the habit of motionlessly seeing. When Jenny Lind was touring America, Barnum had another crew scouring Ceylon for elephants and other natural wonders that, reimported and publicly displayed, became his other great enterprise of 1851, Barnum's Great Asiatic Caravan, Museum, and Menagerie—a show that opened a wonderworld to audiences willing to experience wonders in the passive or spectatorial mode.[19] (Barnum arranged for Lind to review the circus parade in New York City; in other words, to appear in public as an exemplary watcher.) The crowds that mobbed Stowe on her arrival in England were, in her words, "very much determined to look" at her: on this tour Stowe became at once a figure of fame and an object of visual consumption.[20] And what could the proliferation of novel reading at this time reflect if not a mass extension of habits of bodily deactivation and of the reconcentration of self into sight? The reader of every nineteenth century novel made him- or, more likely, herself a Coverdale to the extent that she conferred the status of "characters" on performatively generated others (Little Eva, Zenobia, Ruth Hall) while consigning herself to the category of perceptual faculty or *reader,* enterer into others through an action of the eye. Ellen Montgomery, the heroine of Susan Warner's *The Wide, Wide World,* begins the novel à la Coverdale, looking out the window: shut into a world of enclosed domestic idleness, she scans the space across its boundary for something for her eye to inhabit. When she enters the ideally constructed domesticity of the Humphreys household, she finds an object for this visual appetite in reading: in Warner's account, novels offer adventure via the eye for the residents of immobilized private space.

Quite as interestingly, there is abundant evidence that the form of mass entertainment new in America around 1850 held its audience in the position *of* audience by seeming to embody consumable "life." N. P. Willis's further-information-for-the-curious *Memoranda of the Life of Jenny Lind* (1851)—a book built on press releases supplied by Barnum, and so aimed to create the interest it pretended only to address—treats Lind as a public figure whose celebrity invites inescapable curiosity about her personal life. "The private life of Jenny Lind is a matter of universal inquisitiveness," Willis informs the reader in a chapter on her "Private Habits and Manners"; then, instructing us in how such inquisitiveness might be mounted and targeted, he muses on the love life of this great singer: "One wonders, as one looks upon her soft eyes, and her affectionate profusion of sunny hair, what Jenny's heart can be doing all this time. Is fame a substitute for the tender passion? She must have been desperately loved in her varied and bright path."[21] (The relation to Coverdale's speculations on Zenobia's sexual history or his urge to peep behind the petals of Priscilla's erotic bud will be clear at once.) Through such promotion Lind is made into a public embodiment of a fascinating private life, and her audience is invited to try to bring some fascination into its own life by consuming the public spectacle of hers: no wonder interested spectators actually invade this female performer's private dressing room in a Willis incident uncannily like *Blithedale*'s "Tale of Theodore."[22] *Ruth Hall* is as personal a work as the 1850s produced. It tells Fern/Parton's personal history of struggles and triumphs with a hot display of her personal loves and resentments (resentments above all against her brother, N. P. Willis, the villain of the piece.) But this book's intimacy of record was inseparable from its public or market life. What *Ruth Hall* offered its readers was the chance to "live" a public figure's "hidden," private life by buying and reading a book—and lest the public not be in on the opportunity for vicariousness the book embodied, Mason Brothers publicized its "obscure" personalness, running ads that tantalizingly asked: "IS *RUTH HALL* AUTOBIOGRAPHICAL?"[23] So it is that a buried commercial publicity operation, by producing the sense that a rare "life" lies veiled inside the most public of performances, could further its audience's disposition to seek "life" through the consumption of such performances, and so convert private men and women into a huge paying public: in other parlance, a Westervelt creates a Veiled Lady and thereby produces a Coverdale, and by extension a literary mass market as well.

The strategies by which "life" is made to seem available in consumable objects and experiences and the appetite *for* "life" is used to draw publics into stabilized bodies of consumer demand are as familiar as daily life itself in modern consumer culture. The products or productions that draw Coverdale by their apparent "surplus of vitality" (96) have their successors (to name no more) in the mass-circulation magazine that sold itself not as pictures to look at but as *Life;* or the soft drink that has offered not to quench our thirst but to help us "come alive"; or the car that, at this writing, is inviting us to buy it as a way to discharge our obligation (the ads quote Henry James) to "live all you can; it's a mistake not to."[24] One historical use of *The Blithedale Romance* is to take us back, if not to the origins, then at least to the early history of a social system held together by the public simulation of "life" as a marketing art and a private imperative to remedy deficiencies of "life" in one's life—a system, *Blithedale* tells us, that has its first large-scale social manifestation in the 1840s and 1850s, and that begins its operations in the entertainment sphere. But if the hunger for a "life" felt as alienated into other lives drives the man or woman of this time into spectatorial dependence on commercial entertainment, we might ask at this point, what gives rise to this driving sense of lack? *Blithedale's* answer, I take it, is privacy: that this need is a product *in* the self of a socio-historical construction of privacy as the self's living "world."

Quite as much as he is an observer, Coverdale is a figure of private life. The spaces he seeks out are always strongly bounded off from the public or collective realm: an apartment (the name itself equates dwelling space with separation); a hermitage; the single-family dwelling "just a little withdrawn" (80) that is this communitarian's dream of a utopian social space. At home in the private, Coverdale also carries the private within him as a structure of habitual understanding. The self, this character assumes, is "inviolate" only in the world of its "exclusive possession" (99): to live in the communal, by parallel assumption, is to have one's "individuality" (99) in continual danger of violation. Other characters claim the public—or the public *too*—as their proper theater of action; but when they do so Coverdale's privatizing mind instinctively reads back from their public assertion to the state of private or "individual affections" alleged to "cause" such assertion: "I could measure Zenobia's inward trouble, by the animosity with which she now took up the general quarrel of woman against man" is Coverdale's understanding of Zenobia's feminism (121). A privatized and privatizing mind, the privacy Coverdale embodies is defined not just through its cult of confinement within the "safe" private sphere but also through its attenuation of the erotic in private life—Coverdale's "apartment" is a "bachelor apartment"— and its exclusion of active, productive labor from the private world: Coverdale is the "idle" (247) or "half-occupied" man (133), his apartment the scene of "bewitching, enervating indolence" (19). This is to say that Coverdale represents a human self constructed upon the same social plan that we have seen imaged in the Veiled Lady: the nineteenth-century middle-class construction that locates the self's home or fulfilled state in the enclosed, physically attenuated, leisured, *private* world of domestic life.

But as the veil imprisons the lady condemned to wear it, so the social construction of the private that Coverdale embodies has the peculiarity of being at once desperately clung to and deeply self-impoverishing. Safe at home, his adventures in communitarianism now far behind him, Coverdale finds the private home a sheer emptiness: "Nothing, nothing, nothing" (245) is the weary tale his private life has been able to generate. And it would be easy to guess that what has established this home as a space of deficiency are the very acts of exclusion that established it in the first place. Having shut out the collective world, Coverdalean privacy has *made* itself the place of "loneliness" (70); having sealed itself in from the public, the overtly erotic, the productive, and the active, it has made those modes of life into an "other life" apart from itself and has replaced them, within itself, with a positive sense of their lack. Life in certain of its primary and potent forms, *Blithedale* says, is what the nineteenth-century cult of domesticity insists on not having *in* its life *and what it therefore also* hungers to repossess. At least as *Blithedale* figures it, this is why the contemporary structure of privacy imaged in Coverdale at once closes in on itself and builds, at the heart of private space, the means for a surrogate, spectatorial relation to the life it has put outside. Coverdale's hermitage functions at once to protect a self that feels inviolate only in private and to make that self a watcher, a spectatorial participant in Zenobia and Westervelt's richer intimacies. The private bedroom that shields Coverdale at Blithedale becomes, in its enclosure, an auditorium, a place to listen in on the "awful privacy" (39) of Hollingsworth's adjacent intimacy. The city apartment that guards Coverdale's privacy also drives him to seek entertainment by converting the world of others into a domestically viewable visual field[25]—and so leads him to become, at the moment when he is most fully *at home* in the book, first a reader of novels, then a viewer of the Veiled Lady being readied for the stage.

The Veiled Lady, I began by saying, images the constructions of a certain version of private life and a certain version of public spectacle as two sides of a single process. We are now in a position to say what the logic is that holds these two historical developments together. We could speculate that a more publicized and spectatorial entertainment order and a more leisured, privatized domestic model arose at the same time in America because it was the nature of that domestic model to create a *need for* such entertainment: a need for a now-foregone life to be made repossessable in a form compatible with the deactivations this new order prescribed. By learning how to aim its products toward this life-hunger, a new entertainment industry was able to mobilize domestic privacy as a mass-entertainment market. But that industry could insert itself in the domestic realm because it met needs produced by that realm: chief among them the need to acquire extradomestic life in the spectatorially consumable form of *other* or *represented* life.[26]

What I have been speculatively reconstructing here—with *Blithedale*'s aid because this history has not proved fully knowable without its aid—is the situation of literature in antebellum America, a matter that includes the histories of literary production and consumption but that is not wholly external to literature itself. Literary works, it might be worth insisting, do not produce their own occasions. They are always produced within some cultural situation of the literary, within the particular set of relations in which literature's place is at any moment socially determined. Literature's situation in America in the late 1840s and early 1850s was that it was being resituated: placed into the new and intertwined relations to publicity, to domestic privacy, to the commercial and the promotional, and to vicarious consumption that I have described here. When this change took place, writers could exploit its new structure of literary opportunity in various ways. What they could not do was to ignore the cultural conjunction it produced: they could not ignore it because it set the terms for their work's public life.

If we ask the long-postponed question of why this set of relations should be so much on Hawthorne's mind in *Blithedale*, then, the most forcible answer would be that they preoccupy him at this time because they define his own new literary situation. Hawthorne himself, after all, found a newly enlarged public for his work around 1850, after more than twenty years of writing in obscurity. He also acquired an augmented public life at this time at least in part by being taken in charge by his own producer-promoter, the publisher James T. Fields. Hawthorne began to have his "private life" advertised at this time as part of the creation of his allure: literary mythologizings of his "reclusive" personality and tours-in-print past his private home began in the early 1850s, with full cooperation from his promoters. And Hawthorne too entered into the predicaments of high visibility at this moment: how, in coming before a large, impersonal audience, still to keep "the inmost Me behind its veil"[27] becomes this privacy-loving public figure's problem in 1850 just as much as it is Catharine Sedgwick's or the Veiled Lady's.

The Blithedale Romance, accordingly, should be understood not just as a depiction of self-evident cultural realities but more specifically as an act of reconnaissance into an emerging cultural form. In writing this book Hawthorne uses his work to *work out* the shape of the field that writing has now been placed in, and to measure the meaning of his work's new situation. But the novelists of this time all faced the same situation, which they explored in works of their own. *The Wide, Wide World* is in one aspect a fictional history of this same entertainment revolution. In a central scene, Warner memorably contrasts the bee characteristic of an older social order—an entertainment in which the private is not split from the communal, pleasure not split from productive labor, and the performers not other people than the audience—with reading, the passive, leisured, privatized entertainment form characteristic of modern domesticity, the scene of its own consumption. Melville, who repositioned himself as an antipopular author in face of the same emerging situation that Hawthorne and Warner embraced on other terms, wrote his history of this development in *Pierre* (also 1852), a book that finds its threefold adversary in the cultural organization that encloses sympathy within domestic confinements, a literary market that hypes talent into literary celebrity, and a cultural order that sets the literary in opposition to unrepressed bodily life.[28] Fanny Fern, unlike Melville a courter of popularity and unlike Warner a relisher of fame, made a different accommodation to the literary situation she too found around her. She takes her more sanguine measure of the same ground in *Ruth Hall*, a book that plots the birth of the popular writer at the junction of a business of literary production and a domesticity in need of its wares. Ruth's fan mail—the proof of her celebrity status— makes clear that a home audience consumes her work to help satisfy the cravings that domestic life has not allayed.

Not long after this moment, American literature had other situations created for it. Erastus Beadle's dime novels already in full commercial flower by 1860 embodied a quite different world of popular writing, organizing a mass audience on other terms than a domestic one. By that year a nonpopular "serious" literary zone was successfully institutionalized as part of the establishment of a self-consciously high culture in America, a development that laid the ground from which a quite different figure of the author would later emerge. But those structures were not yet in place a decade before. The dominant world of writing in mid-nineteenth-century America was the highly vicarious, highly managed, privacy-addressing, mass-public one that came together around 1850; and the central fact of literary life then was that a writer who hoped to reach a significant public would have to engage a communication system structured on those terms. Small wonder that the author's *work* at this time is to figure out what this situation means: a work performed, among other ways, through the writing of the story of The Veiled Lady.

3

Starting Out in the 1860s

Alcott, Authorship, and the Postbellum Literary Field

We learn, *we don't know how,* the arts of domestic life—
the manual of a woman's household duties.
—CATHARINE SEDGWICK, *Home*

When Flaubert undertook to write *Madame Bovary* or
Sentimental Education, he situated himself actively within the
space of possibilities offered by the [artistic] field. To understand these
choices is to understand the differential significance that
characterized them within the universe
of possible choices.
—PIERRE BOURDIEU, "Flaubert's Point of View"

I

A FUNNY YET PAINFUL scene takes place near the beginning
of Louisa May Alcott's last novel of the March family, *Jo's Boys*
(1886). Jo March, now Mother Bhaer and the mistress of the
happy asylum-school Plumfield, has returned to writing under the
pressure of hard times. "A book for girls being wanted by a certain
publisher" (Alcott is telling the story of her own writing of *Little
Women* in 1868), Jo has encountered an unforeseen success, her
attempt coming "home heavily laden with an unexpected cargo of
gold and glory." Since that debut she has learned to regularize,
even routinize, this successful literary-commercial venture: "after
that it was plain sailing, and she had merely to load her ships and
send them off on prosperous trips, to bring home stores of comfort
for all she loved and laboured for." [1] But if this traffic in writing
has won a new level of material comfort for Jo's family, it has entailed an equally unforeseen downside, namely, that in becoming

the supplier and exploiter of "the demand always in the mouths of voracious youth—'More stories; more right away!'"—Jo has made herself the object of a parallel demand. The public she courts wants not just to read her works but to see and symbolically possess the author of her works. In *Jo's Boys* an especially enthusiastic fan from Oshkosh pushes her way into Jo's dwelling, snatches a "peep at [the] sanctum" of her study while Jo pretends to be her own maid, and pockets objects from Jo's desk as relics of "the spot where she wrote those sweet, those moral tales which have thrilled us to the soul!" [2]

Like most of the episodes in the March family chronicles, this scene has its proximate cause in Alcott's biography. With the publication of *Little Women*, Alcott was added to the list of celebrity authors to be sought out in Concord—"this sight-seeing fiend is a new torment to us," she wrote in her journal; [3] and in the fan of *Jo's Boys*, Alcott wreaks a special vengeance on the nervy admirer who pressed herself on Alcott—"worked my arm like a pumphandle" (*J*, 196–97)—and invited her to come to be lionized in Oshkosh at an 1875 Woman's Congress. But if it has this real-life occasion, the scene will also have other antecedents for a reader of the last chapter of this book. Alcott's mother from Oshkosh perfectly recreates the Theodore who peeped into the sanctum/ dressing room of the Veiled Lady in Hawthorne's *The Blithedale Romance*. She equally reincarnates the overwrought admirer who, by N. P. Willis's account, invaded Jenny Lind's private withdrawing room and provoked Lind's retort: "Your uninvited presence here is an intrusion." [4] In other words Alcott's scene enacts a standard scenario tied to a certain phase in American literature's social history, and it shows Alcott's engagement with an organization of authorship that we have seen centered at a somewhat earlier time: the situation in which private, domestic women came to appear in public and to capitalize on a paying public in the entertainment sector but thereby also courted an invasion of their privacy, exposing themselves to—if not in fact inviting—the public's vicarious consumption of their "personal lives."

Alcott's tie to the cultural configuration sketched in the first chapter of this book is more striking yet. For the works of Alcott's that continue to be read not only reactivate a philosophy of disciplinary intimacy little changed from its classic articulations in the 1840s and 1850s: they make this philosophy their founding mythology or privileged system of truth. The little women of Alcott's first famous novel live, as the domestic manuals of the previous generation would prescribe, within a loving parental presence, in an enclosed family space warmed by maternal affection and so oriented toward the mother's beliefs. This enveloping presence, operating without the aid of overt or physical coercion, has the power almost magically to mold character in the direction of parental ideals, to transpose parental preference into an imperative from within. Self-centered and acquisitive, the March sisters grumble over their missing Christmas presents until they remember Marmee, which makes them wish to give her a gift rather than get anything for themselves. They are here literally disciplined through love, made other-directed and self-denying by the force of their mother's love for them. When Jo falls into that heavily proscribed mixture of self-assertion and rage that domestic ideology labels "temper," she is again disciplined through the agencies of intimacy and affection. Confessing her own anger to her wayward daughter instead of punishing her, Marmee opens up a new closeness between mother and daughter, then uses the intensified bond between them to draw Jo toward her religious beliefs and the cult of self-control they sponsor. (In *Little Men* we learn that Marmee once tried to spank Jo but that the exercise taught them both the limits of corporal punishment.)[5] Through the mastery of such love-borne discipline, in the sequels to *Little Women* Jo becomes the Marmee of the next generation, performing the mother's work of character making in the extended family of Plumfield. In *Little Men* and *Jo's Boys*, her chief labor is to tame boys as wild as she once was through the methods that worked with her. Jo extends herself to the orphan-urchin Dan, thus, as a loving mother, investing the bond with several kinds of affection simultaneously: "You shall be my oldest son," Jo tells him "with a kiss that made Dan hers entirely."[6] By exploiting his new dependence on her love *for* him she can now plant her expectations as a force *within* him:

"I saw in your room the little Bible I gave you long ago; it was well
worn outside, but fresh within, as if not much read. Will you promise me to read a little once a week, dear, for my sake? . . . You will
do it, for love of mother Bhaer, who always loved her 'firebrand'
and hoped to save him?" [7]

Jo asks with a moral-emotional suasion that would make Little
Eva proud.

The scenario of right character formation and value transmission that I have named disciplinary intimacy survives in Alcott's
fiction with an extraordinary precision of conservation. And her
work perpetuates this philosophy not just in the shape of its narrative episodes but in its understanding of itself as a cultural
agency. The normative mother projected in the domestic ideology
that an earlier chapter of this book has sketched operates not only
directly through her personal presence but also through the mediation of a regular set of substitutes—through motherlike friends
and advisors, through teachers and other social welfare officers,
and not least through books. When Mrs. Montgomery in *The
Wide, Wide World* withdraws herself from her daughter, she cere-
monially delegates her presence to the Bible she gives Ellen, making the book an instrument to draw Ellen into the covenant of her
values. The March family mothers use the book in just this way,
Marmee investing *Pilgrim's Progress* with the weight of a mother's
expectations, Jo giving Dan a Bible and *Undine and Sintram* as a
portable version of her love and exhortation; and Alcott clearly
understands her own books as maternal supplements in this sense,
works that open up a space of heightened pleasure and sharing
and thereby help instill, in young minds, the authority of a domestic ethos. Like the lady from Oshkosh, Alcott's imaginings of
disciplinary intimacy show a structure of literary and moral understandings attached to an earlier nineteenth-century phase of
social history installed deep in a body of work written a generation
later. The question might then be asked: How did it get there?

The answer to this apparently innocuous question might seem
almost trivially easy to obtain, for couldn't we just say that disciplinary intimacy fills Alcott's work because she was a product of that

philosophy? The young Louisa recorded in Alcott's early journals forms a major historical exhibit of a real child of the 1830s–1840s generation (Alcott was born in 1832) being brought up on this culturally sponsored plan. Her journals make clear that the adolescent Louisa was (in her repeated words) cross, moody, willful—or rather they make clear that she was the object of a constant parental attention that invited her to see traits and energies that might have been given very different names under the aspect of these self-critical terms. Alcott's early life was so arranged that out of love of her parents, and in grateful response to the love they showed her in caring for her moral welfare, she was led to identify with the parental view of her character as morally problematic and to find a desired new self in the project of controlling herself on their behalf. Life with father, for the young Alcott, was life with self-reformation as the continuing agenda. An 1843 journal entry shows her celebrating her eleventh birthday in this way: "Father asked us in the eve what fault troubled us most. I said my bad temper" (*J*, 47). She has recourse from this tutelary intimacy to the privacy of her journal, but the journal itself turns out to have been parentally infiltrated for the same strategic ends. Abigail May Alcott wrote the following in Louisa's journal in 1845 (more peeping!):

> MY DEAREST LOUY,—I often peep into your diary, hoping to see some record of more happy days. "Hope, and keep busy," dear daughter, and in all perplexity or trouble come freely to your
> MOTHER [*J*, 55]

This solicitous surveillance prompts a daughter grateful for such attention to covenant with the mother for her own self-improvement:

> DEAR MOTHER,—You *shall* see more happy days, and I *will* come to you with my worries, for you are the best woman in the world.
> L.M.A. [*J*, 55][8]

Coaxed through such heightened solicitude toward a selfhood that has embraced self-management as a virtual career—"the wilful, moody girl I try to manage" (*J*, 61), in her 1850 journal's phrase, is herself—Alcott stands as a striking model of an actual, historical individual constructed on a culturally organized plan for identity formation disseminated in the antebellum decades. It might seem to follow that if this acculturation model so deeply informs her writing, it is because it was first inscribed in her character. But part of the interest of Alcott is that this explanation fails to fit her case. The edificatory or moralizing intention clear enough in the March family novels is conspicuously absent from much of her early work: writing and this possible intention *for* writing have no inevitable relation in Alcott, this is to say. When it does come to govern her writing, the maternal-tutelary mode is, for this author, a sign more of the alienatedness of her literary labor than of her self-expression *in* that labor. "Only a literary nursery-maid who provides moral pap for the young," Alcott's stand-in calls herself in the literary autobiography of *Jo's Boys*, identifying her literary-nurturing functions with the disparagement of her status.[9] The assumption that an author's work flows in some more or less direct way from an authorial self prior to that work breaks down in Alcott's instance and compels us to look for other forms of explanation. I want to argue that Alcott's relation to the domestic literary ethos was a product not of unmediated biography but of the particular way she constructed herself as an author, which was in turn a function of the conditions for literary self-construction set in the literary field of her time.

Alcott's bio   II

If we did not know of it from other sources, Alcott might be enough to convince us that there is such a thing as a primitive will to write. Early and late, Alcott was always scribbling; when overwork led her to lose the use of her right thumb, she trained herself to write with her left hand and wrote on. But on its way to producing the realized author we call Alcott, this originary urge passed through a host of mediatory circumstances that gave her conception of "the writer" a more specified form.

Writing as Louisa May Alcott understood and practiced it was

defined, for instance, against a background of economic circumstances. The daughter of transcendental philosopher who was not
just improvident but virtually antiprovident—one remembers the
story of Bronson Alcott returning home from a season's lecturing
with his net earnings of one dollar[10]—Alcott grew up in a family
(as she put it) "poor as rats" (*J*, 65): needy, economically almost
wholly insecure, and humiliatingly dependent on the charity of
well-wishers. In the domestic economy of what she called "the
Pathetic Family" (*J*, 85), the women and children were recruited
to the role of economic supporter left vacant by an otherworldly
father; and Alcott inherited the dependence of her family on de-
pendents like herself with the particular family she was born into.
Alcott was thus bound to work, in the sense that she was obliged
to earn an income for the intimates who came increasingly to depend on her. But she was also "bound to" work by strictures less
material but not less compelling—strictures that reinforced the
economic necessity for her labor in complex ways. A person whose
early world was rich in occasions for resentment and despair,
Alcott inhabited a High Victorian culture that proposed work as
the spiritually privileged therapy for personal unhappiness.[11] Culturally situated as she was, her search for a meaningful life led
her to embrace work as the ground for her moral self-validation;
and within the little culture of her family this valuing of her work
received a further boost. As a result of her success at working and
earning, she hazards in a journal entry from her early twenties,
"people [have begun] to think that topsey-turvey Louisa would
amount to something after all" (*J*, 73). The discipline of her labor
and the altruism of her support of others, such a passage suggests,
became the chief proof she could offer that she had "become" the
properly managed self her upbringing had urged on her. In this
way the acculturation scheme of her childhood conspired to require her adult wage earning: Alcott had to work to establish her
successful reformation of an originally unacceptable self.

When Alcott came of working age, the available jobs through
which she could discharge this complex obligation were the work
forms marked as suitable for women in her time, the careers that
extended women's domestic labors of homemaking and nurture

out beyond the home. In the 1850s and early 1860s Alcott found paying jobs in housework, as a servant or "second girl"; in sewing; in nursing (her Civil War career); and in teaching, as a governess and in a succession of schools. But working the literary market was established as another women's work at the time of Alcott's childhood; and Alcott first came to writing as another of the work forms through which she could meet an obligation at once economic, familial, and moral. In her personal literary economy, writing was first defined not as a separate aesthetic labor but as a functional parallel to these other careers: Alcott in these years commonly sewed, taught, and wrote as almost interchangeable money-making activities.[12] Writing was differentiated from these adjacent careers, in her emerging experience, primarily by the different working conditions it afforded. When, at the behest of a patron needing a school for his nephew and a tireless educational experimenter (Elizabeth Palmer Peabody) who wanted to "try the new system," Alcott was roped into teaching an early kindergarten in 1862, she was reduced to "visiting about, . . . as my school did not bring enough to pay board" (*J*, 108–9). In the same year she quickly wrote one story that earned her $30, her whole year's school income, and another that paid $100.[13] For Alcott, such circumstances defined writing as the available career that produced the maximum independence: the greatest income, therefore too the greatest self-justification, and the greatest freedom from coercion and exploitation by others.

When Alcott came to centralize her previously more variegated work life in her writing activities around 1862–63, she could do so in part because she found a growing market for her wares. Within a year of her kindergarten debacle she had had her Civil War letters, *Hospital Sketches* (1863), published by the abolitionist-lecture entrepreneur James Redpath, who sought further works from her. Her letters and stories were sought by the *Boston Commonwealth* and the *United States Service Magazine*. She had begun placing stories in *Frank Leslie's Illustrated Newspaper*, whose interest in her was soon to be joined by the Boston-based *Flag of Our Union*. She sold stories as well to the *Atlantic Monthly*.

It is possible to think of these titles as the set of more or less interchangeable outlets that Alcott found for her prose; but from the point of view of literary history, the list has a different meaning. For the array of publications available to Alcott represents a historical phenomenon, a profound evolution in the cultural organization of American letters. The publishing instruments Alcott could avail herself of were recent inventions in the early 1860s: the *Atlantic Monthly* had only begun to publish in 1857, and *Frank Leslie's Illustrated Newspaper* in 1855. The growing number of outlets she personally had access to reflects, more generally, the proliferation of literary vehicles that is a great fact of American literature's social history in the years after 1850, and that helped make literary writing a commercially viable career. (In his reminiscence of these years in *Literary Friends and Acquaintance*, William Dean Howells dwells on the fact that "there were then such a very few places where you could market your work" in the United States before 1860, then rehearses the names of the new journals founded at this time—*The Nation, The Galaxy, Scribner's,* in addition to the ones just mentioned—that gave American writing its first sound commercial base.) [14] At least as crucially, Alcott's early 1860s array of writing outlets reflects the historical emergence, at around this time, of new sorts of internal differentiations within the American literary system. For the particular instruments Alcott wrote for were the foci around which separate literary cultures of the later nineteenth century came to coalesce.

Frank Leslie's Illustrated Newspaper; The Flag of Our Union; Frank Leslie's Chimney Corner, which invited Alcott's contributions when it was founded in 1865; Robert Bonner's *New York Ledger* (founded 1855), which Alcott tried to interest in her "wares" [15] and which later paid her for an advice column—these titles exemplify a new kind of publishing device that was first elaborated in the United States around 1840 but whose strong incarnations were established in the mid- and late 1850s and continued to flourish throughout the century: the story-paper, the large-paged, newspaperlike bearer of column upon column of closely printed fiction (usually with lurid illustrations) often published in tandem with the pamphletlike dime novel. (Alcott did not write for Beadle and Adams, the dime novel house born in 1860 which ran seven story-papers of its own, but her 1865 *Flag of Our Union* serial, "V. V.: or, Plots and Counterplots" was reissued in that journal's dime novel series, Ten Cent Novelettes of Standard American Authors.) By the 1860s instruments with an enormous public—the *New York Ledger* had a circulation of 180,000 by its second year (a number that later doubled), and *The Flag of Our Union* blazoned itself as "A Paper for the Million" [16]—story-paper/dime novel publishing emerged almost contemporaneously with the mass-market form of domestic literary publishing in the 1850s, and the two were at first not sharply differentiated. Bonner published Fanny Fern, a classic 1850s domestic author, in his story-paper the *New York Ledger;* Erastus Beadle printed a magazine called *The Home Monthly;* the full form of *The Flag of Our Union*'s motto was "A Paper for the Million, and a Welcome Visitor to the Home Circle." But if they were not conceived in opposition to one another, story-paper fiction had different characteristics from domestic fiction that help account for their eventual divergence. Story papers favored the genres of high-colored romance and sensational adventure, not the edifying writing of everyday life. (Some sample titles from *The Flag of Our Union* are "Rosalette; or, The Flower Girl of Paris: A Romance of France," by Lieutenant Murray; "The Wandering Guerrilla; or, The Infant Bride of Truxillo: A Mexican Romance of Troublous Times," by Sylvanus Cobb, Jr.; and "The Police Spy; or, The Secret Crimes of Paris: A Romance of the Seventeenth Century," by Francis A. Durivage.) [17] At a nickel or dime an installment, story-papers also formed—and advertised that they formed—a cheaper entertainment than the magazine or hardbound book of more genteel reading cultures. Their print formats geared them to readers poor in cultural as well as economic capital: in their materials and layout, story-papers produced literary writing into a likeness with the most everyday reading matter of the most rudimentary literacy levels, the newspaper—a likeness reiterated by their emphasis on the series, the weekly renewal of standard formats, rather than the individual work of writing.

For these and other reasons, story-paper fiction and dime novels came to supply the reading materials or "literature" of a different social grouping from popular domestic fiction in the later nineteenth century. The demographics of historical audiences are impossible to establish fully, but such evidence as survives suggests a marked divergence in the social character of these two publics. Mid-nineteenth century domestic fiction had its audience centered among people (often women) already possessing, or newly aspiring to, or at least mentally identifying with, the leisured, child-centered home of middle-class life. Story-paper fiction, while no doubt overlapping with domestic fiction's readership in part, is known to have incorporated many groups situated outside such feminized ease: farmboys, soldiers, German and Irish immigrants, and men and women of a newly solidifying working class.[18]

The *Atlantic*, fashioned shortly after the mass-circulated story-paper and domestic bestseller, helped bring together a literary culture constituted on other terms. The *Atlantic* too did not, at its outset, segregate itself in a militant way from the already well-established world of domestic writing. Readers who associate this journal with other things will be surprised to find its first issues featuring Rose Terry Cooke, Harriet Beecher Stowe, and "Life in the Iron Mills," by Rebecca Harding (later Davis), to name no more. But already at its inception, the *Atlantic* sent a different message about the values and interests it represented. By conspicuously featuring the New England authors it had helped make canonical, along with the high arts of contemporary Europe that were surveyed in its reviews, the *Atlantic* affiliated itself with a zone of artistic, cosmopolitan, and classical production that it had itself helped culturally to demarcate. (Howells, still a country boy in 1860, already knew to think of the *Atlantic* as representing "the fine air of high literature"[19] in that year.) By the 1870s the *Atlantic* had established itself as the premier organ of literary high culture in America, projecting a selection of writing organized around high-cultural literary values to an audience centered in the upper social orders (matters returned to in the next two chapters of this book). It helped institutionalize the nonpopular "high" culture that came to exist "above" the domestic or middlebrow world of letters in the later nineteenth century just as the new story-papers of the 1850s helped organize the "low" one that came to exist "below" it.

The publishing circumstances of Alcott's early career, this is to say, are particularized by-products of a larger cultural drama, a major rearticulation of the American literary field. Alcott emerged as a writer at a moment when writing itself was being reestablished as a social activity in America, made the subject of a new scheme of institutional arrangements that stabilized the relation of authors to readers and solidified the writer's public support. But the same reorganization that stabilized institutional support for writing in America in the 1850s and early 1860s also stratified the field of writing—laid the basis for separate modes of literary production to produce separate bodies of writing to separate social publics. Reconnected to this history, Alcott's debut can teach us that late nineteenth-century literary cultures typically studied in isolation from one another came into existence together, through a unified process of cultural development. She can also teach us that at the moment of their joint emergence, writers were not in any necessary way aligned with one or another of these distinct cultures but faced an array of literary possibilities and had several publics and several models of authorship equally available to them. Alcott wrote, for three or four years in the 1860s, for both the *Atlantic* and Frank Leslie; she had it in her power to be both a proto-high cultural and a proto-low cultural author; but that is not to say that the two were interchangeable. For these different literary instruments modelled different conceptions of the writer and his or her labor, and through Alcott we can get some sense of the different work lives the newly stabilizing literary cultures of the mid-nineteenth century invited writers to embrace.

While it was later joined in this role by other "quality" journals, the *Atlantic Monthly* supplied the chief base for the new high-literary professional writer who emerged in the United States after the Civil War—the form of writer represented by Henry James, who started publishing in the *Atlantic* in 1865 and serialized virtually all his novels there through the end of the century; or William Dean Howells, who edited the *Atlantic* and published his novels and reviews there from 1866 to 1881; or Sarah Orne Jewett, whose ties to it will be explored later on. The *Atlantic* supported such writers in the sense that it paid them and built an audience for their work. But it also supported this sort of literary figure in the sense that the cultural ethos the *Atlantic* helped hold together gave them the means to envision the idealized writer they then tried to be: the writer as single-minded devotee of a highly specialized craft whose work derives value from its mastery of its art. We do not think to join Louisa May Alcott to the company of James and Howells and Jewett, Alcott having been consigned to an almost wholly separate zone of cultural memory and value. But there was a time when she appeared just *where* such writers did, and thought of herself as a writer of the same kind.

For this Alcott, as for the other writers I have named, the *Atlantic* both provided a place for paying publication and supported a certain sense of the literary career. If not so self-abasingly as the young Howells, who approached the *Atlantic* and its cultural affiliates as so many shrines, Alcott associated the *Atlantic* with aesthetic values hierarchically conceived. In an early journal she writes:

> I feel as if I could write better now,—more truly of things I have felt and therefore *know.* I hope I shall yet do my great book, for that seems to be my work, and I am growing up to it. I even think of trying the "Atlantic." There's ambition for you! . . . If Mr. L [James Russell Lowell, the *Atlantic*'s first editor] takes the one Father carried him, I shall think I can do something. [*J*, 92]

In the neighborhood of the *Atlantic,* Alcott begins envisioning herself as a writer in a highly distinctive idiom: in the language of hierarchies of merit ("better now"), exalted vocation ("my work"), the gradual attainment of high proficiency ("growing up to it"), and culminating achievement ("my great book"). This magazine attracts such a writer's most ambitious ventures ("I even think of trying the 'Atlantic'"); and acceptance in it validates her sense of high powers: if Mr. Lowell takes it "I shall think I can do something." Alcott had from the first a certain amount of frustration with the *Atlantic* as a publisher, and she had a considerable ambivalence toward the *Atlantic*'s second editor, James T. Fields, and the sense of cultural superiority he projected: "the great James"

(*J,* 120), she dryly calls the Maecenas of Bostonian high-literary culture, publisher-patron of the New England classics and host of Boston's choice literary salon. (It was Fields who helped administer the rites of literary initiation to Howells, the young man from the provinces: "this is the apostolic succession, this is the laying on of hands.")[20] Nevertheless, throughout the early 1860s Alcott thought of the *Atlantic's* judgment as the authoritative measure of what was "best" of her work, and she continued mentally to direct a self-differentiated high grade of work toward the *Atlantic* and its publisher, Ticknor and Fields.[21]

The post-1850s story-paper and pamphlet novel supplied the base for another new kind of author who appears in America in the mid-nineteenth century, the author not as artist-professional but as something like industrial hand. With their heavy demand for fiction, such outlets gave work to hundreds of writers whose names have been lost to memory: the previously mentioned Sylvanus Cobb, Jr., and Francis A. Durivage; Ned Buntline (the pen name of E. Z. C. Judson); J. F. C. Adams, Captain Bruin Adams, Boynton M. Belknap, J. G. Bethune, E. A. St. Mox, and Emerson Rodman, all pseudonyms of E. S. Ellis; Mrs. Metta V. Victor; Mrs. Ann Emerson Porter (Ralph Waldo Emerson's cousin); and many more.[22] The new cheap fiction formats created a paying place for such writers' work, and so allowed them to become authors. But such outlets' organization of literary production also set tight limits on the kind of work they would publish, so that they enforced a particular version of authorship as the cost of their support. Such publications were founded on the frequent reproduction of preestablished generic formulas: the competent performance of a set generic formula, not some idea of originative artistic individuality or abstract aesthetic quality, is their criterion for the acceptable. For this reason the authorship they sponsored minimized individuated self-expression, making the publisher's formula the work's creator and the writer the more or less interchangeable performer of a prespecified task. (Such publishing could carry the separation of the literary work from any real individual "author" to great lengths. Street and Smith's popular author Bertha M. Clay never existed except as a house-controlled name

various unnamed others were hired to publish under. Edward L.
Wheeler, the author of Beadle's hugely popular Deadwood Dick
series, apparently died around 1885, but the firm continued to
publish new work in his name long after his death.) The other
principal requirement such literary institutions set was that very
many stories be published very frequently; and this organization
of demand tended to enforce a certain ethic of writerly productivity. Such records of story-paper writers and dime novelists as
survive tend to be silent about their artistic aspirations for their
works but highly explicit about their work schedules: we know,
for instance, that Joseph E. Badger, Jr., commonly completed an
80,000-word novel in a week, writing in six-hour shifts with two-
hour breaks for sleep; that Prentiss Ingraham, author of over one
thousand such works, wrote a half-dime novel in a day and a dime
one in five days; and that Upton Sinclair, who started such employment at age fourteen, wrote something near the equivalent of
the output of Sir Walter Scott in a year and a half's work for the
firm of Street and Smith. Such records suggest an extreme subor-
dination of writing to values of maximized productive efficiency:
William Wallace Cook called his memoir of dime novel writing *The
Fiction Factory.* [23]

When Alcott wrote for *Frank Leslie's Illustrated Newspaper* and
The Flag of Our Union, as when she wrote for the *Atlantic,* she
wrote within the conception of the writer's work that such journals sponsored. This Alcott, like her confreres, met writing as
something externally specified in format: "can you furnish me
with a sensation story of about 145 to 150 pages . . . so that I can
have it by the middle of July?" James R. Elliott, manager of *The
Flag of Our Union,* wrote Alcott in June 1865. [24] And like her fel-
lows, the Alcott who wrote these bespoke stories always thought
of this kind of writing in terms of speed of production: "I reel off
my 'thrilling' tales" (*J,* 109), she says of such work, or again: "I
intend to illuminate the Ledger with a blood & thunder tale as they
are easy to 'compoze' & are better paid than moral and elaborate
works of Shakespeare, so dont be shocked if I send you a paper
containing a picture of Indians, pirates wolves, bears & distressed
damsels in a grand tableau over a title like this 'The Maniac Bride'

or 'The Bath of Blood. A thrilling tale of passion,' &c."[25] (Alcott's
attunement to the different material properties of her potential literary outlets is a striking feature of this letter.) But no culturally
enforced model of authorship can wholly dictate the experience
an author can attach to it, and Alcott suggests as well the more
personalized meanings that working in this literary economy could
be made to carry.

As Madeleine Stern and Judith Fetterley have emphasized,
story-paper writing brought Alcott an elsewhere-unavailable degree of imaginative freedom together with its specifications and
constraints.[26] The generic rules of the "blood and thunder tale" in
effect required imaginative indulgence of Alcott, a deep release of
sensationalism and exoticism, and so permitted the expression of
drives elsewhere banked in her work: female rage, aggression, de-
viousness, and so on. (Such expression was in part protected for
Alcott by the prevailing cheap fiction convention of pseudonym-
ity: Alcott published this work under the name A. M. Barnard, a
"person" in the same sense as Ned Buntline, Captain Bruin Adams,
or Bertha M. Clay.) Quite as important, Alcott also associated this
phase of her work—in strong contradistinction to high-cultural
writing—with infinite demand easily met. Alcott could not re-
submit to the *Atlantic* until they published her previously accepted stories, which was commonly done after long delay; but
"Mr Elliott wants tales, poems, sketches & novelettes, so I can spin
away ad libitum" (*J*, 139). In her internalized self-hierarchization
of her work, Alcott thinks of sensation fiction as a low achievement and low-grade genre—"rubbish" is her constant term for
such work. Yet this same feature made such writing carry for
Alcott the meaning of unanxious labor, work not exposing aspiration to the possible mortification of failure. "Mr. L[eslie] says my
tales are so 'dramatic, vivid, and full of plot,' they are *just what he
wants*" (*J*, 109; emphasis added), Alcott writes in her 1862 journal, with the joy of one exempted, for a rarity, from being found
wanting.

The two historical models of authorship that I have shown Alcott
entering into in the early 1860s were strongly opposed to one another, both in the world and in Alcott's practice. But a notable

similarity between the two is that neither of them encouraged the kind of authorship this chapter began by considering: writing as a tutelary activity in support of the domestic ethos. Historically, part of the significance of the high- and low-cultural literary establishments I have been sketching is that they established literature around other values than the domestically inflected ones of American literature's first successful institutional establishment; and the Alcott whose work is defined in other than domestic terms adumbrates the otherwise-defined *forms* of authorship these cultural developments enabled. The domestic-tutelary model of writing came to preside over Alcott's work at a later stage than these alternative models. And it came into her writing through her finding of another literary market.

It is a well-known fact that in 1867 Thomas Niles, a partner in the publishing house Roberts Brothers, asked Alcott to write "a girl's book" (*J*, 158)—the book that became *Little Women*. This request invited Alcott to a new genre. But the array of genres operative at any historical moment is always bound together with other cultural organizations and differentiations, and at Alcott's moment the girl's book like other "kinds" known to her—"great book," "blood and thunder tale"—was inscribed in its own circuit of social relations. The cultural processes that organized a reading public around the middle-class values of domestic privacy and sentimental child rearing in the antebellum decades also brought into being the first separate institutions for children's literary production in the United States.[27] (Fanny Fern's father, Nathaniel Willis, parodied as a mere antediluvian meanie in *Ruth Hall*, was a pioneer of this movement and founder of the early children's magazine *The Youth's Companion*.) The 1850s domestic best-sellers were not written specifically for a children's market, but one by-product of the reorganization of the American literary economy in the late 1850s and 1860s was that the child-centered cult of domesticity, previously focussed through such popular adult reading, came to be specialized to the children's department of middle-class reading, freeing up a middlebrow reading zone less tightly defined by that now-older ethos. When Niles asked Alcott to do a girl's book, he was inviting her to write a work with different literary properties

from other works she had attempted: this genre, she grasped, set
domestic realism—writing "not a bit sensational, but simple and
true" (*J*, 166)—as its generic requirement. But in 1867 the genre
with these literary features was attached to the literary market
with this social location and this moral mission. It was in taking
up a form of writing with these social connections that Alcott embraced a "work" of writing with a domestic-edificatory program.
Alcott found her since-familiar character as an author by finding
this position to work within.

The more general point to be made here is that no author
comes to be an author in an unmediated way. A writer can only
become a writer by first constructing some working idea of what a
writer is and does. Such definitions in turn are never merely self-
generated but are formed in and against the understandings of this
role that are operative in a particular cultural space. Louisa May
Alcott came to her career at a time when a profound reinstitution-
alization of the literary field was changing the terms on which this
career itself could be imagined; and at this moment, she shows,
later separate career forms took the form of simultaneous alternatives. She became the kind of writer she did by choosing among
contemporaneously generated modes of literary work that were
at first equally available. The other writers of her time that she
eventually seemed to have so little to do with—the Jewetts and
Jameses on the one hand and the Cobbs and Clays on the other—
became the different kinds of writers they did by making different
use of the same socially structured field of available positions.[28]

Alcott found her eventual identity as a writer, to repeat,
through the way she chose to situate herself in a historical field of
writerly possibilities. But it remains to say how exactly her choice
got made: how she came to invest herself in one alternative organized around her and not another.

After the success of *Little Women*, Alcott did come to accept
this sort of work as her "line" and to discontinue her earlier,
other forms of authorship. To grasp the logic of ·this act of self-
establishment many factors must be considered. We need to remember, for one thing, that little as she initially thought so (she at
first thought this book "*dull*" [*J*, 166]), Alcott had a real gift for

the sort of writing *Little Women* embodies. If it does not represent everything she had it in her to do, Alcott was at least good at this sort of work, and found some measure of self-realization in it: the notion that the only "real" Alcott was the author of story-paper sensation is a sentimental reduction.

Second, this form of writing brought Alcott material rewards of an altogether different order from her earlier work. Widely read, earning thousands rather than hundreds of dollars, enjoying royalties that came in year after year, known and celebrated by her own name, Alcott "walked into a niche" with *Little Women* (in Stern's words) that was "too comfortable to abandon"—the more so because of her complex need for material rewards.[29]

Such an account leaves the question why Alcott could not have continued working on all her literary fronts even if one of them became most profitable. The answer here, a third factor in her decision, is that Alcott's other niches became less tenable at the time of her juvenile-domestic success. If Alcott was a proto-high-cultural author (among other things) during the Civil War years, it can be added that she always had a tenuous footing in that literary world and was admitted to it on disparaging terms. James T. Fields, publisher-patron of Hawthorne and Emerson and designated anointer of new entrants to the new world of high letters, told Alcott in 1862, two years after his very different welcome of Howells, to "Stick to your teaching; you can't write" (*J*, 109). (It was Fields who had funded the kindergarten into which Alcott was forcibly enlisted in 1862.) Alcott had occasional access to James and Annie Fields's salon, the institution that helped initiate so many writers into the nineteenth-century high culture of letters; but she was greeted there more as poor relation than artistic "find" (she and Annie Fields were cousins), and she seems to have felt largely humiliated by the social attentions of "the great publisher."[30] In any case, the *Atlantic* underwent a palpable stiffening of its selection criteria in the mid-1860s, as evidenced by the fact that Rebecca Harding Davis, whose "Life in the Iron Mills" and *Margaret Howth* it had featured, was now dropped and left to the drudgery of popular-commercial writing.[31] At the time of this hard-to-document change, the *Atlantic* also began not finding

Alcott an author of its sort. Having taken four of her stories between 1859 and 1863, the *Atlantic* ceased accepting Alcott's fiction after 1864—a mortification of the fragilely asserted "high" level of her aspiration cruelly reinforced when Ticknor and Fields lost the manuscript of a collection of her fairy tales in 1867. Alcott knew what to do with these rebuffs: she shut down a level of ambition that had left her painfully exposed.

If this world of letters closed itself to Alcott, she herself closed the door to the literary netherworld she had previously enjoyed. When Street and Smith's story-paper the *New York Weekly* asked for a serial from the celebrated author of *Little Women* in 1870, she was told to "Name your own price." Alcott refused this big bribe on grounds not mainly economic; she wrote to her publisher Niles:

> I did not like the list of contributors Ned Buntline, Lu Billings, Spaulding, Philander Doesticks, and other great lights, so I could not think of it, and prefer the "heavy moral." [32]

This letter reveals how much Alcott thought of edifying writing as a product line affiliated with a certain literary market: her lack of moral attachment to the "heavy moral" mode is this letter's great surprise. But it also suggests that she came to embrace that mode and market because of the level of dignity they could afford in comparison with competing literary systems. If such writing helped seal her exclusion from the culture she too considered "high," it also protected her against an inferior status, the company of story-paper writers being morally freer yet unacceptably "low."

But if these alternatives became less accessible to Alcott, it must be added that there was something about the writing role she embraced that especially appealed to her. Alcott needed things from her work. Acculturated as she was, she needed for her writing to be other things more than she needed it to be gratifying. One of the attractions of the "heavy moral" mode, for Alcott, was that it did not correspond to a personal preference: for an author who needed to demonstrate that she had overcome her selfish will, this writing style had the paradoxical attraction that it signified self-

sacrifice, signalled that she had set aside personal pleasure for socially useful work. Alcott the domestic writer always thought of
herself as coerced into such activity—she wrote *Little Women*, she
always implied, because someone else wanted it and hard times
compelled her; she wrote *Little Men*, she told herself, because
someone had to support the children of her widowed sister Anna
(in fact Anna's husband had been insured); having accepted an
advance from the *Christian Union* for the novel *Work*, "I was
bound, and sat at the oar like a galley-slave" (*J*, 184). But the
deep paradox of Alcott's case is that she needed to *need* to write,
needed to think of her work as not willed but constrained. With
fatal symmetry, mid-nineteenth-century juvenile-domestic fiction
("moral pap for the young"), the literary extension of the mother's
work of sacrificial nurture, perfectly fit Alcott's personal need, a
product of the same social developments that produced such fiction, to fulfill herself through self-denial. Alcott chose what sort of
author she would be—but like every writer, she chose among historically structured choices through the action of a culturally con-
ditioned will.

III

This account of the construction of Alcott's authorship may seem
quite external to her work, and may have raised the question of
what relevance, if any, such a prehistory of her writing has to the
reading of her books. Recognizing the legitimacy of this question,
I want to turn now to *Little Women*, and to ask what difference it
makes for this book that it was written in the circumstances just
outlined.

The answer might at first seem to be that this intervening history makes no difference—that *Little Women* is striking for the
extent to which it is not marked by the cultural changes of its time.
Read one way this book is a kind of miracle of preservation, per-
petuating the conventions of the previous generation's domestic
fiction with a freedom from modification rare in any tradition.
Little Women thus draws its horizon just where a book like *The
Wide, Wide World* did. Its known world is what Stowe called the

family state, the world of private domestic relations, the public or
men's sphere—symbolized by the distant Civil War—being marked
here again as terra incognita. Highly conventional "problems" of
female development get played out again in this space, whose
structure of affection helps bring them to familiar normative resolutions. When the jealous Amy destroys Jo's book, Jo feels the
same rage that Ellen Montgomery knew as a typical by-product of
girls' daily life. But for Jo as for Ellen the home world forbids such
self-assertion, and the authority of a loving mother teaches the
lesson of mandatory self-control. When Jo becomes so engrossed
in her book that she refuses to make charitable calls on the needy
Hummels, she replays another scene from Ellen's life, who became
so involved in her reading that she refused to help an illiterate
immigrant write letters home. But here again a fall into self-
absorption teaches that a woman must put service to others before
indulgence of the self: Jo's selfishness all but kills Beth, who contracts scarlet fever while visiting the Hummels in her stead, as her
anger all but killed Amy before.

    In the classic topoi of nineteenth-century domestic fiction,
family love disciplines the woman-in-training toward the acceptance of her "right" or domestic character. This plot is enacted
most profoundly in the set scene Alcott plays out most precisely:
the deathbed scene, hallmark of the sentimental mode. The saintly
Beth is this book's version of Hawthorne's Gentle Boy, or Dickens's
Paul Dombey, or Warner's Alice Humphreys, or Stowe's Little Eva.
Bound for death for much of the book, Beth, like Eva, seizes her
dying as a moment of worldly power, making her deathbed a pul-
pit and using the grief she inspires to plant her expectant presence
deep within:

> "I'm sure I shall be your Beth still, to love and help you more than
> ever. You must take my place, Jo, and be everything to Father and
> Mother when I'm gone. They will turn to you, don't fail them; and
> if it's hard to work alone, remember that I don't forget you, and that
> you'll be happier in doing that than writing splendid books or see-
> ing all the world." [33]

This speech is so moving that it effects, like Eva's similar one, a conversion: "then and there Jo renounced her old ambition [and] pledged herself to a new and better one" (391); and what follows is no less strictly conventional. When the beloved Alice dies in *The Wide, Wide World* Ellen is moved to perform her daily tasks exactly as Alice performed them. A "new round of little household duties"[34] is made emotionally mandatory to Ellen by her loved friend's lost example, which sanctifies the housewife's career of quotidian chores. In *Little Women* Beth's death precipitates Jo's great moment of despair at women's confinement to "spending all her life in that quiet house, devoted to humdrum cares" (404), arguably the most powerful Everlasting Nay spoken in American domestic literature. But here again grief and loss discipline and domesticate: the emotional imperative symbolically to restore the lost beloved—the urge to take her place or in effect to *become* her—makes Jo too embrace the domestic routine that depressed her:

> Other helps had Jo—humble, wholesome duties and delights that would not be denied their part in serving her, and which she slowly learned to see and value. Brooms and dishcloths never could be as distasteful as they once had been, for Beth had presided over both; and something of her old housewifely spirit seemed to linger round the little mop and the old brush, that was never thrown away. As she used them, Jo found herself humming the songs Beth used to hum, imitating Beth's orderly ways, and giving the little touches here and there that kept everything fresh and cozy, which was the first step toward making home happy. [405–6]

Any reckoning of Alcott's work needs to do justice to the deep conservatism of scenes like these. They are conservative not just in that they are old-fashioned in form or nonprogressive in outlook but in that they keep warmly alive, at a later time, a vision of the right ordering of experience pieced together at an earlier moment. Its conservatism must be assumed to have been a central cause of *Little Women*'s popular success; and this would suggest that in the later nineteenth century, children's writing did the cultural work of conservation, helped perpetuate an ethos no longer new to adults.

But if much in *Little Women* is familiar from the previous generation's domestic fiction, some things have changed, and one change is a new liberality of tone. Without departing from highly traditional conceptions of women's character formation, *Little Women* brings a mirth to the plot of female domestication not found in the novels of the 1850s. Fun has a license in the March family unknown to Ellen Montgomery: any reader of Warner's dour novel will note by contrast how game-filled and play-oriented Alcott's novel is. More, while this book is always moving toward a quite conventional character ideal as its end—its truant girls are on their way to becoming little women, and its little women on their way to becoming (in the second volume's title) good wives— Alcott makes a new allowance for, and takes a new pleasure in, the phase where such goals are not yet achieved. Girls must be girls at the end of Alcott's book, but meanwhile they are allowed to be boys: *Little Women* tolerates deviations from normative gender identities unknown to earlier works in the domestic genre. These same girls must eventually become good housekeepers, but before that happens they regularly—how else to put it?—mess up: spill salad dressing on their clean dresses, swamp their kitchens with batches of failed jelly, and so on.

The new liberality that sees the humanness, even the fun, in otherwise-censurable error travels together with a new relaxation on the part of authority-figures in *Little Women*. Unlike Susan Warner's Mrs. Montgomery, who is always there in force with an arsenal of parental sanctions, Alcott's Marmee backs off from the children in her charge, leaving them unprecedentedly free. The mother has left the daughters home alone in *Little Women*'s opening chapter. When Meg wants to engage in social climbing at the home of the wealthy Moffats, Marmee lets her. When Amy wants to impress the high-toned girls in her drawing class, Marmee helps her prepare an absurdly pretentious luncheon. When the four daughters decide to live totally idly during their vacation, the mother not only tolerates their idleness but joins their abdication of household chores. The softened or humanized author-

ity of antebellum domesticity has permuted itself, here, into an
astonishing permissiveness; but Marmee pursues highly regulatory goals through this strategy of nonauthoritarianism. She allows her daughters their free experience on the understanding that
it will teach them the lessons she might have enforced—as, allowed her folly, Amy learns that she has been a fool about her
luncheon; and left in idleness, the girls learn the misery of idle-
nesss and reinvent the domestic work ethic for themselves. Marmee
does not abdicate the work of maternal tutelage so much as she
relocates its agency—makes experience teach what was once pa-
rently enjoined.

This reinvestment of authority characterizes the book quite
as much as the mother within the book. For the prose of *Little
Women* has made its own mitigations of traditional maternal sway.
Alcott called juvenile-domestic fiction the "heavy moral" mode,
but "heavy moral" is what her own writing is not. Her text
has dropped the habit of mustering high-voltage ethical charges
around the rules of everyday conduct that made life in earlier domestic novels one long risk of transgression: what the doctor tells
Ellen early in *The Wide, Wide World*—don't burn the toast or your
mother will die—is a kind of thinking Alcott has largely relaxed.
(Not entirely of course: "be angry or selfish and your sister will
die" is a rule this book still enforces.) In particular, *Little Women*
has put in abeyance the ultimate enforcer of the 1850s literary
generation: the threat of divine displeasure and promise of heavenly reward. Except for rare moments—the proscription of anger
in chapter eight and Beth's death in chapter forty—whose transcendent importance is indicated just by the invocation of religion, *Little Women* is a remarkably secular text, a de-evangelized
domestic text, so to speak. The book's deactivation of such older
authority systems is what creates the possibility for its brand of
domestic realism. The foibles of everyday life can be caught in their
funny human familiarity here because they are not being nailed to
heavily sanctioned moral meanings. (Amy's irritable-charitable
disposal of her failed luncheon—"Bundle everything into a basket
and send it to the Hummels: Germans like messes" [248]—would
be something else than laughable in a more authority-haunted

book.) But this textual leniency does not mean that Alcott has given up the cult of domesticity's tutelary program. Rather, the book, like Marmee, has licensed a now-"free" experience to teach requisite lessons in authority's apparent absence.[35]

The new liberality of a book like *Little Women* has been taken as a sign of a more general liberalization of middle class culture in the postbellum nineteenth century. Behind this book it is possible to read the history of a social class now socially established, and so not needing to insist on the group values it had used to define and justify itself in its insurgent phase. Bernard Wishy and Daniel Rodgers have suggested that such children's writing marks a further reorientation in nineteenth-century middle-class culture from the highly disciplined self-denials of the work ethic to the now-tolerated (even mandated) indulgences of an emerging ethic of consumption—a suggestion that will find further evidence later in this chapter.[36] But to think *Little Women* back into its historical world is also to have another salient feature of the book come into strong focus: namely, the new way it charts the geography of adjacent social space.

The domestic value system that informs *Little Women* has, as always in the domestic tradition, a quite definite social base. Meg's life ties the book to the single-family household in which the man goes out to work at a white-collar job and the wife stays home to run the house (with help), with both parents earnestly involved in the drama of child rearing—ties it in short to the idealized norms of middle-class life, domestic fiction's traditional ground. But the historical group that projected this idyll of insular family privacy did not live by itself in reality. It lived in sight of other social formations and experienced itself in relation to them; and a major function of its group literature was imaginatively to specify its relation to neighboring groups. The older domestic novel typically situates its ideal family over against a schematically represented lower class, often of immigrant origin, that is domestically disorganized and an object of social welfare. (The Phelans fill this role in Sedgwick's *Home;* the equally minimally-sketched Hummels, objects of charity and sources of infection, are the Phelans of *Little Women.*) This class is usually balanced, at the other side of middle-class self-definition, by an equally alien upper class seen as idle, luxuriously wasteful, and devoid of proper virtues of self-control—like the business partner-speculator of *Home*, whose bankrupt home is awash in champagne bottles. But the social adjacency that most deeply interests 1850s domestic fiction is the older household economy based on domestic production and unsentimentalized family bonds. The rustic life so intricately recorded in the Aunt Fortune chapters of *The Wide, Wide World* shows this older order as a menacing proximity to that book's ideal domesticity, which in Ellen's case collapses back upon and must win its way out from this "world we have lost." The nightmare in-laws of Fanny Fern's *Ruth Hall*, also affiliated with an older culture of multigenerational families, homemade commodities, nonsentimental bonds, and in-difference to privacy, pursue the model couple Ruth and Harry and criticize their private life—testimony again to a new social order's anguished sense of interinvolvement with an earlier form from which it has not yet managed to separate fully.

In *Little Women* the household economy still so vividly present to these mid-century books has largely vanished. But now another social rival has become comparably absorbing. A different culture of greater affluence and status is always right at hand in Alcott's book, so close that when her little women go out they are at once in its midst. When Amy goes to school, she is immersed in the lime-exchange cult of more free-spending girls. When Jo and Meg go to a dance, it is to a house where people wear expensive and showy clothes. Meg's principal contacts outside the home are the Moffats, walking embodiments of conspicuous consumption. Amy later mixes with the well-to-do Chesters; Laurie's well-heeled college chums (who are rich enough to buy out the Chesters' fair); the fabulously wealthy Fred; and the luxury set she meets in her art class. I take this change to mean that by 1868 the middle-class audience no longer needs to differentiate itself from the household economic order it was once imperfectly separated from but now needs to deploy its tools of self-definition against another threatening adjacency—the emerging leisure class world of the post-bellum years. Alcott's work, at this obsessively revisited social juncture, is to write a boundary-maintaining moral difference be-

tween the "right" world of Marmee and this more affluent surround. When Meg (for instance) falls, in the positively Dreiserian
chapter "Domestic Experiences," into such a fit of fashion-envy
and consumeristic desire that she buys a dress she cannot afford,
the experience teaches her (and us) the necessity of family fru-
gality. But at the same time that it is erecting an ethic of poor but
honest virtue against the temptations of affluence, *Little Women*
opens an unobtrusive commerce between old-style virtuous domesticity and a new-style lavishness. The Laurence mansion is
right next door to the March house (so proximate are these orders
in *Little Women*), and the daughters who learn homely virtues at
one place nevertheless receive covert aid—luxuries like pianos and
ice cream—from the other. Having ritually reasserted the reign of
traditional values, similarly, this book indulges in its own version
of upward mobility. Amy March renounces the plutocrat Fred only
to land the quite sufficiently wealthy Laurie. Wielding a motherlike character-making power, she convinces Laurie to work for a
living rather than live off his income; but the industrious idyll they
look forward to is full of upper class consciousness: Amy becomes
at last a "true gentlewoman" (418); she and Laurie contemplate
the special pleasures of altruism on behalf of "poor gentle folk"
(429); and Jo's school looks forward to including "rich pupils" as
well as "a ragamuffin or two" (it sounds like a prep school with a
scholarship plan), since "rich people's children often need care
and comfort, as well as poor" (452).

   In the Amy plot especially, *Little Women* is profoundly concerned to negotiate between an older, more heavily moralized
version of middle-class life and the more affluent and enjoyment-
oriented version of that life becoming socially pressing at the
book's time. But Amy's path is toward not just a new social situation but specifically a new base for cultural activity. In the primitive distribution of March family gifts, Amy is marked as the
artistic child or "Little Raphael" (38). Her castle in the air is to "go
to Rome, and do fine pictures, and be the best artist in the whole
world" (134), and her selfish wish, on the book's opening page, is
for art materials—Faber's drawing pencils. Adept at the arts of
pleasing, specifically those who are socially above her, Amy wins

her way not just into a wealthy or classy milieu but into a space with profound relevance to her art. What Amy most essentially wins, through her winning ways, is Europe—a long stay in Europe at someone else's expense. This "Europe," in turn, is something with a perfectly definite meaning in the American culture of this book's time. As a later chapter must explain more fully, the reformulated upper order of the postbellum decades took Europe as a group-defining value in a double sense. European travel became one of the chief ways of displaying upper-class prerogatives of wealth and leisure for Americans after 1860, and so became a status-bearing class pastime; concurrently, the newly articulated high culture this group affiliated itself with made initiation into European art a chief mark of cultural value—a value displayed in the new gentry-founded art museums full of European masters, among other ways. With the establishment of an American high culture with this social constituency, the knowledge of touristic-artistic "Europe" became the chief requisite for American artists seeking high-artistic careers, and in America in the late 1860s the ability to display this knowledge became the chief literary ticket in. Near the moment of *Little Women,* William Dean Howells launched himself into the assistant editorship of the *Atlantic Monthly* and his subsequent career by presenting Italy to an American readership. (Howells's first book was *Venetian Life* [1866], and his first novels were romances of international tourism.) Henry James toured Europe in the same year as the fictional Amy March, strenuously appropriating Europe and its art and thereby binding himself more tightly to American high-cultural circles: "I find myself tending more and more to become interested in the things for which you have said so much—art and the history of art and multifarious Italian matters," James wrote Charles Eliot Norton, high priest of the Bostonian cult of high-art appreciation, in 1870.[37] Mark Twain launched his American career in 1869 with another rehearsal of the possession of Europe: the satire of American culture-mongering and status-seeking "innocents abroad." May Alcott, Louisa May Alcott's sister and original of Amy, followed the same culturally organized career path with less ambivalence than Twain. A talented painter praised by Ruskin for her copies of the Turners

in the National Gallery, this forgotten artist had art lessons with
the same drawing master as Henry James, William Holman Hunt,
and expatriated in pursuit of her artistic goals within a year of
James, in 1876.[38]

In *Little Women*, Amy does not attain to an artistic career. Approached with the hierarchical plan of aesthetic value she brings
from home, Europe shows Amy the difference between "talent"
like hers and "genius" (378) like the great masters', and like the
Hilda of Hawthorne's *The Marble Faun* or the Rowland Mallet of
James's *Roderick Hudson,* she renounces her own ambitions as a
tribute to the artistically great. She becomes, instead, a patron of
the arts, putting her wealth and trained taste to the service of supporting fine art's cultural presence—her "white pillared mansion,"
the Mount Parnassus of *Jo's Boys,* is "full . . . of music, beauty, and
the culture young hearts and fancies long for."[39] What Alcott images in Amy is a contemporaneous development we have touched
on from the author's side. Her plot figures the emergence, to one
side of the old-style domestic world, of a new social support for
artistic activity, the high-cultural world stabilized after 1860 with
leisure-class or owner-class backing (she and Laurie must have
subscribed to the *Atlantic*); and her plot suggests how this new
world's boundary mechanism works. In *Little Women,* Amy gets out
of the world of domesticity and self-denial because she gets to
go to Europe, and she gets to go to Europe because she curries
favor with her wealthy Aunt. As this book understands it the
new high culture organized around nondomestic values accepts
and even seeks recruits from the middling orders, but it requires
them to have had certain formative "experiences"—like European
travel—only open to the well-to-do and their adherents: to the
upward-looking Amy, but not the favor-shunning Jo; in real life
to self-gentrifiers like William Dean Howells or Bernard Berenson
or even Mark Twain, but not to Louisa May Alcott. (Alcott first
went to Europe as a paid companion to a neurotic invalid—as an
extension of female servitude, in other words, not an adventure in
leisure and privilege.)

If I am right here, one project of *Little Women* is charting the
field of specifically artistic spaces that have opened up at the time

of its writing. What makes this hunch more plausible is the fact that the book attends much more overtly to another new literary economy: the reading culture centered on the story-paper. Jo is a publishing author in *Little Women* and in the chapter "Literary Lessons" she finds a new outlet for her work, which the book characterizes rather complexly. At a public lecture Jo sees someone reading "a pictorial sheet" illustrated with "an Indian in full war costume, tumbling over a precipice with a wolf at his throat, while two infuriated young gentlemen, with unnaturally small feet and big eyes, were stabbing each other close by, and a disheveled female was flying away in the background with her mouth wide open" (251): unmistakably, a story-paper. The story-paper, Jo apprehends, features a certain "style" of writing (252)—the exotic and elaborately melodramatic "sensational story" (253). But it also binds such writing to a particular system of literary production, centered in a business office—a nondomestic space and very much a men's world—where sharp-eyed editors freely alter work with an eye to its popular sale. It ties writing as well to a certain economics of authorship—Mrs. S. L. A. N. G. Northbury, Alcott's rendition of the staple producer for the *New York Ledger,* Mrs. E. D. E. N. Southworth, is known to "make a good living out of such stories." It ties writing to a socially differentiated audience—it is notably a "lad" (251), not the feminine reader of domestic fiction, whom Jo sees reading the *Blarneystone Banner.* And it ties writing as well to a highly particular social ethos. This journal's productions "belong to that class of light literature in which the passions have a holiday"—conspicuously not, in other words, to the literary culture of self-control and self-restraint. Its editor mercilessly cuts "all the moral reflections" (326) Jo has put in her work: edification, staple and end of middle-class fiction, has no place in this differently conceived prose entertainment.

The story-paper is grasped as a literary-social institution in *Little Women,* an organized place for writing that enmeshes writing in a definite set of social relations. This socially structured writing world is another of the new presences *Little Women* knows to be adjacent to itself; and another work of this novel is to bound its world off from this newly encroaching neighbor.

This bounding is enacted through an extraordinarily elaborate textual activity in *Little Women*. Story-paper writing first appears in the book simply as an available career, a kind of work that is open to Jo. But the book then manufactures a strongly negative ethical charge around this apparently indifferent activity. The proscription of such writing is performed first through the narrative voice. Usually tolerant and bemused, Alcott becomes for once intrusively moralistic and heavy-handedly censorious when she approaches this subject: "the means [Jo] took to gain her end were not the best" (324), she writes; and again: "wrongdoing always brings its own punishment, and when Jo most needed hers, she got it" (328). The narrator's exposition of the "wrong" of such writing runs as follows:

Mr. Dashwood rejected any but thrilling tales, and as thrills could not be produced except by harrowing up the souls of the readers, history and romance, land and sea, science and art, police records and lunatic asylums, had to be ransacked for the purpose. Jo soon found that her innocent experience had given her but few glimpses of the tragic world which underlies society, so regarding it in a business light, she set about supplying her deficiencies with characteristic energy. Eager to find material for stories, and bent on making them original in plot, if not masterly in execution, she searched newspapers for accidents, incidents, and crimes; she excited the suspicions of public librarians by asking for works on poisons; she studied faces in the street, and characters, good, bad, and indifferent, all about her; she delved into the dust of ancient times for facts or fictions so old that they were as good as new, and introduced herself to folly, sin, and misery, as well as her limited opportunities allowed. She thought she was prospering finely, but unconsciously she was beginning to desecrate some of the womanliest attributes of a woman's character. She was living in bad society, and imaginary though it was, its influence affected her, for she was feeding heart and fancy on dangerous and unsubstantial food, and was fast brushing the innocent bloom from her nature by a premature acquaintance with the darker side of life, which comes soon enough to all of us. [327–28]

The genres of story-papers require certain forms of knowledge of their would-be writers, the experience needed to project their generic "reality." This experiential horizon is "dark," a "tragic" dimension, Alcott's last phrase implies, that characterizes all human life. But her prose also suggests that this "darker" life corresponds specifically to the life of a lower, and a fearfully lower, social stratum: a social "underside" characterized by crime, sexual license and the nonprotection of women's "innocent bloom," poor nutritional habits, "folly, sin, and misery." Alcott presumes, here, that story-papers are the literary emanation of lower-class culture, such that to "enter into" such writing even imaginatively is tantamount to going into "bad society." A woman can cross over into this genre and social culture, but not without violating the shieldedness from indecent knowledge that establishes the proper "women" of middle class society. For a woman to write such work, in short, is to become unwomanly: to desecrate "some of the womanliest attributes of a woman's character."

In this paragraph an apparently universal term in fact linked to the norms of one social group gets deployed against a literary form known to belong to a different social group. The very idea of the decently domestic "little woman," the concept on which the ethos of middle-class domesticity is founded, is mobilized against story-paper fiction here; and the subsequent narrative reinforces this effect. As Alcott continues her story, Jo's secret writing career turns out to have been detected—by Professor Bhaer, the husband destined for this "good wife." Generations of readers have been groaned over this final match. But the disappointment Bhaer engenders is just what makes him right for Jo, within the thinking of the book's dominant ethos. In an ethos that sets the transcendence of untutored personal desire as a primary value for women, Bhaer's nonattractions—his poverty, his age—become positive qualifications in a husband. (Jo knows better than to accept the proposal of Laurie, who is wrong for her just because he is so right for her: so young, so wealthy, so high-spirited, so much fun.) Bhaer's further "attractiveness" lies in his moral superiority, and even more in the confident authority with which he projects it. In the nineteenth-century culture of domesticity, the insistence that the child take a morally authoritative parent as its love-object strongly disposes the child to find its lovers in parentlike figures: it is not accident but the fulfillment of her upbringing that Ellen Montgomery finds her adult love in John Humphreys, who stands to her as older to younger, teacher to pupil, and moral regulator to morally regulated.[40] This is just the relation Professor Bhaer occupies toward Jo; but to fit him for the role of love-object the book needs to let him assert himself toward her in a morally authoritative form.

This is what happens in the story-paper subplot. Bhaer is only a teacher in the same house with Jo, a learned man known to be in need of a good wife (Jo's peeping has taught her that he darns his own socks) and known as a public defender of old-time religion, until the scene where he weighs in against her writing. Story-paper fiction, he informs her here, is "bad trash" (333), not just a vacuous entertainment of innocent manufacture but an active agent of social debasement. When Jo tells him that "many very respectable people make an honest living out of what are called sensation stories," he turns on her and takes higher ground: "If the respectable people knew what harm they did, they would not feel that the living *was* honest. They haf no right to put poison in the sugarplum, and let the small ones eat it" (333). In taking this high tone, Bhaer associates himself with "that Father and Mother" whose moral insistences laid "sure foundations" for Jo "to build character upon in womanhood" (334); and the narrative organization of *Little Women* gives this otherwise unrelated development extraordinary literary implications. For as the story is constructed, Professor Bhaer qualifies himself as parent substitute and potential beloved through his censure of story-papers; and Jo attains to her mature womanly life by accepting his lesson, renouncing her sensation-fiction writing, and converting to a more morally acceptable genre. The juvenile-domestic writing she turns to now, exemplified in the text by the *Little Women*-like poem "In the Garret," brings Jo to her husband and her own married self.

If more evidence were needed, this sequence shows how little the social situation of Alcott's authorship is external to her work. *Little Women* is a book written in full awareness of the places for writers and writing structured in its surrounding culture, and weighing their different meanings and accessibilities is one of its chief imaginative projects. The way Alcott differentiates among writing worlds within *Little Women* sheds considerable light on her own choice of literary position. But the book's great interest is that it affords a glimpse, as well, of a larger process of cultural discrimination.

This chapter has had as its subject the segmentation of American literary cultures in the decades after 1850, the articulation of hierarchically arrayed literary "levels" that is a newly insistent fact of American life in the later nineteenth century. One of the points Alcott has helped demonstrate is that these cultures were not truly separate but lived together; but that is not to say that they were undifferentiated. Their difference, rather, was not a given but an action: a relation established *for* them against the fact of their possible continuity. How were these literary levels separated? By the different literary features—styles, genres, voices or tones, mimetic modes—of the work they supplied, potentially (though literary features never by themselves establish the cultural placement of a work); by the separate social audiences they colonized and served, eventually. But before these bodies of writing could be bounded off in practice, the difference between them needed to be socially designated and weighted; and this is the process Alcott exposes. *Little Women* shows new lines of literary division being drawn as part of a larger action of social division. In it a middle-class ethos anxious to differentiate itself from a lower order projects the value terms it uses to organize that difference into the literary realm: fastens the opposition domestic fiction/sensation fiction to the larger oppositions good society/bad society, respectable/nonrespectable, womanly/unwomanly, morally self-controlled/licentious. Through this process an aesthetic difference between once equally acceptable modes is made to express the moral difference between "us" and "them," and the choices people make between now-separated writing worlds come to tell what "kind" of people they are.

The larger reality Alcott shows the inner workings of—the correlation of newly severed literary worlds with newly sharpened class divisions, and the resultant conversion of literary taste into a

✳ prime sign of class difference—is a decisive feature of American
cultural organization in the Gilded Age. Dee Garrison has studied
how the librarians of the Gilded Age associated the taste for "low"
fiction with the "lowness" of the lower orders, and how they
used their leverage over lower-class reading choices to enforce extraliterary social decorums. (Professor Bhaer would have made a
splendid librarian.) From the popular side, Michael Denning has
studied how the boundary drawn between genteel and sensational
literature in the later nineteenth century helped both parties for-
mulate the difference between the middle and working classes as
those groups became more decisively divided.[41] Such organizations of the cultural realm shaped the understandings actual indi-
viduals acted on—what is Alcott's rejection of story-paper writing
but a repudiation of a form she fears will declass her?—and they
also shaped the lives individual works could lead. When lines of
literary-cultural demarcation first sketched in the 1860s began to
dry, Alcott's own work began to have its social place determined
by these schemas. Harriet Beecher Stowe wrote Alcott in 1872:

> In my many fears for my country and in these days when so much
> seductive and dangerous literature is pushed forward, the success of
> your domestic works has been to me most comforting. It shows that
> after all our people are all right and that they love the right kind of
> thing.[42]

Stowe here all but overtly amalgamates the literary opposition
domestic fiction/sensation fiction to the social opposition "our
people"/lower class ("dangerous" was a prime name for that class
in the nineteenth century). As Stowe reads them, Alcott's books
stand on one side this opposition and help show the power of that
side: if *Little Women* and *Little Men* can be popular too, then "our
people" are not done for yet.

Later still, when now-hardened cultural divisions began to produce real differences of class experience, Alcott's writing suffered
the fate Stowe foresaw: that of becoming the loved property of
some of "us." Alcott's children's books continue to be read with a
depth of absorption perhaps unequalled by any other nineteenth-

century American text. But at least one piece of evidence suggests that this audience has been partial, not universal. In her turn-of-the-century study of the lives of women workers, Dorothy Richardson amazes her interlocutors by her ignorance of the story-paper authors Laura Jean Libbey, Charlotte M. Braeme, and Effie Adelaide Rowlands, canonical writers in their circle. "What kind of story-books do you read, then?" they ask, only to have her discover that they are equally ignorant of Charles Dickens, Oliver Goldsmith, and Louisa May Alcott. Richardson continues:

> I spoke enthusiastically of "Little Women," telling them how I read it four times, and that I meant to read it again some day. Their curiosity was aroused over the unheard-of thing of anybody ever wanting to read any book more than once, and they pressed me to reciprocate [they have just narrated Libbey's "Little Rosebud's Lovers" to Richardson] by repeating the story for them, which I did with great accuracy of statement, and with genuine pleasure to myself at being given an opportunity to introduce anybody to Meg and Jo and the rest of that delightful March family. When I finished, Phoebe stopped her cornering and Mrs. Smith looked up from her label-pasting.
>
> "Why, that's no story at all," the latter declared.
>
> "Why, no," echoed Phoebe; "that's no story—that's just every-day happenings. I don't see what's the use putting things like that in books. I'll bet any money that lady who wrote it knew all them boys and girls. They sound like real, live people; and when you was telling about them I could see them as plain as plain could be—couldn't you, Gwendolyn?"
>
> "Yep," yawned our vis-à-vis, undisguisedly bored.
>
> "But I suppose farmer folks like them kind of stories," Phoebe generously suggested. "They ain't used to the same styles of anything that us city folks are."[43]

In this astonishing passage, social divisions focussed through different reading habits have become an unbridgeable gap. Two literary cultures stare at each other in mutual incomprehension, with what passes for literacy in each signifying illiteracy in the eyes of the other. In this divide, Alcott's book, the cherished possession of one group, is a complete mystery to the other. Implementing as it does a "foreign" principle of mimesis, the domestic realism of "just everyday happenings," it appears to the working-class women as incompetent fiction: "that's no story at all." Or the charity of incipient pluralism suggests that it might not be "no story" but someone else's story: to the taste of some remote other, denizen of a different world. *Little Women* has become a marker, here, of real-world social separations; and in her conclusion, Richardson, good user of literature for social management that she is, looks to *Little Women* as a tool of social reform. She proposes to make the culture of working people less alien by injecting her kind of book into the acculturation of their children. Some philanthropist, she writes, should "make it his business that no tenement baby should be without its 'Mother Goose,' and, a little later, its 'Little Women,' 'Uncle Tom's Cabin,' 'Robinson Crusoe,' and all the other precious childhood favorites."[44]

Having come to her career at the time when literary boundaries were being socially organized, and having chosen a certain social audience and social ethic with her choice of work, Alcott would have understood the process that produced Richardson's divided world. But she would also have known that that process made a different world from one she had seen: a world in which a writer could write across generic boundaries; could be an author of all kinds, at once "blood and thunder" writer and high-literary aspirant and "the Thackeray, the Trollope, of the nursery and the school-room;"[45] and so could write toward the whole audience that was divided up in her time.

The Reading of Regions

For a History of Literary Access

W E LIVE in the presence of a new wish toward the literary. This wish, not found in significant concentrations before the modern Civil Rights movement, is that literature be no party to the play of social discrimination, indeed that literature be the exemplary social institution opened to the human in its full range. This wish has chosen, as its means for seizing its goal, the assault on literary canons, a strategy that has met with notable success. Ten years ago it would have been hard to predict the achievements this movement has already registered both in exposing the partiality of previously authoritative literary constructions and in discovering work implied by the received canon not to exist. But as it comes closer to success, canon revision begins to reveal certain problems with itself as a way to realize the wish that drives it, one of which I want to speak to here.[1]

Canon revision, like the entitlement movements that are its social cognates, turns on a critique of exclusion. Over against a representation that says some works are justly enfranchised as literature and others justly disenfranchised or forgotten, this movement labors to demonstrate the interest and power of neglected works, thereby baring the systematic suppressions of a hitherto "complete" account of the literary and opening it to modes of experience it had shut out. Such a critique implies that for every gap

in the official literary record there is a body of literary expression
in the state of being denied, and successful retrievals in the early
phases of extracanonical exploration—Oxford University Press's
Schomburg Library of Nineteenth-Century Black Women Writers
is the most recent—have done much to warrant this assumption.
But as canonical extension presses beyond its initial rediscoveries
it also helps expose that its dream of a potentially full literary record has a utopian (not to say illusionistic) side.

For the same effort that has restored what Whitman calls
"many long-dumb voices" to literature begins to reveal that there
are many more long dumb voices not available for historical recov-
ery by audio equipment however sensitive. In *A Room of One's
Own*, Virignia Woolf asked of the Elizabethan Renaissance "why
no woman wrote a word of that extraordinary literature when
every other man, it seemed, was capable of song or sonnet,"[2] and
while a nearly obsessional critical attention has produced the
names of lost women writers of this time, there is no denying that
it has not retrieved a female Spenser or Shakespeare, or even a
female Surrey or Nashe. For any historical period we could make
a list of kinds of authors of whom we cannot find representatives,
a list as long as we have patience to make it. Joiners and weavers
appear in *A Midsummer Night's Dream*, but where are the plays
written by Elizabethan joiners or weavers? The song of an agricultural laborer inspires Wordsworth's "Solitary Reaper," but where
(except in Burns) are such a laborer's own poetical utterances?
American literature from "Song of Myself" and *Huckleberry Finn*
to *All God's Dangers* and *The Color Purple* delights to give voice to
the socially voiceless, but where—except in such retranscriptions
by others in different social positions—is the literary output of
semiliterate delinquent boys of the Mississippi River valley, or of
unlettered black sharecroppers of the Deep South, or (to name a
category no one has yet thought to miss) of the "mash'd fireman"
whose sufferings Whitman superbly enters into in "Song of Myself," or the travelling salesman Dreiser knows as Drouet, or the
mental defective Faulkner brings to written life as Benjy?

Such figures—and hundreds of others—fail to show up in literature as makers; in Woolf's words, their literary genius (what-

ever it may have been) "never got itself on paper."[3] And we should not forget to add that the figures who did get onto paper and into print are not for that reason each other's equals *in* the literary. "There shall be no difference" is canon revision's other Whitmanian motto; but differences of expressive power, if not the specific value differences a traditional canonical system once ascribed, are what the display of a whole field of writing necessarily reveals. Susan Warner's rediscovered domestic novel *The Wide, Wide World* restores an intensely interesting work to American fiction, and the whole field of mid-nineteenth century American writing—not only the women's domestic branch—is better understood in the light of Warner's case. But we get this book wrong if we deny the restrictions of expressive range within which Warner writes: that the terms on which she gets to write also restrict her range of motion *as* a writer is part of Warner's meaning as a historical exhibit. Jack London exemplifies a working-class autodidact successfully pressing himself into the ranks of authors at the turn of the century. But to note the poverty of the literary resources London's writing knows how to command is not only to engage in social or literary snobbery. It is to identify the specific difference in seized competence and realized power (every author possesses such a difference) that is his literary mark.

Fully surveyed, the literary field reveals that literature is exactly not fully representative, but instead that literature has been differentially available throughout its history: available on some terms at some periods to some figures and groups of figures, but available on other terms—including not at all—to others. Before such a recognition, the wish for inclusion that has fueled recent canon interrogation will need to shift its question: will need to stop asking how some writing came to be forgotten and ask instead why only some writing exists to be remembered in the first place; will need to ask not only how discriminations among works have been made after the fact in canonical selections but what it is about different works that endows them with different literary resources at the point of their creation. Pressed far enough, the will to literary representativeness will require, as a sequel and supplement to the labor of canon revision, an inquiry into the history of literary access.

a systematic asking by what means and by virtue of what circumstances different potential authors have been able to lay claim to different powers in the literary realm.[4]

The issue of literary access is a densely historical subject, not knowable except through the local circumstances of particular literary-historical situations, and especially not knowable through the unhistoricized aid of present-day prejudices of whatever stripe. But if the subject of access must quickly become particular to be interesting, a few general statements might be hazarded in advance. For one, the study of literary access must insist at its inception that the history of access is never wholly external to authors and their achievements, never wholly the product of contextual or cultural determinants. No one appears in authorship without the prior achievement—funded by just that specificity of will and imagination that makes that figure a distinctive being—of thinking him- or herself over from a person in general into that more specialized human self that is an author. No candidate for authorship is ever so advantaged that he does not need to be able to seize that advantage or wish to turn it *to* advantage. Henry James came to literature from the leisure class, but being of the leisure class has never of itself been sufficient to make anyone a Henry James. The seventeenth-century "mob of gentlemen who wrote with ease" (in Alexander Pope's phrase) no doubt wrote more easily than the nongentlemen of the same time who had more rudimentary literacy skills, but even they did not become writers merely by being gentlemen, whatever weight that must have carried as an enablement. Conversely, no external disadvantage has yet proved so total that we can say for sure that it absolutely prohibits the attainment of authorship to figures as crafty and willful as humans in all known social grades have proved to be. The system of Southern slavery that outlawed the imparting of literacy to blacks withheld, in an external or institutional way, the most elementary means of literary access (and so circumscribed most slaves' literary expression to the oral realm). But Frederick Douglass's ability (among others) to appropriate the knowledge of reading and writing from a system bent on denying him that knowledge shows that a severely deprived figure can still become a writer given enough will and ingenuity; and Douglass can stand for the writers in every cultural configuration who succeed in making themselves writers in excess of such configurations' plans for figures of their sort.   *human agency*

The history of access cannot be grasped without reference to the act by which some human agent, equipped with some set of drives and gifts, not others, asserts himself in the realm of writing. But assertions of authorship are always staged within particular cultural settings, which belong to this history just as much. Any act of literary accession finds the conditions of its possibility set in a social situation defined by a multiplicity of interconnected factors. The ease or obstruction of the way into writing is set from far back by questions of education and acculturation, by the differential social dissemination of relevant skills and of the encouragement to embrace them. Virginia Woolf's fictitious Judith Shakespeare, still our greatest imagining of the problem of literary creativity as a social problem of access, is shut out of authorship at the point of achievement because she has been shut out of the settings that would have enabled eventual achievement. Kept home while her perhaps no more gifted brother is sent to school, "she had no chance of learning grammar and logic, let alone of reading Horace and Virgil," and the upbringing thought suitable for girls not only limits her knowledge but teaches her that the written is not for her: "She picked up a book now and then, one of her brother's perhaps, and read a few pages. But then her parents came in and told her to mend the stockings and mind the stew and not moon about with books and papers." [5] Woolf's recovered writer Lady Winchilsea also sees herself excluded from enabling education by social organizations of gender and knowledge, "debarred from all improvements of the mind," and so afflicted with anxiety at the point of aspiration. Of "a woman that attempts the pen" she writes:

> And if some one would soar above the rest,
> With warmer fancy, and ambition pressed,
> So strong the opposing faction still appears,
> The hopes to thrive can ne'er outweigh the fears. [6]

Lest we think that "woman" is an invariant category invariably linked to disadvantage, Eudora Welty might be cited as a writer whose way into writing was eased at every step. In *One Writer's Beginnings,* Welty remembers a childhood home furnished with books. (This home is a direct descendant of the insular, child- and book-centered home of nineteenth-century middle-class domesticity.) Welty remembers being continually read to by loving parents; being given books of her own in early youth; being given blanket permission at age nine to "read any book she wants from the shelves [of the Jackson, Mississippi, Carnegie Library], children or adult;" later, going to colleges where gifted teachers initiated her into "the immediacy of poetry" and opened up the English literary tradition. This chain of social settings made writing a completely familiar possession to Welty, and gave her will to write the character of a supported activity. "It was my mother who emotionally and imaginatively supported me in my wish to become a writer. It was my father who gave me the first dictionary of my own," the grateful Welty writes.[7]

But the case of Richard Wright, who lived for part of his childhood in the same town as Welty, would show how a different social positioning in the same world can produce a different literary initiation. As a black boy in the segregated town in which Welty was a white girl, Wright grew up in the culture of deprivation organized as the social opposite of her world of security and abundance, a culture of *literary* deprivation among other forms. The laws of segregation shut Wright out of the library that honored Welty's note of permission from her mother. (Wright eventually got to use the Memphis public library by forging requests from a white patron and pretending to be his illiterate servant.) Excluded from such whites-only institutions of the written word, Wright was doubly debarred from literature by his fundamentalist grandmother's fierce animus against secular entertainments or "worldly books," which he alleges she burned. (By his account the young Wright unknowingly peddled a segregationist newspaper because its magazine supplement gave him his unique access to printed fiction.) In this situation Wright's own writing was more than discouraged. Writing itself was rendered almost inconceivable: the very idea of literary writing as a desirable or valuable act was made almost impossible to frame. "My environment contained nothing more alien than writing or the desire to express one's self in writing," Wright memorably writes. When he reads his first written composition to the girl next door, she asks, bewildered: "What's that for?"[8]

Wright found his own surrogate institutions of literary education after leaving Mississippi, and his beginning did not keep him from writing any more than Welty's guaranteed her writing. But his different acculturation gave him a different relation to this act: made writing a foreign power to be seized over against the world that denied him that power, not, as with Welty, an extension of home security. And even Wright's disadvantage was only comparative. When, hired as an amanuensis by an illiterate black insurance agent, the city-bred (and schoolteacher-mothered) Wright visited the black culture of the rural Mississippi Delta, he met a literary deprivation much more fundamental than his own: "I had been pitying myself for not having books to read, and now I saw children who had never read a book. . . . I would fill out insurance applications, and a sharecropper family, fresh from laboring in the fields, would stand and gape,"[9] he writes in *Black Boy.* The authors to have emerged from this unleisured and unlettered setting are not to be named.   *a ll his analytic question*

Schemes of training and transmission are one social form mediating the possibility of literary careers. Another lies in the history of literary institutions. Earlier chapters of this book have insisted that the literary sphere is the subject of plural and changing cultural organizations, determining what forms of writing are in cultural operation at any time or place, what mechanisms of production support such forms, what publics such forms are brought to and what value they have attached to them. Here it can be added that every literary institution projects a profile of the authors it can support through its prescription of the competences required to produce its forms. Lady Winchilsea's couplets remind us that she wrote in the setting of late seventeenth- and early eighteenth-century English Augustanism, a literary culture that organized itself against an insurgent mass-print culture by attaching high

all the variants needed to understand howt why texts get produced

how Texts come To be + mean

value to knowledges not available to the popular orders, classical
learning above all. It was this historical organization that made
gentlemanly classical education such a crucially requisite literary
knowledge at her time—and that, conversely, made her exclusion from such "improvements of the mind" such a crucial de-
barment. (Literary institutions discriminate not crassly or overtly
but through the knowledges they presume.) But the prerequisite
scheme Lady Winchilsea encountered is by no means invariant.
One of the meanings of the nineteenth-century domestic culture
of letters this book has been surveying is that it institutionalized
a writing world in which classical education had relatively little
value and knowledge of home management—what Lady Winchilsea calls "the dull manage of a servile house"—constituted a
major resource. In the 1869 essays in *Hearth and Home* that Woolf
would have found fascinating, Harriet Beecher Stowe asks the
question, "Why is it . . . that the best writing is done by men?"
and gives a social, institutional answer: "the education of the
woman stops short at the point where the boy's education really
begins," with the result that women are made "deficient in the
very first requisite of a good writer—namely, something to say
which is worth saying." But the always upbeat Stowe then argues
that if "the experiences of woman in real life" all come "to her in
her domestic capacity," that very knowledge may constitute a peculiar literary resource, a "subject matter which woman, and only
woman, could possibly be able to present;" and Stowe urges
would-be women writers to seize on "domestic and rural subjects," "the simple and homely scenes of every-day life," as the
way to begin their careers.[10] Stowe makes a classic contribution
here to the American literature of self-help. But what makes her
advice practical is a literary-institutional fact: the mid-nineteenth-
century stabilization of a literary culture centered on domestic
lore. This fact made the housewife's experience pertinent literary
training, and so opened the door for middle-class women into
letters—into one zone of the literary field, to be more precise.

I do not pretend to have exhausted, here, the list of institutional
factors bearing on artistic careers. In a moment I will be turning to
a historical case study, where the nature and operation of these

factors can be more fully considered. This excursus has meant only
to raise a subject and—so to speak—to trumpet its importance.
The history of literary access, conceived as the history of the processes by which literary writing has had different cultural places
made for it, and so has had different groups placed in different
proximities *to* it; the history of access, conceived at the same
time as the history of the acts—successful, failed, and partially
achieved—by which potential authors have made themselves into
authors within the opportunities and obstructions of particular social situations: this is the history we need to begin to compose if
we would understand the relation of the whole of humanity to the
whole field of letters. In place of the paired positions toward this
crux that entrap us now—an egalitarianism whose social politics
makes it deny that differences of literary achievement exist in spite
of their manifest reality and a residual classicism that insists that
literary works are not equal but that makes their differences an
affair of individual genius, while distributing its sympathies toward
genius in suspiciously limited ways—the study of literary access
offers to recognize the reality of literature's different availability but
also to understand that difference historically, as a culturally mediated historical product. Such a study would ask of every literary
attempt what sense of literary empowerment it illustrates and proceeds from, then what conditions enabled its writer to envision his
power in that form and not another: a way of putting the question
that makes the whole field of possible writing the object of inquiry,
but that seeks to establish *how in* that field differences arise.

history of literary opportunity

The Reading of Regions: A Study in the Social Life of Forms

In American literature in the second half of the nineteenth century,
regional fiction presents an especially instructive instance of the
history of literary opportunity. Focused on the ground of literary
forms, this familiar if rather tepidly admired genre presents an
easily identified set of formal properties. It requires a setting outside the world of modern development, a zone of backwardness
where locally variant folkways still prevail. Its characters are eth-
nologically colorful, personifications of the different humanity

produced in such non-modern cultural settings. Above all, this fiction features an extensive written simulation of regional vernacular, a conspicuous effort to catch the nuances of local speech.
Edward Eggleston tells his reader in the preface to *The Hoosier
Schoolmaster* (1871) that his labor in writing has been "to preserve
the true *usus loquendi*" of "the provincialisms of the Indiana back-
woods." Thomas Nelson Page's *In Ole Virginia* (1887) begins by
underscoring that "the dialect of the negroes of Eastern Virginia
differs totally from that of the Southern negroes, and in some material points from that of those located farther west," then offers a
pronunciation guide for the dialect it records.[11]

But focused within the history of authorship, the genre defined
by these place-centered literary features also possesses an unexpected further feature, namely, that it served as the principal
place of literary access in America in the postbellum decades. Regionalism was not the career vehicle for Henry James and William
Dean Howells, the most heavily professionalized among post–
Civil War writers. But virtually every other writer of this time who
succeeded in establishing himself as a writer did so through the
regional form. Eggleston became an author by becoming the literary recorder of rural Hoosier culture. Twain (admittedly a more
complicated case) became the author of a midwestern life only
somewhat further west. George Washington Cable established his
literary self by taking what his first book called *Old Creole Days*
(1879) as his subject. Sarah Orne Jewett and Mary Wilkins (later
Freeman) made themselves writers by making remote New England villages their literary concern.

But more interestingly for my purposes, this genre did not just
create a place for writers: in the later nineteenth century, regionalism was so structured as to extend opportunity above all to
groups traditionally distanced from literary lives. Regional fiction
set as the competence required to produce it the need to know
how to write, but it set this entry requirement unusually low: since
this form was heavily conventionalized in formulas that barely
changed from the 1860s to the century's end, it did not require the
more highly elaborated writerly skills that other forms asked for
their successful performance. (The fact that authors in this mode

typically had their first efforts published suggests how little special training the form required, how adequate it was found in its most conventional versions.) The other knowledge this form required was familiarity with some cultural backwater, acquaintance with a way of life apart from the culturally dominant. In this respect regionalism made the experience of the socially marginalized into a literary asset, and so made marginality itself a positive authorial advantage. Through the inversion of customary privilege built into its formal logic, this genre created a writer's role that women were equipped to perform, especially women from from small towns and peripheral locations—like Mary Wilkins, of the nonmetropolitan Randolph, Massachusetts; Rose Terry Cooke, from rural Connecticut; Tennessee's Mary Noailles Murfree; Iowa and Arkansas's Alice French ("Octave Thanet"); or Louisiana's Grace King. Ann Douglas has noted that local-color writing provided the door into literary careers for women in the postbellum decades that the domestic-sentimental novel had afforded in the antebellum years;[12] but women were by no means the only socially disparaged figures that this form paradoxically advantaged. The vernacular requirement of the local-color form made the folkways and speechways known to African Americans—heretofore a mark of their inferior "civilization"—into a valuable literary capital; and by trading on the value this form gave to the knowledge of black vernacular, members of America's principal subjugated minority—Charles Waddell Chesnutt and Paul Laurence Dunbar, in particular— broke into the ranks of American authors. The form extended a comparable opportunity to those disparaged in other ways. Hamlin Garland, the first farmer to have entered American literature, felt humiliatingly handicapped for authorship by his provincial origins and immersion in manual labor. But in Garland's case a farm worker was enabled to become an author by the regional form, which converted his rural background into a career-funding resource. American literary writing in all its branches was a monopoly of the native-born throughout the nineteenth century. But when an ethnic immigrant first succeeded in establishing himself as a writer outside his ethnic group, it was again with the assistance of the regional mode. I am thinking of Abraham Cahan, who won a general American audience with *Yekl: A Tale of the New York Ghetto* (1896) and *The Imported Bridegroom, and Other Stories of the New York Ghetto* (1898) by figuring out how to adapt the dialect tale formula to the "region" of the Lower East Side.

Historically, then, nineteenth-century literary regionalism yielded more than a place of access. It effected a revision of the traditional terms of literary access, a major extension of the literary franchise. This fact gives the genre its importance for the history of access at large. But if we place it within that history we will right away face a question: Why should this genre have made the difference I have discussed, what was it about this form that let it so re-form the field of possible authors? I have said that regional fiction could alter the demographics of authorship because it en-franchised a new set of social knowledges as a source of literary expertise. But this reasoning cannot say why the genre should have entered the literary field when it did, or how it won the power, there, to establish its practitioners in careers. Those matters are functions of its cultural life and standing; and to know how this form created enablement we need to inquire into the terms of its historical social life.

One reason regionalism could win public places for those who wrote it in the later nineteenth century, we might begin by observ-ing, is that this genre was an object of special demand. A kind of writing that has been the target of much milder interest at other times and places was the focus in America, from the 1860s well into the 1890s, of intense and steady readerly desire. Sample cir-culation histories—the fact that Sarah Orne Jewett's first volume, *Deephaven* (1877), went through twenty-three editions in its first nineteen years, or that Mary Noailles Murfree's *In the Tennessee Mountains* (1884) went through seventeen editions in its first two years—attest to the market for such wares in these years. In rec-ognition of this market, American publishers of the Gilded Age not only eagerly received but actively encouraged the production of this commodity. In 1867 one publisher contracted to pay Bret Harte, the pioneer creator of local-color fiction in its far western variant, $10,000 for exclusive rights to whatever he might write in the coming year. Regionalism, this publisher clearly believed, was

the current form of limitless demand, the work for which a publisher could not pay too much. In the wake of Murfree's 1878
discovery of Southern Appalachia for local color (regionalism's
nineteenth-century history is that of a search for new locales by
which to renew a standard formula), another publisher sent another would-be author—Sherwood Bonner, or behind her pseu-
donym, Katherine Sherwood Bonner MacDowell—on a flying visit
to learn how to "do" Tennessee mountain folk and cash in on
Murfree's success. Bonner was raised one county seat away from
Faulkner's Oxford, Mississippi, but her life story more nearly re-
sembles Scarlett O'Hara's. After the war this strong-willed belle left
her weakling husband and child to parlay her charm into a more
powerful career, as an author. The terms of her success show the
opportunities for the ambitious that regionalism's demand created.
Virtually recruited into authorship by the need for local color, she
found a comparably ready market for her tales of black life south
of Memphis and of downstate Illinois.[13]

Bonner's case demonstrates how the public demand for regionalism produced the opportunity it offered. During the time when
readerly desire attached to such fiction, virtually anyone who
could supply this commodity could get his or her work into print,
and so win public recognition for an asserted literary self. But if its
popularity was the condition for the opening it afforded, this fact
only drives our inquiry back a step. What was the condition for its
popularity, we would now need to ask: what gave this of all genres
such appeal at this time? *why appeal of regional lit.?*

A historiography long attached to regional fiction offers one explanation for the interest it held.[14] Regionalism became a dominant
genre in America at the moment when local-cultural economies
felt strong pressure from new social forces, from a growingly
powerful social model that overrode previously autonomous systems and incorporated them into translocal agglomerations. This
genre's great public flowering began with the Northern victory in
the Civil War, in other words with the forcible repression of sec-
tional autonomy in favor of national union and the legal supplanting of the locally variant by national norms of citizenly rights.
Regionalism's heyday was in the years of rapid corporate-capitalist

industrial development in America, with its reinsertion of agrarian
and artisanal orders into a new web of national market relations.
(The national brand and national corporation—Coca-Cola and
Standard Oil—are other inventions of regionalism's years.) The
linkage of American railroads into a transcontinental network
helped further incorporate once self-enclosed social communities
into a national commercial grid. The great American cities that
grew up at the new junctures of transportation and commerce in
the Gilded Age—Chicago, Cleveland, Pittsburgh, and the rest—
embody another supersession of an older localism. Such cities
drew population from small towns and the rural countryside, a
now-"older" world they helped devitalize and deplete.

Such familiar Gilded Age histories have an obvious relevance to
the regional genre, and in their light it has seemed easy to say what
office it must have performed. The cultural work of nineteenth-
century regionalism, the emotional and conceptual service this
writing performed that made it meet a profound social *need*—for
the historical demand for regionalism bespeaks not just taste but
need—has been assumed to be that of cultural elegy: the work of
memorializing a cultural order passing from life at that moment
and of fabricating, in the literary realm, a mentally possessable
version of a loved thing lost in reality. Nineteenth-century regionalism can be said to have manufactured, in its monthly-renewed
public imaging of old-fashioned social worlds, a cultural version of
D. W. Winnicott's transitional object: a symbol of union with the
premodern chosen at the moment of separation from it. Certainly
the works of nineteenth-century regionalism read their function in
these terms. Many of them specify the incursion of forces of modern development upon once-autonomous cultural islands as the
occasion for their recording of local lifeways: in *Oldtown Folks*
(1869) Harriet Beecher Stowe announces that she wants to register
the New England village order of "ante-railroad days" because
those days are "rapidly fading"; in *In the Tennessee Mountains* the
imminent arrival of the railroad drives Murfree to want to capture
endangered Cumberland Mountains ways.[15] Many of these works,
similarly, offer themselves as a surrogate memory of a life now
passing into the past. Their memorial function is announced in

their titles: *Oldport Days; Oldtown Folks; Old Creole Days;* "Old Times on the Mississippi"; *In Ole Virginia;* "The Old Agency "; and so on.

There is no reason to doubt that the regionalist genre had the array of forces bound together under the word "development" as a prime historical referent; and it would not be wrong to assume that this form's ability to articulate the dislocations that development engendered was a major cause of its nineteenth-century popularity. But it is worth at least wondering, I think, whether this familiar account tells the whole story of regionalism's cultural operation. This account's general historiography, after all, is not inevitable. The recent historical work affiliated with the label "new rural history" has shown that there was no unilinear or invariant suppression of local-cultural economies in the period of intense capitalist-industrial development in the United States, indeed that such cultures persisted, adapted, and even established themselves during the years of their purported demise.[16] Such work reminds us that nineteenth-century regionalist fiction—the form of rural history operative in its time—did not simply record contemporary reality but helped compose a certain version of modern history. Its elegaism, further, has a clear and suspicious relation to what recent anthropologists have seen in traditional ethnographic writing (regional fiction is also a nineteenth-century ethnography): the habit while purporting to grasp an alien cultural system of covertly lifting it out of history, constituting it as a self-contained form belonging to the past rather than an interactive force still adapting in the present.[17] For the United States, regionalism's representation of vernacular cultures as enclaves of tradition insulated from larger cultural contact is palpably a fiction. This would suggest that its public function was not just to mourn lost cultures but to purvey a certain story of contemporary cultures and of the relations among them: to tell local cultures into a history of their supersession by a modern order now risen to national dominance.

Further, the received account of regionalism's cultural operation implies that it helped readers in general work through the emotional difficulties of a shared contemporary history. But if we were to track it to the scene of its historical operation we would find that this genre was highly localized in in its late nineteenth-century life, active in some cultural places and not others. In nineteenth-century America regional writing was *not* produced for the cultures it was written about, which were often nonliterate and always orally based. It was projected toward those groups in American society that made a considerable investment in literary reading; but even here we can discriminate. In its early avatars, such writing most often appeared within the middle-class domestic reading world that early chapters of this book have considered. Susan Warner wrote early regionalism in the Aunt Fortune sections of *The Wide, Wide World* and elsewhere; Stowe, the triumphant "literary domestic" of the antebellum decades, shifted into regional writing with *The Pearl of Orr's Island* (1862) and *Oldtown Folks;* Eggleston's *The Hoosier Schoolmaster*—a regionalist classic whose cultural provenance is marked by its concern with graded elementary schools and noncorporal discipline—was serialized in *Hearth and Home,* a family entertainment and instruction magazine that Stowe helped edit. But beginning in the 1860s, then decisively after 1870, regionalism shifted its mode of cultural production and began to be featured in a different kind of place. The Bostonian *Atlantic Monthly* gave Bret Harte the celebrity contract for his fables of California. It also serialized Twain's "Old Times on the Mississippi," the stories of Murfree's *In the Tennessee Mountains,* and the bulk of Jewett's tales of coastal Maine, to name no more. The New York-based *Harper's Monthly* sent the Mississippi-born Sherwood Bonner to soak up the color of eastern Tennessee. It also printed Wilkins Freeman's tales of insular New England villages and Constance Fenimore Woolson's stories of rural Ohio, rural Michigan, and rural Florida. George Washington Cable's tales of New Orleans Creole society were sought out and printed not in New Orleans but in the North, in *Scribner's Monthly* and its successor, *The Century Illustrated Monthly Magazine.* This New York-based magazine also serialized *The Adventures of Huckleberry Finn* (1884) and Thomas Nelson Page's *In Ole Virginia,* among other regional works.

The names of such places of appearance are not a neutral fact of publishing history. These journal titles specify a highly particular provenance: they say that regional fiction was published within a certain historical formation of the literary, and beyond that, of culture at large. Lawrence Levine and others have documented the profound reformulation of "culture" as a social and artistic category that took place in America after 1850. These historians have reconstructed the process by which a previously more unitary culture, in which artistically mixed programs played to mixed social audiences, got broken apart, and a now-separated "high" culture asserted over against a now-distinct "low" opponent. The segmentation and stratification that produced a separate high culture is seen in the splitting off of a nonpopular "legitimate" theater from the older theater that had played Shakespeare with farcical interludes; in the midcentury remaking of a museum from a popular hall of miscellaneous wonders (like Barnum's 1841 American Museum) to a monumentalized shrine for classical masterpieces (like the 1870 Metropolitan Museum of Art); and in the supplanting of popular band programs by the newly institutionalized symphony orchestras that specialized performance to the classical repertory—the Chicago Symphony, the Boston Symphony, and the like.[18]

This stratification in the cultural realm happened not alone but in complicated interaction with a parallel stratification in the social realm, the articulation of a new-style "high" social class. Ronald Story, E. Digby Baltzell, Burton Bledstein, and others have told the story of the formation of a translocally incorporated social elite in place of an older, locally based gentry order in the the mid-nineteenth century. (Story calls this process "the shaping . . . of a durable upper class within a capitalist order.")[19] The new elite of the post–Civil War period was composed of various subgroups—inheritors of older wealth and of older local-gentry status, mercantile and managerial groups grown rich in the new corporations, the new-order professionals of this professionalizing period; and elements of the earlier self-articulated middle class eager to distinguish themselves from a now more clearly defined working class strongly identified with this new elite formation as well, especially after the 1860s. The point about the postbellum upper class is that it was not an already integrated "group" but a group in the process of self-grouping, a coming-together of elements with a common need to identify themselves as superior. And in this process of self-definition. Culture played a crucial role. In the 1860s and later, the newly formed elite identified itself very centrally through the artistic culture it enjoyed. In consequence, in the postbellum United States, a now-segregated high culture became a chief sign of elite status and chief weapon of elite social sway. In this period it was the social segments just described that devoted themselves to high art and founded its social institutions. This group turned out the audience for such art and trained itself to appreciate such art—so that the young Jane Addams, like most upper-middle-class girls of her generation, was brought up in a self-devotion to Culture that would have been aimed toward domestic or religious goals a generation earlier. In the late nineteenth century this group also promoted the culture it valued as a means to subordinate the differently cultured *to* its values—as genteel librarians used their institutional control over reading habits to try to change the living habits of the lower sort, or as genteel art patrons strove to recivilize the public through the public display of classical works.[20]

In the years between 1860 and 1900, the *Atlantic Monthly, The Century Magazine,* and *Harper's Monthly Magazine* achieved an identification as the three American "quality journals." This means that these three journals produced the same high or distinguished zone in the literary realm that the classical museum or symphony orchestra produced in art or music, a strongly demarcated high-status arena for high-artistic practice. And though actual audiences are notoriously hard to establish, there is reason to think that they produced literary writing toward a similarly constituted social public. Sometimes these periodicals say whom they address quite overtly: the 1878 *Atlantic* article "Three Typical Workingmen" speaks of its readers as "cultivated" people and explains how the textual format of such journals' articles—particularly their length—sets them outside the world of working class reading.[21] But these journals specify their assumed audience just as overtly on every page of every issue, in the work they elect to publish. The nineteenth-century *Atlantic, Harper's,* and *The Century* can be searched in vain for articles that address the interests of factory workers, immigrants, farm laborers, miners, clerks, shopgirls, and secretaries. To a student of mid-nineteenth-century domestic per-

iodicals they will seem equally notable for their nonaddress to
classic middle-class interests: the discourse of evangelical piety,
the child-rearing essay, and the lesson in good housekeeping, the
staple genres of that group's reading, are wholly absent from their
pages. Instead, their selections speak to interests highly particular
to the new upper class and its imaginative adherents. The great staple of these journals, the virtually mandatory item
in their program of offerings, is the short piece of touristic or va-
cationistic prose, the piece that undertakes to locate some little-
known place far away and make it visitable in print. The mental
habits these pieces rehearse are, in sociohistorical terms, quite
strongly localized. It is pertinent here to remember that the late
nineteenth-century American elite, self-defined through its care
for high art, was also identified by its other distinctive leisure practices—its new sports, for instance: golf, tennis, yachting; and particularly its arts of leisure travel. The postbellum period is when
the American elite perfected the regimen of the upper-class vacation: the European tour, for the whole family or, if the father's
business pressed, for the wife and daughters, of the length of four
months or more; or the comparable summer in the country, at
seashore or mountain resorts. The American abroad—a rarity in
the 1830s but commonplace in the 1870s—is one manifestation
of this Gilded Age class phenomenon. The gentry summer resorts
newly colonized after the War—the Berkshires, Massachusetts's
North Shore, Cape Cod and Martha's Vineyard, the Maine and
Jersey shores—are another sign of the same historical process. The
building style of the postbellum summer "cottage"—the shingle
style Vincent Scully has studied—is the architectural manifestation
of the same social development. Howells's documentary *The Rise of
Silas Lapham* (1885) notes that in the contemporary world the hereditary upper class and industrial nouveaux riches both make it
their duty to "summer," and Howells implies that such vacationing
sets the social ground on which these class fractions can meet: the
industrially rich Laphams first meet the Brahmin Coreys when
their wives and children summer on the St. Lawrence.[22]

Evolved *at* this time, elite vacation habits also took on a heavily
symbolic function *in* this time in dramatizing this group's social

superiority. As Thorstein Veblen, the great theorist of the post–Civil War leisure class, would argue, the upper-class vacation, with its conspicuous requirement of surplus funds and large leisure, made an especially "serviceable evidence" of a socially differentiating freedom from need. (It is worth remembering that a week's paid vacation became the norm for American white collar employees only in the 1920s; for others it came later yet.)[23] For this reason, vacationing, like the high-cultural competences that required an equal ability to have devoted time to the training of nonproductive tastes,[24] became a piece of an upper-class habitus highly expressive of social distinction. When the historian of post–Civil War Hartford's gentry establishment notes that for "Hartford people of the dominant prosperous class . . . it was almost a social necessity to go to Europe every two or three years" and that "after 1875 it was a social necessity in any case to get out of the city in the summer" (practices widely shared elsewhere), his reiterated word "necessity" is fully apt. The better-off of this time invested themselves in vacation travel not only because they liked to or were free to but because such travel was a chief means to establish elite social standing. Twain's *The Innocents Abroad* (1869) knows that a prime contemporary reason for going to Europe is that it marks one "select" back home.[25]

It would be wrong to assume that all readers of the "quality" journals of the Gilded Age were necessarily members of the "quality" socially. Nevertheless, these journals do address an upper-class-centered social interest. And the principal proof is that they speak so insistently to the class-signifying leisure habits I have been describing. These magazines speak to "us" on the condition that "we" are the kind of people who attach almost unlimited value to vacation travel. Typical *Harper's* illustrations show "us" to ourselves if we either actually engage in gentry vacationing or mentally identify with those who do: in *Harper's* people like "us" appear promenading at the Jersey shore, having their vacation baggage carried by servants, being paddled in canoes by ungenteelly dressed locals, interviewing a cook for the yacht. Charles Dudley Warner's *Atlantic* serial *The Adirondacks Verified* meets one of "our" needs if our needs include verifying the attractions of newly

ARRIVAL AT FORTRESS MONROE.

Sample illustrations from *Harper's New Monthly Magazine*, 1875–1890

ON THE PIER, CAPE MAY.

YOUNG LADY IN A CANOE, PADDLED BY A GUIDE.

INTERVIEWING THE COOK.

THE GOVERNMENT WHARF, FORTRESS MONROE.

colonized vacation spots and verifying that they carry suitable social meanings: Warner assures his readers that only the cultivated will enjoy Adirondack primitivism. (The *Atlantic* article "A Cook's Tourist in Spain," by contrast, makes clear that package tours are déclassé.) Warner's *Harper's* serial *Their Pilgrimage*—an almost unbelievably thorough tour of the resorts of the contemporary elite—is a valuable vade mecum if our group ethic mandates ritual travel to vacationing's sacred spots.[26] The same logic holds for scores of similar features.

The writing marked as literary in the Gilded Age appeared in these journals together with the prose of vacation travel, and not just together but in virtually fixed conjunction with such prose. Murfree's celebrated "The Dancin' Party at Harrison's Cove," thus, ran in the same volume as Warner's *The Adirondacks Verified*, Henry James's international novel *The Europeans*, and James's nonfictional "Recent Florence." Murfree's Cumberlands tale "Way Down in Lonesome Cove" ran together with Howells's Florence novel *Indian Summer*, and with travel essays on Persia and "The Blue Grass Country of Kentucky." Mary Wilkins Freeman's "A Humble Romance" was originally flanked by a feature "The North Shore" (of Lake Superior)—with picturesque illustrations of the cliffs above Duluth—and another on Biarritz. Freeman's "Revolt of 'Mother'" ran together with "Across the Andes," "Mountain Passes of the Cumberland," and "The Social Side of Yachting."[27] If we take these insistent conjunctions seriously (and the list of them could be greatly lengthened), they can teach us two things. They tell us that nineteenth-century literary genres we are used to thinking of as freestanding were not autonomous in their original cultural production but formed mutually supportive parts of a concerted textual program. And they say that the literature included in this program—like the nonfictional adjuncts that give this message more overtly—must also have been produced for an elite-based reading world.

The larger point at stake here is that writing's historical publics have always been socially localized. Such publics are always established on some principle of inclusion from among those who have leisure to read and attach value to this entertainment. But the groups that have come together into literary audiences have never been grouped by their reading tastes alone: their reading interests are always bound togther with the set of extraliterary interests that unite them as a group. Earlier chapters of this book have studied one such culture of letters: the antebellum domestic reading world that conjoined literary reading with other identifying cares of middle-class domesticity. Here we are witnessing the emergence of another American reading culture that gave literary writing a differently constituted social base and so enmeshed it in a different set of ancillary concerns: not child rearing and home management but the high-cultural values and vacation arts that identified the postbellum elite's more sumptuous leisure. Post–Civil War literary regionalism circulated almost exclusively within the historical reading world constituted on these terms. Accordingly, if we would understand the grounds for its demand, we need to grasp how it met imaginative needs particular to this literary-social situation.

The way forward from this point can only be opened up by speculation. Nevertheless, to see nineteenth-century regionalism within this more tightly specified social situation is to have some of its possible functions seem obvious. For one thing, its place of cultural production would clearly seem to link regionalism with an elite need for the primitive made available as leisure outlet. The "social necessity" that made European travel and countrified summering interchangeable practices established paired needs for resort to the most highly evolved contemporary civilization (as "Europe" was conceived) and to a civilization equidistantly lower, primitive, or underdeveloped. (So it is that the Loire and the Adirondacks, or Gloucester, England, and Gloucester, Massachusetts, could become substitutable summer alternatives.) This pairing of high-cultural European and rustic-domestic vacation spots finds its reflection in the quality journals' nonliterary writing array: in their complementary featuring of Persia and Kentucky, northern Michigan and Biarritz, and so on. It is equally reflected in such magazines' selection of literary features: in their coproduction of international theme novels and American regional fiction, genres that typically ran side by side. The symmetry of these categories

strongly implies that regionalism worked as a literary supplement
to a more general production of inhabitable backwardness, as the
international novel supplemented the production of visitable "Europe." The fact that Constance Fenimore Woolson's early tale "In
Search of the Picturesque" was published together with a pioneering account of the just-discovered vacation spot Mount Desert
Isle,[28] a wholly characteristic conjunction, suggests that such fiction and nonfiction literally *co-operated,* in the realm of reading, to
produce the unmodernized picturesque. In its first context, this
genre offered freshly found primitive places for the mental resort
of the sophisticated. A genteel vacationer conducts us into the
country folk world in "The Dancin' Party at Harrison's Cove."

But if regional fiction gave exercise to a sophisticate-vacationer's habits of mind, we might speculate that it also rehearsed a
habit of mental acquisitiveness strongly allied with genteel reading: All reading, it may be, plays into the drive to appropriate experience vicariously, as Hawthorne and Henry James believed. But
the appropriative mind appears to have been especially highly
developed in the nineteenth-century leisure class (for which we
could read *owner* class), where it was deployed along certain characteristic lines. This historical grouping is especially identified by
what might be called its cultural or cross-cultural acquisitiveness.
In distinction from other contemporaneous formations, the postbellum elite and its adherents made other *ways of life* the object of
their admiration and desire, objects which they then felt free to
annex: the upper class vacation, thus, entails crossing out of one's
own culture into another culture (not just place) to the end of
living another way of life. Regionalism can be guessed to have
ministered especially effectively to the imagination of acquisition.
The paradox of this genre is that it purports to value a culture for
being intactly other at the very time that it is offering outsiders the
chance to inhabit it and enjoy its special "life." Twain's Hartford
neighbor Charles Dudley Warner called another of his travel pieces
"Our Italy"[29]—showing how the travel writing of this time both
makes apparently distinctive places functionally interchangeable
(*California* is our *Italy*) and textually reprocesses them into possessible property (California is *our* Italy, the Italy we own).

But if reading nineteenth-century regionalism back into its
original scene of operation links it to this sort of experiential im-
perialism, it also ties it to deep class anxieties. The elite formation
defined in part through its high-cultural affiliations and vacation
practices was of course defined in other ways much more fundamentally. In the 1860s and after, the elements of this coalition
were brought together not just by their shared pleasures but by
their shared opposition to other groups, especially to the newly
antagonistic working class that postbellum industrialism also produced. That class was growingly peopled with the newly arriving
immigrants that capitalist development lured, so that the elite that
was another by-product of the same development found itself increasingly surrounded by foreigners in its formative years. (In Boston, the spiritual home of late nineteenth-century high culture,
thirty percent of the population was foreign-born in 1900, and
seventy percent born of foreign parentage.) To this elite at this
time, as many studies have shown, the immigrant became a kind
of iconic representation of the lower classes thought of as class
antagonists. The immigrant became a phobic embodiment of all
imagined threats to elite superiority, from cultural mongrelization
and racial dilution to political anarchism and class war.[30]

Paradoxically, then, an often virulent nativism was another defining feature of the late-century group that loved "the foreign" in
other capacities; and the components of the upper class habitus
assembled in the later nineteenth century served not just statically
to symbolize superior status (as Veblen and his unknowing successor Bourdieu imply) but actively to manage the socially foreign's
threat. The since-characteristic American elite institutions elaborated between the 1870s and the 1890s—the residential suburb,
the private day school and prep school, and the country club—
aimed not just to mark an "exclusive" zone in status terms but
actively to exclude, to shut the elite in from its social "others."[31]
The rustic vacation, similarly, served not incidentally to reconstitute a homogeneity disturbed in the larger world. E. Digby Baltzell,
the principal historian of upper class self-incorporation practices,
writes with satiric glee:

Just as the white man, symbolized by the British gentleman, was roaming round the world in search of raw materials for his factories at Manchester, Liverpool, or Leeds, so America's urban gentry and capitalists, at the turn of the century, were imperialists seeking solace for their souls among the "natives" of Lenox, Bar Harbor, or Kennebunkport. Here they were able to forget the ugliness of the urban melting pot as they dwelt among solid Yankees (Ethan Frome), many of whom possessed more homogeneous, Colonial-stock roots than themselves. . . . All one's kind were there together. . . . When J. P. Morgan observed that "you can do business with anyone, but only sail with a gentleman," he was reflecting the fact that a secure sense of homogeneity is the essence of resort life.[32]

As a social construction, late-century high culture too served to project the aristocratically based arts of Northern and Western Europe as "civilization" and to consign those of other classes and regions to the category of the noncivilized. (One remembers here the turn-of-the-century high-cultural practice of having Italian opera, in the original uncomfortably popular and ethnic, performed in German).[33] Culture so constituted could function as an apparently purely aesthetic agent of social exclusion, as the specialization of the musical repertoire to its high-classical portions specialized audiences to the educated minority acculturated in such tastes.[34] But high culture could also work as a force of coercive *in*clusion, of social management on the elite's behalf. Horace Scudder's widely successful plan to install classic American literature as mandatory reading in American public schools was overtly designed to counter the menace of the un-American. With that social ulteriority so commonly coupled with professed worship of disinterested artistic "quality" at this time, American literature as the native-born upper class selected it was here deployed as an Americanizing agent, a means to bring the immigrant young out of their hereditary ethnic cultures and into an "American" culture synonymous with elite tastes.[35]

Nineteenth-century regionalism was produced as an upper order's reading at a time of heavy immigration and the anxieties associated with such immigration. (Jewett's initial volume, *Deephaven*, was published in 1877, the year of the Railroad Wars, the Molly Maguires, and unprecedented industrial strife.) This conjunction invites us to consider literary regionalism as another of the leisure pastimes that dealt with the threat of the foreign from within an apparently detached entertainment realm. Regional fiction too could be considered as an exclusion mechanism or social eraser, an agency for purging the world of immigrants to restore homogeneous community. The extremely rare appearance in such stories of any of the ethnic groups associated with contemporaneous industrialization—Irish immigrants appear for a rarity in Jewett's "Between Matins and Vespers"—would seem to warrant our considering regional writing (like the summer resort or country club) a *haven* for readers, a space of safety constructed against an excluded threat. But in a sense, regionalism's peculiarity is exactly that it did *not* exclude the foreign; so that a more complex reading of its function is required. Perhaps the deepest paradox of the subject I am discussing is that the late nineteenth-century class that saw polyglot America as a social nightmare and that made purity of speech a premier tool of social discrimination should have cherished, as one of its principal entertainment forms, the dialect or local color tale, definable after all as the fiction where people talk strangely.[36] Ethnically deformed speech—what else is dialect?—is the most fundamental requirement of the regional genre; and as a social institution this genre's action was to immerse readers in a cacophony of almost-foreign ethnically inflected tongues: Creole ("You t'ink it would be hanny disgrace to paint de pigshoe of a niggah?"); New England rustic ("Thar's Mis' Bliss's pieces in the brown kalikee bag"); backwood Hoosier ("It takes a *man* to boss this deestrick. Howsumdever, ef you think you kin trust your hide in Flat Creek school-house, I ha'n't got no 'bjection"); eastern Virginia negro ("'Well,' sez he, 'I'm gwine to give you to yo' young Marse Channin' to be his body-servant,' an' he put de baby right in my arms—it's de truth I'm tellin' yo'!"); Mississippi Delta negro ("'Onymus Pop, you jes take keer o' dis chile while I'm gone ter de hangin'"); Tennessee mountain ("I dunno *how* the boys would cavort ef they kem back an' found the bar'l gone"); and so on.[37] Through such writing, we can surmise, an audience that identified its own nonethnic status with its social superiority could nevertheless bring itself within hearing distance of the "stranger in the land," so that regionalism was a means to acknowledge plural Americas. Yet this fiction produced the foreign only to master it in imaginary terms—first by substituting less "different" native ethnicities for the truly foreign ones of contemporary reality: crusty Yankee fishingfolk for southern Italians or Slavs, Appalachian hillbillies for Russian Jews and Chinese;[38] then by writing the heterogloss into the status of variant on or deviant from a standard of well-bred educated speech. Nineteenth-century regional writing produced a real-sounding yet deeply fictitious America that was not homogeneous yet not radically heterogeneous either and whose diversities were ranged under one group's normative sway. Its performance of such important wishful thinking must have contributed profoundly to its historical public demand.

There is, it should be insisted, no necessary relation between the regionalist form and any of the social forces I have been discussing. This literature has been created in quite other social situations, where it has had other issues at stake in it: we would need to compose a very different description of the social life of such cognate forms as the nineteenth-century Spanish and Latin American custom sketch (*cuadro de costumbres*), the early twentieth-century South African *Plaasroman*, or the revived American regionalisms of the 1920s and 1930s and the 1980s. But if it has no necessary relations, this literary form had certain actual relations in nineteenth-century America, relations *created for* it by the history of its cultural production—the process that sets every form the terms of its public life.   *limited access*

If we now recall that this genre also created roads into authorship for would-be writers, it will be clear that this statement requires emendation. Regionalism, we could now say, made places for authors but made them *in a certain position*. By virtue of its historical situation, when writers came into authorship through this genre they were placed in inevitable relation with the field of forces that structured its social place: found their literary roles

bound together with the high zone in a steeply hierarchized
plan of culture, with correlative class prerogatives of leisure and
consumption, with a certain socially based appetite for under-
development, and with a related will to renew the dominance of
culturally dominant groups.

The social organization of literature's public life never deter-
mines literary creation. Literature is only produced when some
actual author realizes the possibilities of some historically structured literary situation; and writers have been able to realize the
same situation variously, even in contradictory ways. A full social
history of regional authorship would want to stress the extraordinary range of powers and interests to which authors found their
way through the medium of this form. Joel Chandler Harris, author of the enduring regional work *Uncle Remus: His Songs and His
Sayings* (1881), was rendered almost speechless by shyness in his
everyday social life but spoke easily when he spoke in black vernacular dialect. In this quite literal sense Harris could be said to
have found a voice through the conventions of dialect fiction.[39] To
cite one more case only, George Washington Cable found his way
to the politics of his liberal racial polemics of the 1880s, the important Civil Rights essays "The Freedman's Case in Equity" and
"The Silent South," at least in part through his regional writing,
through the exploration of cross-racial injury and cross-racial justice in *The Grandissimes* (1880) and other works. But if writers can
make different things of the enabling conditions of their work,
they become writers in circumstances not wholly of their making.
And a full history of regional authorship would show that the authors who won literary identity through this form achieved that
identity in and against the particular array of forces that specified
this genre's social place.

If we were considering the case of Constance Fenimore Woolson, for instance, we would be struck by the quite fundamental
ways in which her personal construction of an authorial career
implies the social history of the regional genre. Woolson was in
the most direct of ways enabled by this form. Its emergence in the
early 1870s established a literary use for the kind of places where
Woolson had spent her life, and the market that developed for

such work meant that this person from "nowhere" could get her writing published.[40] And published not just anywhere: Woolson was able to place her early work in *Harper's Monthly,* and the essential fact of her career is that her regional writing won her a specifically high-cultural literary position. The company whose fellowship sustained her in her desperately lonely life was the inner circle of American literary high culture: Thomas Bailey Aldrich, Edmund Clarence Stedman, Henry James, and the like. High cultural status—inclusion in the world of serious writers— also gave Woolson crucial inward sustenance, the ability to take herself seriously as a writer in a life devoid of more traditional validations.[41] Had the regional form not been given this form of status, as it would not have had it been culturally situated on other terms, Woolson would have won such support against almost infinitely greater odds. And she could only have made with great difficulty the career move she made with relative ease, the self-transformation from a writer of country districts to literary American abroad—literary worlds apart were it not for the fact that their late nineteenth-century cultural placement made them adjacent and complementary genres.

If we turned from Woolson (for instance) to Hamlin Garland, we would find a different model of authorship, but one achieved by working out a different relation to the same set of literary-social facts. Garland was much more heavily disadvantaged for a life in letters than the poor but genteel Woolson. The son of a farmer and himself a farm laborer, Garland felt set by birth and labor beneath the dignity of the cultivated classes; indeed Garland's sense of social inferiority is as aggravated a case as American literary history has to show. Yet the market for literary regionalism in the late nineteenth century made a place for Garland too in letters—but this time at the price of more painful psychic dislocations. As *A Son of the Middle Border* records, Garland desperately desired to acquire mental culture to lift himself from the disparagement of manual labor into the higher ranks of mind workers. Given the organization of culture in his time, this meant in practice that Garland tore up his roots in Iowa and South Dakota to transplant himself to the East of high culture: his autobiography, a kind of nonfiction *Jude*

the Obscure, shows him in his mid-twenties virtually starving and
freezing in order to keep reading in the Boston Public Library. Garland's first literary dream had been to write short stories in the
manner of Hawthorne. But in this different cultural world he became acquainted with a different target for his aspiration, the regionalist form. Armed with this form, he returned to the upper
Midwest in the late 1880s and "discovered" both its literary potential and the subject matter of his own future art, the hard-bitten
farm stories that became *Main-Travelled Roads* (1891).[42]

Garland too was enabled by the regionalist genre. Garland too
found a chance to exploit his outsider's social knowledge through
the workings of this form. And Garland too (if a little less securely
than Woolson) won a prized "insider" status through this mode of
work. When editors like Howells of *Harper's Monthly* or Richard
Watson Gilder of *The Century* approved of his stories of rural life,
this parvenu of letters won the feeling of election into the culture
of his dreams.[43] But Garland could only win the literary status that
attached to regionalism in his time at the cost of more or less vio-
lently estranging himself from the culture of his origin; and the
violations his authorship entailed put their distinctive mark on his
work. In his most powerful early story, "Up the Coulee," the impoverished midwestern farm world is revisited by a prodigal son
who has become a member of the Eastern art world and leisure-
vacationing class (this character was yachting abroad when he
missed the news that the family farm was about to be lost). Not
Garland's own condition except in his wishes—leisure-class life is
the only thing this story describes unconvincingly—this social position is the one Garland feels himself to have become aligned with
in taking up his literary career. The cultural relocation attached to
his choice of genre has its triple yield in a gloating desire for the
life of prestige, a corresponding guilt toward the home world he
has so willingly escaped, and a rage against the system of social
difference that makes elite pleasures be purchased at country people's expense. Garland's farm stories find their sequel, accordingly,
in his rampant 1890s populism and his rage against literary centers
in the screeds of *Crumbling Idols* (1894)—a conjunction that makes
no sense except in a situation where literary regionalism, class

privilege, and high-cultural hierarchy have been bound together.

Other regionalist careers display other permutations; but by now I hope a general point has been established. Literary forms, I have been contending, create different sorts of literary access; but no form creates access unconditionally. Such forms are always placed in some determinate set of literary-cultural relations, and the place they create for authors is inevitably a place *within* this specification of their work's life and use. But how the conditions of literary practice actually condition literary production—how such apparent externalities mediate the will to write—is a question still largely unanswered. In the chapters that follow I turn from the description of nineteenth-century regionalism's public life to see how this form was engaged on the author's side, and with what consequences for authorial self-realization.

Jewett, Regionalism, and Writing as Women's Work

I

Sarah Orne Jewett, best known for her book *The Country of the Pointed Firs*, has been unfairly considered a minor regional writer of vivid descriptions of the simple life of rural Maine in the late nineteenth century. Sarah Sherman has taken steps toward correcting this injustice by enabling us to see Jewett as an artist whose stories, focusing on women's lives and relationships, contain the prevalent symbols and myths of a culture struggling to find expression.[1]

THIS JACKET COPY from the best book on Jewett, Sarah Way Sherman's *Sarah Orne Jewett: An American Persephone*, gives a good condensed history of Jewett's literary fortunes. Unlike the recently recovered nineteenth-century women authors who had been marked as subliterary and erased from the literary record, Jewett has been perpetuated in official literary memory, indeed has held a steady reputation as a literary artist: witness the fact that F. O. Matthiessen, the author of *American Renaissance*, wrote a biography of her in 1929. But Jewett's traditional recognition was achieved within terms that covertly delimited her status—she was honored within the minor-sounding category of "regional writer"—and for this reason her modern rehabilitators have needed first to rescue her from the belittling associations of this mode. The expected path of revision would be to claim that Jewett had been unfairly consigned to the regionalist category, but in her case this move would hardly be possible: few authors of any time or condition have clung to a single genre more tightly than Jewett adhered to the local-fiction form. Accordingly the revisionary gambit in Jewett's case has been to claim that the genre itself has been read "unfairly," and to correct this "injustice" by making the seemingly minor regionalist form the site of major cultural transactions.

As this blurb also suggests, feminist criticism has supplied Jewett with her most successful rescue plan to date. Critics in this mode have argued that in the nineteenth century, regionalism had a since-forgotten status as a women's literary work space, was not a lesser suburb of the literary domain but a separate precinct in which women used a woman-transmitted form to express a vision specific to women's lives. In this reading women regionalists grasped literary hold of self-enclosed rustic enclaves not out of sociological interest but as an imagery for projecting a woman-centered world, a world where strong women were still in charge of essential functions and where women's values as the nineteenth century identified them—values of family and community in particular—socially prevailed. With the meaning of her genre respecified in these terms, Jewett's critics have been able to lift her out of the "minor" project of regional genre painting and into the "major" one of articulating women's culture. A book like *The Country of the Pointed Firs* is now said to detail the particulars of simple life in rural Maine to the end of realizing a world where women are capable and men are dysfunctional; where children stay bound to their mothers and inherit their mothers' powers; where female community supplants self-assertive masculine individuality; and where the feminine is seen as the outlet to the divine.[2]

This way of reading the meaning of regionalism has produced an irreversible change in our understanding of both the genre and

Jewett's work in it. The work of Marjorie Pryse, Elizabeth Ammons, Sarah Sherman, and others has reminded us that the historical audience for regionalist fiction was predominantly composed
of women readers, and that this form must have operated in the
service of women's concerns. By suggesting that the regional en-
clave and the female domestic sphere were socially homologous
(and so figuratively interchangeable) as antitheses to a dominant
culture of competitive individualism, this work has also equipped
us with a practical-critical tool for locating women's cultural issues
within the "mere" description of rural life. But the feminist reconception of regionalism has tended to repeat the autonomy fantasies
of the nineteenth-century ideology of separate spheres. In grasping
the sense in which local color fiction forms a "women's tradition"[3]
this criticism has tended to ignore the fact that women's writing
never exists only in relation to itself, never fails to be defined in
relation (even if only a relation of difference) to other writing by
other groups. Similarly, in disclosing concerns specific to nineteenth-century women's life, this criticism has tended to forget that
no culture is ever specified by its gender dimension alone: that in
the real historical world there has been no "women's culture" but
plural and divergent women's cultures, each defined by a host of
other social determinants. With the success of the feminist rehabilitation of regionalism so nearly consolidated, it is time to remember that there were other historical terms of this genre's
existence and to try to grasp what they might have been.

    In the previous chapter I sketched a different account of the re-
gionalist genre from what feminist studies have proposed. I placed
this genre in a literary culture projected toward an American upper
class coming together as a social entity in the later nineteenth century; and I argued that regionalism played to this audience by re-
hearsing the leisured outlook that differentiated it as a social
group. If, for an experiment, we were to focus Jewett on the background not of women's culture but of a nineteenth-century leisure-
class culture "struggling to find expression," we would find for her
writing a more concretely specified social home.

    The first comprehensive appraisal of Jewett's oeuvre saw her
social base in these terms. Reading back from her work to the au-

thor implied in it, a 1904 *Atlantic* reviewer supposed Jewett to be a "gentlewoman" "in close touch with humbler country-folk" who wrote about the "humble and homely" to "people of her own social and intellectual class." This reviewer, Charles Miner Thompson, also guessed that it was the emergence of gentry-class vacation practices that created Jewett's literary audience: "In the early seventies the summer boarder, so soon to develop into the summer cottager, was born, and with him a new audience for any writer who could describe the scenes in which he found so great a pleasure. Miss Jewett seized this opportunity."⁴ The grounds for this surmise in Jewett's work are not far to seek. Her first volume, *Deephaven* (1877), is wholly overt in linking the regionalist literary "visit" with the vacationing habits of an urban upper class: the Boston girls who frame this volume come to the Maine shore as a relief from the tedium of summering in Europe, having declined other invitations to Newport and Lenox. (They are to take two of their apparently numerous servants with them, and so are sure of "jolly housekeeping," while the obviously Irish "old Nora" will take care of the house in town.)⁵ Jewett's culminating volume, *The Country of the Pointed Firs* (1896), marks the class dimensions of the regionalist project much more lightly; but it builds the class logic of vacationing into itself in an even more fundamental fashion.

To particularize a little: Dunnet Landing in *The Country of the Pointed Firs* may function in one aspect as a female utopia, but it is no less centrally a world realized in a vacationer's mental image. This work is oriented toward a place, but it establishes this place not in its own terms but as a place to come *to,* a place literally of resort for a narrator who comes from afar. The asymmetrical characterization scheme practiced in *Pointed Firs* effaces this narrator and her home world as it glorifies Maine coastal folk, but the few facts we learn tell very efficiently where this unnamed speaker comes from. She is an urbanite, a native of the world of "anxious living" (213)—the world of stressful modernity and its social arrangements. She is affiliated in the city with Veblen's "superior pecuniary class," the people of large wealth and the leisure accoutrements that testify to that wealth: she discovered Dunnet Landing "two or three summers before in the course of a yachting cruise" (2). (It was of the price of a yacht that J. P. Morgan said: "If you have to ask, then you can't afford it.") How she supports herself—is it by her writing?—we never learn. But she has the resources, by no means shared in a town where forty-two-cent debts are remembered, to make "choice of a summer lodging-place" (3). She can command someone else's home as a second home for her leisure, and does so with a confident exercise of her rights.

As in the plan of vacation, the requirement of the place of resort in *The Country of the Pointed Firs* is that it should have no relation to the world left behind. But in practice this vacation world is defined through constant reference to the home world, realized not in its independent reality but as the antitype of the one left behind. Part of the imaginative labor of this volume is to produce coastal Maine as antithesis of 1890s urban modernity.[6] Over against the historical facts of the more "foreign" immigration from southern and eastern Europe and the compounding of class tensions with new ethnic strains, prominent sources of "anxious living" in American cities in the 1890s, this volume projects a counterworld of magical social homogeneity, a society of old-stock families descended from northern European roots. Mrs. Todd's home-brewed spruce beer may link her to an older scheme of household production in which women had productive roles, but it also functions as fantasized antitype of contemporary industrial production: this magical brew carries symbolic weight as a negative image of the new mass-produced, nationally marketed commodities of the 1890s, for instance Coca-Cola and Hires' Root Beer. (The fact that the narrator's presence in Dunnet Landing might mark this place's incorporation into a new interstate commerce—the tourist economy—is conveniently forgotten in *Pointed Firs,* where the summer person comes as a single figure transported by unseen means.)

As she renders it a counterworld to 1890s modernity, Jewett's literary labor also makes Dunnet Landing fit the other prerequisite of the vacation site, that it be a restorative place. Through Mrs. Todd's herbal medicines Jewett characterizes the summer landlady as a curative figure, indeed as the embodiment of the therapeutic.

And throughout *Pointed Firs* Jewett endows Maine life with a sanative quality of life. The natives of Dunnet Landing live in an exemplary state of strong feeling, and they have lived their passions into their objective world to such an extent that every object bespeaks a history of human association. Elijah Tilley's teacups are not cups only but memorials of his dead wife, "poor dear," and symbols of his unceasing love and grief for her; the place "where pennyroyal grew" (46) is so instinct with the memory of Mrs. Todd's courtship that to revisit it is to relive her early love and loss; the "thick striped-cotton shirt" that Mrs. Blackett made for William—unlike the ready-made garments that are its historical contemporaries—shows the "loving stitches" (54) of a mother's labor and so continually bespeaks its maker's love for its user. (Jewett follows Wordsworth and George Eliot in this cult of an object world humanized through continuous association.) Through such representations Jewett's Maine becomes a place healed of the alienations that prevail in the world of social mobility and mass-produced commodities, and a place to which cityfolk can resort to find health. The words of the later Dunnet Landing story "William's Wedding" describe the visitor-narrator becoming whole again beyond confusion:

> The hurry of life in a large town, the constant putting aside of preference to yield to a most unsatisfactory activity, began to vex me, and one day I took the train, and only left it for the eastward-bound boat. . . . But the first salt wind from the east, the first sight of the lighthouse set boldly on its outer rock, the flash of a gull, the waiting procession of seaward-bound firs on an island, made me feel solid and definite again, instead of a poor, incoherent being. Life was resumed, and anxious living blew away as if it had not been. I could not breathe deep enough or long enough. [213]

But within the vacation mentality at the same time that one seeks to lose one's home self in the vacation place, that place is all along being annexed as a recreational extension of the home world; and this is so in *The Country of the Pointed Firs* as well. Jewett imputes to Dunnet Landing a life so pure that she calls it simply

"life"; but in her stories this apparently intrinsic property of the
place offers itself to visitors remarkably freely. After a few nights
under the Maine coast's "spell" Mrs. Todd tells the narrator "all
that lay deepest in her heart" (7). Soon after, Mrs. Todd shows her
lodger the place "kind of sainted to me" where pennyroyal grows,
even though "I never showed nobody else but mother" (48). As
soon as the summerer begins to wish to know "about the inner
life and thought" of the "self-contained old fishermen" (115), Elijah Tilley opens his most intimate thoughts to this virtual stranger.
Through this one-sided (and quite wishful) process of exchange,
a life initially not the narrator's becomes her sympathetic possession; and when she has acquired enough of this life, it becomes
strangely abstractable, generalizable, and portable. By coming to
"know" Mrs. Blackett, Mrs. Todd, and William "in their own habi-
tations," the narrator learns that "their counterparts are in every
village in the world" (218). She learns, in other words, that one
need not stay in their spot to possess their virtue. And carrying the
good of the place *out* of the place—indeed, reprocessing it just for
such exportation—is essential to this book's plan.

   In *The Country of the Pointed Firs* the narrator's urban culture is
also marked as a print-based culture, and the source of her continuing alienation at the book's beginning is that she proposes to
spend her time writing in Dunnet Landing. Part of the healing res-
toration the book charts for this narrator lies in her escaping from
the written and its isolations into an oral culture of "mak[ing] a
visit" (58) and sociable storytelling, a disabstraction of language
that reaches its climax when she eats the name of the family on
the cake at the family reunion. But this narrator returns from Dunnet Landing's fully socialized language exchanges to the "cold
page" (217) her stay has equipped her to write; and the book itself
projects itself *into* Maine life to the end of making it inhabitable by
outsiders in print. In "William's Wedding" Jewett tells the "reader
of this cold page" that "it is written for those who have a Dunnet
Landing of their own: who either kindly share this with the writer,
or possess another" (217). Dunnet Landing is here offered as a
place interchangeable with other places and possessible through
print: reading it, consuming its representation in writing, will ei-

ther remind us of the parallel vacation spot we already "own" or supply us with such a spot if we don't yet "possess" one.

My point here is not that *The Country of the Pointed Firs* is reducible to some preexisting body of vacationing thought. The force of Jewett's work, as I read it, lies in the way she uses the literary medium to produce meaning for this thought beyond what it possesses in existing social usage—as on her harrowing last page, Jewett (before Woolf in *To the Lighthouse* or Wallace Stevens in "Auroras of Autumn") makes the deserted summer house an emblem of the extinction of the human from the scenes of its life. But as she produces such resonances for the topoi of vacationing, Jewett also builds her work almost wholly *upon* those topoi; and this literary act has social coordinates. Since those structures of thought had a precise social placement in her time—since in the late nineteenth century vacation travel marked the leisure class as a class apart—the elements Jewett builds with show her work's origin in that world of social understandings. In its literary figurations her book precisely figures the social habits and anxieties that attach to this group at this moment in its history: its cross-cultural cosmopolitanism; its anxious nativism; its acquisitiveness and sense of its right to own; its care for literary art.

I agree with Jewett's modern critics that finding her full interest requires recovering the social relations of her form. But I would draw the map of those relations differently: I see Jewett's regionalism as produced not in some weakly specified women's culture but in the culture of a quite specific late nineteenth-century upper class, a class that organized a certain world for women (the chief performers of its leisure) but that was defined by a host of other social relations at the same time. But if this claim were granted in even a preliminary fashion, two questions would follow: how did Jewett's writing enter into the social affiliations I have proposed for it, and what (if anything) did this situation do to her work? In this chapter I set out to answer the first of these questions in order to be able to pose the second. I want to reconstruct the situation of Jewett's authorship, then ask what difference it made that she should have organized her authorship in the cultural space she inhabited.

II

One chief fact defines Sarah Orne Jewett's literary career. From her first major work in the early 1870s, the sketches that became *Deephaven*, through the 1880s pieces collected in volumes like *Country By-Ways* and *A White Heron And Other Stories*, through *A Native of Winby* and *The Country of the Pointed Firs* in the 1890s, and into the later Dunnet Landing stories—"The Foreigner," "A Dunnet Shepherdess," "The Queen's Twin," and "William's Wedding"—published after 1900, Jewett wrote about one thing: the life of countryfolk in Maine coastal villages. Jewett virtually identified being a writer with writing *about* a regional *subject;* and if we want to grasp the conditions for her writing life we must first seek this identification's enabling grounds.

The search for antecedents for Jewett's version of authorship leads back to two facts of nineteenth-century literary history. First, the story of rustic places had been well established as a form for women authors by the late 1850s. In the ten years after Jewett's birth in 1849, American readers became acquainted with Mrs. Gaskell's *Cranford* (1853), George Eliot's *Scenes of Clerical Life* (1857) and *Adam Bede* (1859), Harriet Beecher Stowe's *Oldtown Folks* (1869), and the early stories of Rose Terry Cooke.[7] Second, and to some extent intertwined with this development, Jewett's own place became an object of insistent verbal attention in her late girlhood and early womanhood. American literary periodicals featured the New England shore with extraordinary persistence in the 1860s and early 1870s: in addition to the Maine story Jewett later singled out as the inciter of her wish to write, Stowe's *The Pearl of Orr's Island* (1862), the *Atlantic Monthly* and *Harper's Monthly* produced a stream of pieces fictional and nonfictional on Cape Cod and the out islands, the Massachusetts North Shore, coastal New Hampshire, and the seacoast of Maine.

Together, these features perform a collective labor of both publicizing the New England coast and producing a certain public meaning for it. Through their insistent descriptions they articulate this region as lying outside of contemporary economic life and progress, and so as being available for another form of develop-

Dona Brown – *rise
of Tourism*

ment. An 1874 *Harper's* article describes Nantucket and Martha's Vineyard as scenes of decline and depopulation following the collapse of the whaling industry. Their location outside the world of modern economic activity makes them, in this writer's eyes, repositories of a New England order now passing in more developed zones. This backwardness in turn makes them suitable for a second-growth industry of aesthetic "appreciation": *Harper's* pictures the Nantucket studio of Eastman Johnson looking out where whale-ships used to ride, and so invites us to see a former commercial center as a *scenic* place. Celia Thaxter's 1873 serial *Among the Isles of Shoals* similarly memorializes the death of shipping activity in these islands off the coast of New Hampshire but then produces a second life for them through its prose, in which they are notable for their wind and light conditions, their austere landscape, and their superb birds and flowers. The fact that there was a tourist hotel on the Isle of Shoals founded by Thaxter's father and now largely run by her, and that in "naturalizing" the islands she has been covertly creating touristic desire to visit them, is concealed until Thaxter's last page.[8]

It would be by no means easy to specify all the cultural connotations of the prose charting of northeastern coasts in this time. Most obviously, it accompanied and helped facilitate the urban reappropriation of the New England shore as a vacation site in the late 1860s and 1870s, processing real places into sites of suitable attraction. But its aestheticization of an "old" New England also fed into nontouristic (if not nonupper-class) developments: the architects who formed the firm McKim, Mead, and White found the elements for their colonial revival style by visiting Portsmouth and Newburyport, earlier featured in Thomas Bailey Aldrich's "An Old Town by the Sea" and Harriet Prescott Spofford's "Newburyport and Its Neighborhood" in *Harper's*.[9] But this writing had literary consequences as well, and Jewett can be said to embody them. By chance of birth she lived in just the kind of world that this genre featured: a coastal town—South Berwick, Maine—still full of relics of an earlier prosperity but now cut off from modern industrial activity, in this case by the decline of the shipbuilding trade. By virtue of the currency of this genre, at the moment when Jewett

came to her literary ambition she found her lived world presented
to her as a literary subject. In taking Maine's coastal backwaters as
her theme she made a personal self-identification with long-lasting
personal artistic consequences; but she was also realizing a literary
possibility set in the culture of her time.

Jewett's advent shows with classic clarity how nineteenth-
century regionalism created literary opportunities for marginal
groups. The cultural operativeness of this mode made a young
woman from a small town (a well-educated young woman whose
family subscribed to literary periodicals, anyway: the genre was
not comparably helpful to South Berwick's less well-off)—this
genre made a young woman from a town on the edges of cultural
excitement possess a literary capital just *in* that experience. And
the currency of this form meant that when Jewett reproduced her
known world in the contours of this genre, she found a ready outlet for her wares. Jewett had pieces accepted in the *Atlantic* before
she was twenty: taking regionalism as her work gave her an access
to readership and recognition as unobstructed as American literary
history has to show. But the genre she tapped into was also located
in a certain social place; so that when she adopted this form it
drew her into a particular field of social relations.

It is significant here that the *Atlantic Monthly,* already the publisher of *The Pearl of Orr's Island* and *Among the Isles of Shoals,*
should have provided Jewett with her natural market. Of the three
or four "serious" periodicals founded in America in the mid-nineteenth century the *Atlantic* was the one most committed to an ideal
of literary high culture, and by the time of Jewett's debut it had
already established itself as the authoritative discriminator of "literature" in the high-cultural sense. William Dean Howells, its editor at the time of *Deephaven,* attested that the *Atlantic* was "the
most scrupulously cultivated of our periodicals." Twenty years
later, in the year when *The Country of the Pointed Firs* was serialized
there, a new editor with more commercial tastes called the *Atlantic's* traditional fare "angel-cake"—a backhanded compliment, but
a tribute still to the elevations it was known to seek.[10] By virtue of
the reception her writing won her in this journal, Jewett won a
secure place *in* literature and *as* literature at a moment when

a hierarchical reorganization of the literary sphere was pushing other writers—including popular women writers—into a newly disparaged condition.[11] The *Atlantic's* circulation was not large in the later nineteenth century, and its rate of pay was not high by the standards of commercial publishers. For this reason, being produced here broke Jewett out of the highly commercialized and publicized mode of authorship experienced by the mid-nineteenth century best-sellers. But what she lost in popularity and income through this change in mode of production she gained back in status. When Horace Scudder became editor of the *Atlantic* he wrote to ask Jewett to keep up her contributions in order to continue this journal's association with "the most stable and pure American literature"—a new kind of tribute for an American woman author.[12]

Writing in the regional genre brought Jewett into association with the *Atlantic* and its high-prestige form of authorship. Her *Atlantic* connection, in turn, brought her into a new social world, the world of personal relations concretized around this organ and the literary values it professed. Through the editors of the *Atlantic*—in other words, through the literary bonds her writing had established—Jewett was introduced to James T. Fields and Annie Fields, the couple who helped establish the high-literary establishment of the later nineteenth century. As the aggressive partner in the firm of Ticknor and Fields and as editor of the *Atlantic* from 1859 to 1871, Fields had gained monopolistic hold on the writings of Hawthorne, Emerson, Longfellow, and their likes and contrived the means to identify them as classics. He then transferred this cachet to the new authors his publishing instruments brought to public life, for instance William Dean Howells and Henry James. The high-spirited and immensely attractive Annie Fields, his much younger wife, supplemented his business dealings by travelling with him and making literary contacts abroad, then by creating the Bostonian salon where foreign literary dignitaries, still-living but already canonized American authors, and young aspirants to high letters could meet and realize a literary world. (Henry James, who wrote a poignant memoir of Mrs. Fields, met Harriet Beecher Stowe in the Fields salon at 148 Charles Street. Willa Cather, who

wrote another such memoir, met Sarah Orne Jewett in Annie
Fields's house and through her hospitality.) The personalization of
literary relations that Annie Fields performed was especially successful in Jewett's case. Jewett met Annie Fields in the 1870s, but
became more intimate with her during James Fields's final illness;
and when Fields died in 1881 Jewett became Annie Fields's companion or second consort.[13]

Jewett's friendship with Fields brought her into a new way of
life with several interrelated aspects. When Jewett had assumed
the position of a well-to-do urban vacationer in *Deephaven,* she
had not been expressing her own actual relation to her subject—she was still a resident of the world she described as a visitor.
Instead she had been mastering a convention of her genre: fictively
projecting herself into the cosmopolitanized point of view from
which the local is "seen" in local color fiction. One consequence
of Jewett's association with Fields was that it realized, for her, the
social position she had first entered into as a generic fiction. As
Fields's companion Jewett came to spend long periods of the fall
and winter living in Boston—*The Country of the Pointed Firs* was
written, as *Deephaven* was not, by a Maine resident since renatur-
alized as a city person. And this association brought Jewett not just
into the city but specifically into the culture of an urbanized social
elite, with all its self-differentiating social practices. In Boston,
Jewett lived in Fields's famous house at 148 Charles Street, on the
aristocratic Beacon Hill. In Fields's company and as an extension
of their friendship, this regional author made touristic pilgrimages
to Europe, cherished pastime of the American cultured class. And
this friendship brought Jewett on long visits to what Henry James
called the Fields's "happy alternative home on the shining Massachusetts shore,"[14] her summer "cottage" at Manchester-by-the-
Sea—and so made Jewett a vacationer at places not far from her
home.

Jewett, the daughter of the town doctor and occupant of the
principal house in South Berwick, grew up as a member of the
sort of local gentry class characteristic of a village order of social organization. Her connection with Annie Fields might be said to have
given her a bridge into the more modernized version of the Ameri-

can social elite—less place-centered, more citified, more leisure-oriented, and more *culture*-oriented—that emerged together with a postvillage world in the mid-nineteenth century.[15] But what this friendship brought her in a more immediate way was a world of female affection and sharing organized in this social position. Studies of American women's cultures have tended to focus on nineteenth-century middle-class associations of women around values of home, family, and religion. Conversely, studies of the high-culture-promoting upper class have tended to ignore the women's world that it helped to form. But the Jewett-Fields relation can teach us that this social development brought into being its own quite intense female world of love and ritual organized around other values than domestic ones. In an 1890 letter, Jewett writes to Annie Fields: "I have been reading Mr. Arnold's 'Essays on Celtic Poetry' with perfect reverence for him and his patience and wisdom. How much we love him and believe in him, don't we? Do you know this book and the essay on translating Homer? I long to read it all with you."[16] This letter shows how the high-cultural order of the later nineteenth century casts women in the role of idealizing appreciators of such culture, but it also suggests how embracing this role can create new bonds between women: shared reverence for Matthew Arnold fashions a link between his female admirers here, and reading him provides the occasion for their intimate togetherness. In practice, the cultural order Annie Fields helped implement created a place where women of highly developed artistic competences could form a community around their artistic taste. In her association with Fields and their mutual friends—the painter, poet, and writer Celia Thaxter, the cellist Sara Norton (sister of Charles Eliot Norton), the stained glass worker Sarah Whitman, the poet Imogen Guiney—Jewett found a world where shared cultural enthusiasms formed a medium for the exchange of affections and where such affections yielded emotional support for women's artistic endeavors.[17]

The relations that Jewett entered into in the 1880s and 1890s can be thought of as mere biography, a detached backdrop for her writing life. But in fact they are the concomitants of the literary life she chose. In embracing the regional form, Jewett took its at-

tendant culture as her personal world; and if we ask what coming
to authorship through this form meant for Jewett, we need to
reckon what this culture provided her. Regionalism was produced
in a certain social situation in her time, and by embracing this
form, Jewett gained the specific artistic base this social situation
could provide: she won the backing of the high-cultural literary
establishment and of the women's artistic community nested *in*
that establishment for her literary self-assertion. But the culture
attached to regional fiction was a conceptual space as well as a
social one, with its own distinct structures of understanding and
value. And Jewett's way into authorship gave her a certain matrix
for self-conception—set her a certain mental world in which to
build the idea of her work—at the same time that it gave her a
certain base.

The milieu that Jewett's writing brought her into was intensely
literary. In the drawing room at 148 Charles Street, Annie Fields
sat under the portrait of her friend Charles Dickens. Another
friend, William Makepeace Thackeray, had finished *Henry Esmond*
in this house, and another, Matthew Arnold, had read the proofs
of *Essays in Criticism* there. At Manchester-by-the-Sea, Annie
Fields conversed familiarly of the Brownings and Henry James, Jr.,
and entertained one guest (Willa Cather) by reading Arnold's
Scholar Gypsy and *Tristan and Iseult* entire. (Cather adds of this occasion: "Miss Jewett said she didn't believe the latter poem had
been read aloud in that house since Matthew Arnold himself read
it there.") [18] But if this milieu was steeped in literature it was also
literary in a quite distinct sense of that term. "High literature" or
"serious writing" are shorthand names for the formation of this
category in nineteenth-century high culture; the Jewett-Fields milieu lets us see what those terms meant in practice. "Literature" as
it is realized in Annie Fields's surround includes not just the here-
and-now reading of mass-literary culture but works from the past
and from the foreign literatures of the present: Cather recalls Fields
opining "you know, my dear, I sometimes think we forget how
much we owe to Dryden's prefaces" and sending this underread
guest off to read "Dr. Donne." [19] Jewett, like Henry James, trea-
sured Flaubert and Turgenev—one of many signs that James and

Jewett inhabited the same culture of letters. More crucially, the designation "literature" in the Fields-Jewett world involves a prior act of hierarchization and elimination. This term is produced through a stratification in which most writing, including virtually all popular writing, gets marked as nonliterary and unworthy of attention—such writing is usually just not referred to in the Jewett-Fields milieu—while some other writing gets identified as rare or select: in short, as "literature."

After this initial discrimination, the high-quality zone of writing is made, in the Fields milieu as in nineteenth-century high culture generally, an object of something like ultimate value. For Jewett, Arnold is an author and therefore more than an author: she reads him with "perfect reverence." Longfellow is to Jewett literally immortal, and his work a sacred edifice. Upon his death she writes Annie Fields:

> I have just been thinking that a life like that is much less affected by death than most lives. A man who has written as Longfellow wrote, stays in this world always to be known and loved—to be a helper and a friend to his fellow men. It is a grander thing than we can wholly grasp, that life of his, a wonderful life, that is not shut in to his household or kept to the limits of his every-day existence. . . . And now what must heaven be to him! This world could hardly ask any more from him: he has done so much for it, and the news of his death takes away from most people nothing of his life. His work stands like a great cathedral in which the world may worship and be taught to pray, long after its tired architect goes home to rest.[20]

This letter perfectly exemplifies the sacralization produced for literature in nineteenth-century high culture, the investment in secular art of a degree of value saved for the religious in less secularized milieus. Jewett's Longfellow Cathedral has its architectural equivalent (for instance) in Henry Adams's Chartres, an artwork become itself quasi-divine in the absence of faith in the God once worshipped there.

Working together, the stratification of the literary and the high valuation of its highest grade produce another distinctive feature

of the nineteenth-century high-cultural definition of the literary, a
sharp isolation of the literary precinct. We associate Henry James
with a historically new assertion of the autonomy of the literary.
One of James's most powerful creations is the prescriptive redefi-
nition of the "art of fiction" whereby works are made to be defined
by their inward properties of formal arrangement, not their larger
social connections, and so are made to take value through their
deliberated composition or "art," not their service to extraliterary
goods. But James's autonomization of literary art was made thinkable in a certain historical culture, the late nineteenth-century high
culture of letters, and it realized a conception deeply inscribed in
that world.[21] When Cather, the belated perpetuator of nineteenth-
century high-cultural conceptions at the moment of twentieth-
century modernism, writes of her elected precursor Jewett, she
begins with Jewett's remark that certain writing "belongs to Literature." For Cather as for James the defining mark of this "higher
order of writing" is that it is formally highly deliberated and
crafted, "tightly built and significant in design." And for Cather as
for James the mark of the finely composed is that it creates its own
space, insulated, purified, and self-regulating. Cather says of Annie
Fields's salon, a social work of ideal art: "The ugliness of the world,
all possibility of wrenches and jars and wounding contacts, seemed
securely shut out. It was indeed the peace of the past, where the
tawdry and cheap have been eliminated and the enduring things
have taken their proper, happy places."[22] Presented as it was in
Fields's milieu, literature formed a world of artistic rarity bounded
off from the profane or mundane world outside: visitors to her
drawing room invariably described it as a combination of a museum of literature and a literary shrine.[23]

I dwell on the concept of literature specific to a certain cultural-
historical setting because one of the chief consequences of Jewett's
having founded her authorship where she did was that she took in
this understanding as part of her mental universe and framed the
idea of her work in its terms. Jewett abjured the abstraction of
critical writing, and she is nowhere so explicit about her theory of
the literary as James. But an idea of the nature of literary writing

is indicated everywhere in her work, as some comparisons make clear.

It is not for nothing that recent criticism has sought to align Jewett with American women writers of the previous generation. In her focus on enclosed communities bounded off from a masculine world of contemporary economic activity and filled with women's domestic arts and sociabilities, Jewett obeys protocols of inclusion and exclusion very similar to the domestic novelists of the 1850s literary generation. Nevertheless, if we put Jewett's work next to her sentimental-domestic forebears, she shows fundamental differences from these possible kin. The world projected through the writing of Susan Warner or Harriet Beecher Stowe is always child centered. Young children—Ellen Montgomery and Nancy Vawse in *The Wide, Wide World*, Little Eva and Topsy in *Uncle Tom's Cabin*, Moses and Mara in *The Pearl of Orr's Island*—have principal roles in these books, and the work of child rearing—the struggle to instill a mother's values in a child's character—forms their principal drama. (Stowe's regional novel *Oldtown Folks* presents itself as a fictional history of New England child-rearing practices.) By contrast, the worlds Jewett generates through her writing are almost always child free, and the forming of children's characters fails to appear as a source of literary interest. The "children" in *The Country of the Pointed Firs* are over sixty years of age.

Even more strikingly, the literary world of the earlier domestic novelists is always insistently religious, grounded on the structures and values of liberal Protestant religious belief. Their characters are believers more fundamentally than anything else they are, and when they are not believers—as are (in different ways) the unregenerate Topsy, the unconverted Ellen, the skeptical Augustine St. Clare, and the God-hating Simon Legree—their absence of faith still forms the most significant fact about them. And like the characters *in* these novels the writing *of* these novels produces reality within a religious frame of reference. In another book Ellen Montgomery's hyperconformity might mean something else, but in *The Wide, Wide World* it means that she has undergone conversion and entered into the covenant of saving faith. The prose of

Uncle Tom's Cabin makes us read Uncle Tom's physically unresisting death as a sign that he has won the Christian's victory of faith in the face of worldly evil, and this prose makes caring *for* a slave the equivalent of a saving love for the least of these our brethren. But to turn from these writers to Jewett is to encounter an almost wholly secular textual world. Unlike their predecessors in Stowe's *The Pearl of Orr's Island,* the old-timers of Deephaven and Dunnet Landing show virtually no trace of an orthodox Christian heritage, and its absence is not even remarked on; and Jewett's writing virtually never constructs the significance of what it represents in traditional religious terms. Whatever the interest we are invited to feel for the humble folk of Maine (her "lowly"), Jewett does not invite us to interpret our sympathy as Christian caritas. When Jewett moves to intensify the symbolic import of her characters, she does so by linking them to classical literary archetypes, as when Mrs. Todd becomes Antigone-like, not by making them, as Stowe does with Tom and Eva, *figurae Christi.* The last page of *Pointed Firs* rehearses the experience of dying quite as movingly as the death of Little Eva, and for many modern readers more movingly. But this death is no prelude to otherworldly glories.[24]

We might think of these differences as merely individual, as if to say: Warner and Stowe cared about one sort of thing, Jewett cared about another. Or we might think of them as generational differences reflecting historical changes in the world, as: Jewett's world is childless because she writes at a time of declining rural birthrates and the out-migration of the rural young;[25] or Jewett's world is secular because she writes at a later, more secularized phase of the process of religious liberalization that Stowe and Warner knew in its pious-sentimental moment. Such accounts are not unhelpful; but I would argue that what these differences reflect most fundamentally is the fact that these authors wrote on different understandings of what literary writing *is.* The sentimental-domestic fiction of the mid-nineteenth century is literary in a particular sense of the term. Books like *Uncle Tom's Cabin* and *The Wide, Wide World* are written on the understandings that literary discourse is continuous with, not differentiated from, the discourses of piety and domestic instruction and that the *work* of literary writing forms part of a larger project of promoting domestic morality and Christian belief: it is not by chance but in fulfillment of this specific vision of authorship that Stowe wrote novels *and* texts of domestic instruction *and* tracts for the promotion of piety (three modes of authorship not discontinuous for her), or that she and her contemporaries wrote books that are indistinguishably novels, domestic child-rearing manuals, and tracts on Christian duty, like Catharine Sedgwick's multipurpose *Home*. This literary understanding, in turn, was not self-generated by the 1850s cohort of women writers but formed in face of a quite specific situation of letters. Stowe and her contemporaries organized their authorship within the new middle-class literary culture of the antebellum decades, which made a place for novel reading that conjoined it with this group's other distinctive social practices, domestic piety and sentimental family nurture. Such authors realized the literary logic of this situation by *thinking* their writing as a family support system at once novelistic, morally pedagogic, and evangelical in form.

What we encounter in Jewett is an authorship practiced on a radically different plan. Jewett has dissociated the cultural fields that are conjoined for her predecessors: religious and child-rearing issues are almost wholly recessive in her work not just because she cares less about them personally but because in her understanding literary writing is a *different thing* from the work of piety or nurture, an activity they have no part in. If we ask how Jewett came to extricate the literary from connections it was once enmeshed in, the answer is at least in part that she constructed her idea of authorship in a different literary-cultural situation. Jewett's more tightly bounded understanding exactly reflects the late nineteenth-century high-cultural presentation of literature as a sphere of its own of value in itself. To a significant extent Jewett shares James's view that "questions of art are questions (in the widest sense) of execution; questions of morality are quite another affair," a thought unthinkable where Stowe comes from.[26] Her authorial self-identification with this more autonomized or aestheticized un-

derstanding of literary writing is a further consequence of her having come into writing where she did: a consequence with larger
historical resonances.

The historical significance of Jewett's reconception of her work
is that it effected an more general transformation in the figure of
the American woman author. By orienting herself within an up-
per-class-based universe of high-cultural understandings, Jewett
broke the woman author out of the earlier domestic definition of
her work and recreated her as a "literary" artist in the same sense
as her highly reputed male contemporaries. This differentiation in
turn helps to explain the difference of Jewett's later fortunes. It is
not the whole truth to say that only invidious distinctions enforced
by dominant cultures make some writing "literature" and other
not. Works of writing are literary in different senses and to different extents, and not just because we later label them so but because they enact, in their composition, different understandings of
what writing is and does. Working from her different culturally
based model, Jewett *made* her work literary in a different way than
her sentimental-domestic predecessors—produced fiction that
does not engage overtly extraliterary systems of signification
(family values, evangelical Protestantism) to the same extent, and
so seems to generate meanings from within its textual "art." As the
understanding of literature Jewett subscribed to gained in cultural
power, the difference this idea made *in* her work helped create a
different public life *for* her work. Historically, the high-cultural
specification of "literature" was one among several conceptions
operative in the 1850s and 1860s, but through the successful institutionalization of high-cultural schemes in America this definition became the dominant one in the later nineteenth century and
remained so for most of the twentieth. When this severely auton-
omizing conception came to cultural power, works literary in a
different sense, for instance sentimental fiction, came to appear
nonliterary; and by the nature of their textual organizations these
books defied efforts to restore them to literature until an alternative definition of the term, corresponding to their much more socially *related* textual form, could again be made current. But the

fact that Jewett made her work literary in the sense that came into currency meant that she did not suffer the same vicissitudes. When this definition rose to cultural ascendancy it found in her work the kind of thing it valued, and so recognized her as the "literary artist" it could not see in a Stowe.

But the world of understandings into which Jewett's authorship inserted her contained other elements than the one I have been discussing; and if in one aspect this base helped her become (in the sense just described of that variable term) a more *literary* writer, in another it helped render her a *minor* literary figure.

The issue of size or scale has formed part of every reckoning of Jewett. In her essay "Miss Jewett," Cather wrote that "to note an artist's limitations is but to define his talent,"[27] but rarely has limitation been used to define an artist's talent to the extent that it has been used to define Jewett's. In the 1890s Jewett's *Atlantic* editor, Horace Scudder, praised her for "her nice sense of the limits of her art." Twenty years later, Henry James admired the "beautiful little quantum of achievement" Jewett had produced in "minor compass." Later still, Cather, Jewett's great early twentieth-century advocate, wrote that "she was content to be slight, if she could be true." And even Sarah Sherman's important recent rehabilitation begins by likening Jewett to a fragile teacup.[28] In view of this history it would be easy to assume that Jewett has been (as my initial quotation has it) "unfairly considered a minor regional writer," but this invidious judgment has not been only a retroactive product of her reception: the curiosity of Jewett's case is that she shared the judgment of her limitation and, more, made it a founding feature of her literary self-conception. Her letters, thus, are a kind of a diary of a self-belittler. Sometimes she figures herself as a minor in age: in a famous letter, the forty-eight year old-Jewett wrote: "This is my birthday and I am always nine years old." At other times she uses tropes of height to measure (and diminish) her stature: "I seem impressive, but really I only come up to my own shoulder," writes this non-self-aggrandizer. At other times she presents herself as the writer as little creature, producer of small—and shrinking!—objects at best:

I do so like Craddock [Mary Noailles Murfree], who takes time, and
is lost to sight, to memory dear, and writes a good big Harper's story.
So does [Murfree's] Sister, with one for the "Atlantic" called Felicia;
so does not S. O. J., whose French ancestry comes to the fore, and
makes her nibble all round her stories like a mouse. They used to
be as long as yardsticks, they are now as long as spools, and they
will soon be the size of old-fashioned peppermints, and have neither beginning nor end.[29]

Jewett's compulsive self-miniaturization may be thought to display a general syndrome afflicting women authors, the self-under-
mining bred by enculturation systems that mark assertion and
achievement as proper provinces only for men. But the diminution
mechanisms built into Jewett's self-assertion also received massive
reinforcement from the culture of letters she inhabited. To a much
greater extent than other American literary cultures of the nineteenth century, the self-designated high culture of the postbellum
decades organizes the arts around the figure of the Great Artist.
The hierarchizing and sacralizing tendencies of this scheme work
to break a few artists—the great practitioners—out of the community of all who write and to elevate them into a region of
supreme eminence and transcendent authority. We know this culture, accordingly, by its cult of the master, witnessed in a hundred
ways: in its centering of art museums and art education on the Old
Masters; in its composition of new school curricula fixed on canonical authors (a special labor of Jewett's editor Horace Scudder);
in its publication of standard editions of classic authors (the project of the *Atlantic*'s parent company, Houghton, Mifflin); or in its
master-centered critical works, like William C. Brownell's *Victorian
Prose Masters* and *American Prose Masters*.

Canonicity, the recent debate on canons has tended to forget, is
itself no invariant historical structure. Rather, the hierarchizing act
that produces canons has been enforced with different degrees of
strenuousness in different cultures at different times. In nineteenth-
century America the canonical presentation of art and artistic
status was insisted on peculiarly vehemently in the upper-class-
based high culture of the postbellum decades, as part of a more

general defense of social hierarchy; and in that culture the idea of the master entailed yet further stratifications within the ranks of the "artistic." In this ethos—as not, comparably, in other contemporaneous ones—an extremely well-articulated idea of the minor author travels together with the idea of the great one. Henry James is thinking in the idiom of this world when he divides the society of authors into "life-giving master[s]," whose powers strain even the largest readerly receptacles "to breaking," and their littler, lesser companions—for instance Jane Austen, author of "little touches of human truth, little glimpses of steady vision, little masterstrokes"; or Hawthorne, with his "little tales," "little attempts, little sketches, little world"; or Jewett, with her "beautiful little quantum of achievement."[30] One of the great proofs that Jewett and James share the same world of cultural understandings (as they shared the same friends, publishers, editors, and literary favorites) is that she too sees the writer in gradations from greater to lesser. Jewett believes in the master quite as much as James: Cather testifies that Jewett applied the adjective "great" "very seldom (to Tolstoy, Flaubert, and a few others)"; in surviving letters Jewett calls Flaubert "a master writer [who] gives everything weight" and finds another "Master" in "Turguenieff." *And* for Jewett as for James the rank of master entails a lesser rank of the fine or high artist who shares the master's sense of art but is not his equal in achievement: "not a Master by any means, but a story-writer of certain instincts!"[31]

The author Jewett refers to in the last cited line is herself, and this letter poignantly shows the invidiousness the whole system of graded authorship held for Jewett. Before the organizing term *master* she defines herself as not-master, as one whose work calls up the thought of a mastery only to have a certain difference come clear. But what this letter shows most crucially is that the major-minor distinction maintained in Jewett's culture entered the thought of those who inhabited that culture and helped frame their personal understandings—of themselves quite as much as of others. If Jewett and James have literary selves finally very different from one another, it is partly because of the different ways they realized the self-fashioning possibilities of their shared situation.

Before a conceptual structure that marks some writers major and others minor, James powerfully identifies with the idea of the major, and forges a career-governing ideal self in the image of the literary master: "to write well and worthily of American things one needs even more than elsewhere to be a *master*," he is already saying in 1870; and at the time of his fortieth birthday: "I must make some great efforts during the next few years . . . if I wish not to have been on the whole a failure. I shall have been a failure unless I do something *great*."³² In the same situation and before the same field of choices Jewett identifies instead with the idea of the minor, and so embraces a literary self projected on a more circumscribed plan.

As with all hypothetical histories, it is unclear whether Jewett could have been a "major" writer had she aspired to be one. What is clear is that the renunciation of such ambitions formed part of the governing idea of her career; also, that such self-attenuation was both implicit in and reinforced by her choice of genre. Nineteenth-century America had nothing like the officially established hierarchy of genres that in older times marked tragedy higher than comedy and pastoral's oaten flute a lesser thing than epic's trumpet sterne. Nevertheless, Jewett's contemporaries clearly share a consensual understanding of what "great" work is like. James and Howells, the chief aspirers in Jewett's literary generation, associate the major with an act of self-extension, a quite visible setting aside of lesser projects to undertake big things. The marks that qualify a work as major, for these figures, are that it be sustained or long (their self-appointed first "big" novels, James's *The Portrait of a Lady* [1881] and Howells's *A Modern Instance* [1882], are double the size of their predecessors); that it engage the deep feelings attendant on grave issues (Howells crowed of *A Modern Instance* that in divorce he had found "a theme only less intense and pathetic than slavery"); and that it have scope, reading the personal or local within a larger experiential horizon—as *The Portrait of a Lady* makes individual development a transcontinental (and cross-cultural) project; or as *A Modern Instance* grasps a Maine town's apparently static local life as participating in larger patterns of national social change.³³ In face of such understandings, regionalism

could only appear as the point-by-point converse of major writing;
and in embracing regionalism Jewett not only embraced the chief
minor mode of her time but also constrained her work within
boundaries that would ensure its minor status. Regionalism was
established as a form of short story or sketch length in the literary
practice of her time, so that in writing regionalism Jewett wrote
short pieces when long works carried the meaning "major." (Her
longer work, *The Country of the Pointed Firs, her* well-disguised bid
to become "big" and do a "big thing," is small compared even to
James and Howells's smaller novels, and takes the form of a series
of tales and sketches: Jewett herself called it "the Pointed Fir Papers," as if to reduce it back to its small component parts.) [34] Regionalism in nineteenth-century practice was also associated with
a mitigated range of tone and feeling, attenuated from comic and
tragic heights and depths to the mildly humorous and the mildly
pathetic; and in choosing the regional form, Jewett also accepted
its generic diminution of her work's emotional scale. By its formal
operations, regionalism limited the literary work's social horizon
to a self-containedly local world, as Deephaven and Dunnet Landing are shut in from a larger American social history, not, like
Howells's Equity, made another site *of* that history; and through
her adherence to this mode, Jewett rendered herself the fictive historian of the parish or byway (two of her favorite figures), of the
lesser, not the larger, world.

The problem that Jewett has always presented for her admirers
is how to value her achievement without inflating the dimensions
of her achievement. If I am right, these limitations are the product
neither of mere personal lack of "power" nor of a general disable-
ment of women's relation to writing but of Jewett's adherence to
structures of literary self-conception specific to her cultural situation—structures built into her genre through its institutional
articulation in her time. But the contextualization that made regionalism complicit with self-limitation did other things than help
Jewett be content to be slight. It also helped foster an attitude toward literary work in another direction newly assertive.

This attitude can be heard in a letter from Jewett to Annie Fields
written just after Stowe's death in 1883:

I have been reading the beginning of "The Pearl of Orr's Island" and finding it just as clear and perfectly original and strong as it seemed to me in my thirteenth or fourteenth year, when I read it first. I never shall forget the exquisite flavor and reality of delight that it gave me. I do so long to read it with you. [Again, reading as vehicle of intimacy.] It is classical—historical—anything you like to say, if you can give it high praise enough. I haven't read it for ten years at least, but *there it is!* Alas, that she couldn't finish it in the same noble key of simplicity and harmony; but a poor writer is at the mercy of much unconscious opposition. You must throw everything and everybody aside at times, but a woman made like Mrs. Stowe cannot bring herself to that cold selfishness of the moment for one's work's sake, and the recompense for her loss is a divine touch here and there in an incomplete piece of work.[35]

This letter—which for all its generosity might still raise doubts whether women's literary traditions function on a noncompetitive basis—speaks to an obvious feature of *The Pearl of Orr's Island*, the massive nonalignment of the book's first and second halves. At the same time, it also expresses a more general difference between Jewett and her American female predecessors, a different stance toward the question of literary selfishness. For Jewett the aesthetic problem of underdeliberated design in *Orr's Island* signals a prior problem of literary commitment which in turn bespeaks a problem of authorial self-conception, Stowe's insufficient detachment of a self from others to devote to her work. What to Jewett's eyes is a problematic "warm selflessness" in Stowe is something we have learned to understand historically. Mary Kelley has shown that the terms on which women authors of the 1850s generation seized public literary careers required them to define writing as an extension of traditionally determined women's maternal or domestic labor, part of a woman's proper *being for others*, not a counter-domestic end in itself. The heroic female author of Fanny Fern's *Ruth Hall*, thus, writes to clothe and house her children, not to satisfy a mere will to artistic creation. When her daughter (presumably envious of her mother's absorption in her work) asks whether such apparently pleasurable self-investments will be hers when she grows up, her mother harshly corrects her: "God forbid! No happy woman ever writes." Stowe, who in the preface to *The American Woman's Home* declared that woman's "great mission is self-denial, in training [family] members to self-sacrificial labors for the ignorant and the weak," spoke of *Uncle Tom's Cabin* as a *mother's* work, a work too preoccupied with a mother's cares to have attention to spare for formal features: "I no more thought of style or literary excellence than the distressed mother who rushes into the street and cries for help to save her child from a burning house, thinks of the teachings of the rhetorician or the elocutionist," she writes, leaving no doubt about what "selfishness . . . for one's work's sake" would have meant to her.[36] But for Jewett such ulteriority has become a deficiency, not an end required to give writing point; and writing has become an allowable selfishness, an aim both requiring and excusing abstention from the ordinary social world. Here again, Jewett's changed personal thinking clearly reflects the differently articulated logic of a changed literary culture. The culture of letters Jewett inhabits to a peculiar extent locates value within works of art, not in the higher goods art could be said to serve. In its aesthetics the good in a work of art is put there *through its art,* through the disciplined application of a craft specific to that mode of creation; and the perfecting *of* this art therefore both requires and justifies the author's intensely specialized devotion to his art or craft. This ethic of sacrificial self-devotion to the work "for one's work's sake" is best known to us through its Jamesian incarnation, but Jewett, too, strongly appropriates this shared cultural property. Her embrace of it marks a literary development of immense historical resonance: the moment when a publishing American woman author first claims the duty (hence the right) to take her art seriously, and to define her proper self as the maker of her art.

This ethic of legitimated dedication is a last yield Jewett derives from her work's cultural situation, and in its fullest expression the social specificity of its derivation is clearer yet. Late in life Jewett wrote a letter to Willa Cather in which this usual self-effacer reveals a willingness after all to be someone's master, to objectify her practice into an abstract code and to voice the authority of that code to a young aspirant. This letter—Jewett's equivalent to James's contemporaneous prefaces to the New York Edition—is addressed from a woman to a woman, but in it neither woman is legitimately recognized as anything but the artist, an (almost) ungendered figure of self-disciplined professional devotion. Jewett writes:

My Dear Willa,—I have been thinking about you and hoping that things are going well. I cannot help saying what I think about your writing and its being hindered by such incessant, important, responsible work as you have in your hands now. [Cather was still working for the S. S. McClure media syndicate.] I do think that it is impossible for you to work so hard and yet have your gifts mature as they should—when one's first working power has spent itself nothing ever brings it back just the same, and I do wish in my heart that the force of this very year could have gone into three or four stories. In the "Troll-Garden" the Sculptor's Funeral stands alone a head higher than the rest, and it is to that level you must hold and take for a starting-point. You are older now than that book in general; you have been living and reading and knowing new types; but if you don't keep and guard and mature your force, and above all, have time and quiet to perfect your work, you will be writing things not much better than you did five years ago. This you are anxiously saying to yourself! but I am wondering how to get at the right conditions. . . . .Your good schooling and your knowledge of "the best that has been thought and said in the world," as Matthew Arnold put it, have helped you, but you need to deepen and enrich still more. You must find a quiet place near the best companions (not those who admire and wonder at everything one does, but those who know the good things with delight!). You do need reassurance,—every writer does!—but you need still more to feel "responsible for the state of your conscience" (your literary conscience, we can just now limit that quotation to), and you need to dream your dreams and go on to new and more shining ideals, to be aware of "the gleam" and to follow it; your vivid, exciting companionship in the office must not be your audience, you must find your own quiet centre of life, and write from that to the world that holds offices, all society, all Bohemia; the city, the country—in short, you must write to the human heart, the great consciousness that all humanity goes to make up. . . . And to write and work on this level, we must live on it—we must at least recognize it and defer to it at every step. We must be ourselves, but we must be our best selves. If we have patience with cheapness and thinness, as Christians must, we must know that it *is* cheapness and not make believe about it. To work in silence and with all one's heart, that is the writer's lot; he is only the artist who must be a solitary, and yet needs the widest outlook upon the world. But you have been growing I feel sure in the very days when you felt most hindered, and this will be counted to you. You need to have time to yourself and time to read and add to your recognitions. I do not know when a letter has grown so long and written itself so easily, but I have been full of thought about you.[37]

If we did not know it already, this virtual literary testament—one of the most extraordinary pieces of writing in the Jewett canon—would be enough to establish Jewett's cultural citizenship with perfect accuracy. The passage is redolent of Matthew Arnold, idealizer of a "best self" produced through acculturation in "the best that has been thought and said," and so locates itself in the nineteenth-century American social formation that made Arnold its guide, the old gentry and new professional segments that adopted high culture as their project and group ideal. The passage's universalized Arnoldian humanism is shot through with markers of this group's class outlook—an expectation of the availability of leisure; a kind of leering disdain for the workerly "office" and its "companionship" ("vivid, exciting," and clearly not the right set); and hostility in particular to the McClurean or mass media world of writing, continual object, at the turn of the century, of elite fear of a new popular culture's threatened "debasements" of the "best." The opposition the passage turns on at its end—of quality or highly perfected versus "cheap" productions—encodes a structure of value similarly particular to this social group at this time, a value that again functions to make apparently aesthetic discriminations underwrite a larger social invidiousness. Jewett's idiom is echoed in James's ubiquitous distinctions between the "cheap" object "of easy manufacture, showing on every side the stamp of the machine," and the "excellent," "more precious products of the same general nature . . . belonging to the class of the hand-made"; in the disdain of Theodore Thomas, pioneer of the all-classical symphony orchestra playing for "the influential minority," for "vulgar" and "trashy" popular culture; in Harvard literature professor Barrett Wendell's remark to Harvard President Charles W. Eliot that they should leave "Boston University, Tufts, and the other lesser colleges" to educate the "cheap material" of a socially lower clientele, "each in its cheap way"; and in Cather's recoil from the "cheap," "mercenary," "vulgar and meretricious" tastes that join the "young man of foreign descent" with the "new American . . . to whom the old Yankee . . . is almost a foreignor."[38] Nevertheless, in this social location, and by firmly embracing the invidious structures of its thought, something else becomes thinkable for Jewett, something not comparably thinkable in other cultural settings. This world's sharp demarcation of the aesthetic sphere and its investment of moral value in "high" art enable Jewett to conceive of a specialized literary conscience, a kind of aesthetic superego requiring the writer to try to do a "best" now defined wholly in artistic terms. Once this "literary conscience" has been conceptualized and morally funded it becomes a matter of duty for a woman no less than a man to dedicate herself to her work, to withdraw herself from other involvements and give herself to this higher good: "To work in silence and with all one's heart, that is the writer's lot." To be able to think a writerly self on these terms—to have one's artistic career demand self-sacrifice and so to have it free one from more traditionally required female self-sacrifices—is another product of Jewett's having come to authorship where she did; and if through the logic of regional authorship Jewett gave up the will to do major work, she also won the ability to claim what she saw as the major writer's attitude toward her work. "He is the only artist who must be a solitary, and yet needs the widest outlook upon the world," she writes to her protégée—the male pronoun this time designating their own achieved artistic selves.

III

We can attach different meanings to Jewett's achievement of authorship. It is easy to read her into women's literary history told as a story of progress. In this account, with Jewett, women authors escaped the self-vitiating definition of themselves as something other than artists and laid claim to the same vocational seriousness as their male contemporaries. By this means Jewett helped pioneer "the first generation of American women writers who saw themselves as artists,"[39] and she helped prepare the way for a next generation of writers—Edith Wharton and Cather most notably— who could undo the limitations of ambition that she still accepted. But it would be possible to suspect that this narrative elevates into a normative position a conception of "the artist"—professional-istic, formally proficient, aesthetically oriented, and socially neu-tralized or detached—that is historically contingent, not invariant or eternal. In the light of this suspicion we could see Jewett not as climbing up a step on the unchanging structure of "Art" but as conducting an aestheticization of women's writing, the meaning of which is more mixed. As we know, the high-cultural reformula-tion of aesthetic categories in the later nineteenth century created a new attention to the craftedly verbal or *formal* features of the work of art and simultaneously delimited the work in new measure *to* such features, making the "work" of art more a self-contained wrought object and less a form of action in the world. Jewett can be thought of as having incorporated this double transformation into women's writing with an inevitably two-sided result: that as she became a finer artist in the craft-applying sense—her work has a finish unknown to Stowe—she also restricted her art's applica-tion to a fined-down experiential world; and that she became more dedicated to her art at the price of having that art give up larger functions of social edification and political address embraced by the less "artistic" domestic-sentimental generation.[40]

But whichever of these values is attached to it, Jewett presents a single historical exhibit. Whether taken as leading a progress into art or a shrinkage into "Art," Jewett embodies a historical rene-

gotiation of the relation of American women to literary careers,
marks the emergence of a sense of art and of woman's relation to
it with these features inextricably entwined: that its literary aspirations now find substantial social support, *and* that that support
ties it to elite social institutions; that it embraces artistic goals
frankly, no longer cloaking such ambition behind religious or
familial or sentimental-political covers, *and* that its art ceases
to operate in such transliterary cultural registers; that it accepts
its difference from a major work it imagines in detail, *and* that
through its vision of such work it construes a strong ethical imperative to its own career. One may applaud some of these features
and regret others, but Jewett teaches us that they are not so easily
separated: that these interdependent features came all together
into women's literary self-definition is the historical fact Jewett
helps establish. And she shows that literary regionalism gave the
site for the reconstruction of women's authorship on these terms.

How this genre mediated this transformation will now be clear.
There is no necessary relation between regional fiction as a literary
structure and the cultural forms I have tied it to here—class-bound
leisure pastimes, beliefs in literary autonomy, and so on. This
genre's relation to such forms was given not through any intrinsic
propensity of its conventions but through a process of socioliterary
history, through its inclusion in an institutionalization of culture
that conjoined certain genres with a certain formulation of the literary and with certain structures of social value. This cultural history is what made literary regionalism and minor high-literary
authorship (for instance) share common space in late nineteenth-
century America; but the positioning of this genre still had no invariant effect on authors or their careers. Authors *made* themselves
authors of different sorts by the way they accepted or resisted the
values constellated around this form. Jewett, a virtual native of the
social world that sponsored nineteenth-century high culture, profoundly embraced the conceptual structures aligned with regionalism—the religion of art, the autonomization of the aesthetic, the
stratification of high and low, the major-to-minor gradient—and
composed a base for her work by that means. But the nongentry
Hamlin Garland—a regionalist as populist activist in the decade of

The Country of the Pointed Firs—resisted the depoliticization and cultural hierarchizing associated with this mode; and Mary Wilkins Freeman, an author like Jewett, only grimmer, embraced many of the strictures affiliated with this mode but not the Arnoldian cult of cultural uplift.

Jewett made her literary identity through her highly personal way of identifying with the cultural structures surrounding her form. But if her case is worth singling out, it is because the consequences of this act were more than personal. Partly through her power as a writer, partly through the culturally derived structures through which she disciplined and sustained that power (Jewett, like James, sustained her authorship over a whole long career), and partly too through her prominent production within the "quality" literary journals of her time, Jewett's personally achieved authorship took on a more general authority, establishing the normative model for women's high-artistic literary identity in America. The career plan modelled by Jewett set a figure of authorship—aligning women's writing with high-cultural aspiration, with antifamilial careerism and profound artistic seriousness, with self-conscious refusal of the forms of artistic practice marked as "major," *and* with regional subject matter and its richnesses and its self-enclosures—that her successors had to contend with for at least a generation. Wilkins Freeman practiced authorship on Jewett's plan. So did Cather, another devotee of the figure of the artist, whom Jewett urged toward regional subjects and who was, if not content to be slight, still stubbornly resistant to the modernism that made a master in her day. So did Eudora Welty, most Jewett-like of all later writers in her devotions and self-limitations. So did not Edith Wharton, who nevertheless felt the need to avoid Jewett, the sketch-length work, and the regional subject, in order to combat the circumscriptions Jewett's literary model reinforced.[41]

A more influential figure than we even now acknowledge, Jewett's influence was exercised chiefly through the figure she presented of the woman as literary worker. That figure (like all such figures) was profoundly mixed in its ingredients—an affair not of empowerments or restrictions alone but of certain forms of enablement and delimitation seized together. Those ingredients in turn were set in the social conditions of Jewett's work, however idio-syncratically she combined them. Jewett's figure of the author out-lived its own occasion to act in the different literary-historical situations of later times, but it was forged *in* and *from* the late nineteenth-century cultural situation of the regionalist mode. Like the countryfolk she describes, her model of literary identity bears an inescapable mark of local derivation.

CHAPTER

6

"Why Could Not a Colored Man?"
Chesnutt and the Transaction of Authorship

how did regionalism serve/limit minority writers?

I

NINETEENTH-CENTURY REGIONALISM is among other things a work of ethnic imagining, a literary form performing the larger cultural service of imaging Americas different in habits, speech, and appearance from a norm this form helps render normative. In practice, this genre easily took on the related task of imagining American racial differences. The Chicanos and native Americans of Helen Hunt Jackson's *Ramona* (1884), like the black storyteller of Joel Chandler Harris's *Uncle Remus* (1881), fulfill this form's formula for the production of otherness just as neatly as Eggleston's white midwestern rustics or Jewett's north-country locals do; and the enduring popularity of these two works should remind us that the apparently minor genre of regional fiction has generated some of American culture's most persistent images of America's racial minorities.

But in the work of Charles W. Chesnutt, the child of parents on both sides half-Negro and so a man socially consigned to the category of the Negro, the racial difference that is this form's frequent subject matter reverses its position and becomes not the distant object of someone else's literary attention but a property of the author himself. With Chesnutt, local color writing becomes the product *of* the so-called "colored"; and in this development the regionalist form again displays its peculiar function as a site of literary oppor-

177

tunity, a door through which groups traditionally barred from the literary realm have won access to that realm. Chesnutt was not the first author of African-American origin, but he was the first to have a book published as a literary work by a high-cultural literary publisher—so that it was through the regionalist genre that an African-American author first won anything like a position as a mainstream author in American literary culture. Inextricable from this change in public status, in Chesnutt an African-American writer first took possession of the operative understanding of authorship that governed the dominant literary system of his time. Like Henry James or Sarah Orne Jewett and quite unlike his African-American predecessors, Chesnutt conceives of writing as a largely autonomous zone of verbal creation. Unlike black writers of the previous generation, for whom authorship was all but inevitably tied to the slave narrative's generic requirements of personal testimony and real or pretended facticity, for Chesnutt writing means writing fiction, and is a medium of verbal invention. The most powerful writers among Chesnutt's black contemporaries—Booker T. Washington and Frances Harper come to mind—think of writing as ancillary to a primary work of public speaking and they mentally subordinate such speech to larger goals of moral and social betterment. But Chesnutt, like his high-cultural white contemporaries, dissociates literary art from such transliterary aims and makes it more of an end: Chesnutt's aim as a writer, most unlike Washington, or Harper, or Frederick Douglass, or Harriet Jacobs, is to *have a literary career,* through mastery of writing (in his phrases) to "secure a place in literature" and attain to a "successful literary life."[1]

Chesnutt's importance to literary history lies partly in his writing, but partly too in the fact that he embodies a historical renegotiation of the relation of members of his race *to* writing as a cultural activity. And in Chesnutt's case, as in Jewett's not wholly dissimilar one, this attainment of a new relation to writing took place through the mediation of the regionalist mode. But Jewett and Chesnutt come to writing from profoundly different places: Jewett from a long-established social elite, Chesnutt from a group only just freed from slavery and still the object of massive social disadvantage; Jewett from a world where literary writing was a known and valued practice, Chesnutt from a world just learning how to read; Jewett from the group regionalist fiction was produced *for,* Chesnutt (at least in the eyes of others) from the group such fiction was written *about.* These differences did not prevent Chesnutt from making his way into authorship. But they did make a difference in the authorship he attained. In this chapter I want to consider the different opportunities the regionalist literary form afforded when approached from a different position.

II *enabling conditions*

Charles Waddell Chesnutt was an extraordinarily ambitious man whose ambition was directed in significant part toward literary achievement. This is the great fact of Chesnutt's case, and to seek for an explanation of it beyond a certain point is to come up against the mystery of character, the not-to-be-accounted-for process by which one becomes endowed or disposed in one way and not another. But if it is not caused by such circumstances, Chesnutt's literary aspiration (like everyone else's) has its enabling conditions, which are to be found in a historically specific cultural situation.

The early life of Chesnutt could be told as follows. Chesnutt was born in 1858 in Fayetteville, North Carolina, of parents with the status of free Negroes. His family migrated to the free state of Ohio as the Civil War approached, but returned to North Carolina with the beginning of Reconstruction. He was educated at the Howard School, the graded school for Negro children established in Fayetteville by Robert O. Harris, until his mother died and his remarried father moved into the country. When the need to help support his father's growing family threatened to push him out of school and into jobs on the farm or in a saloon, Chesnutt's teachers intervened and found him a series of positions in black schools. In his early teens he became a pupil-teacher at the Howard School. In his mid-teens he taught at Robert's brother Cicero Harris's school at Charlotte, North Carolina, and (in summers) in more primitive black schools in adjacent rural districts. When the first North Carolina normal school for the training of black teachers was established at Fayetteville in 1877 with Robert Harris as principal, Chesnutt became the first assistant in the new school. When Harris died in 1880 Charles Chesnutt was made principal of the Normal School for Colored Teachers, at the age of twenty-two.[2]

These are the facts of Chesnutt's personal biography. But each of these facts also ties Chesnutt to a historically given social situation, situations that put him in a certain relation to letters and (through letters) to the world. The so-called old order free Negroes of North Carolina were greatly more likely to be literate than their enslaved compatriots, whose introduction to reading and writing was forbidden by law. By the chance of his birth within this social division, then, Chesnutt came into literacy as a family inheritance when he could more easily have inherited its lack. His formal education bespeaks his involvement at every point with another social development, the postbellum history of black education. From the age of seven on, Chesnutt lived amidst the massive drive by emancipated blacks to realize their freedom by repossessing the education that had been denied them; and the social structures designed to accommodate what Booker T. Washington called the "experience of a whole race beginning to go to school for the first time"[3] form in the most literal possible way the *scenes* of Chesnutt's childhood. Chesnutt could go to school in Fayetteville after 1867 because a school for blacks had just been founded there by one of the idealistic Northern educators (in this case a black one) with Northern philanthropic backing who came south after the war to teach in the new freedman academies. When Chesnutt taught in rural black districts in his teens, he was working in another institution new at this time: the ill-funded and irregularly maintained schools that poor rural blacks insisted on holding to the extent that they could to give their children some share of a previously withheld resource of knowledge. (Booker T. Washington and W. E. B. Du Bois also taught in these characteristic institutions of the Reconstruction decades.) Chesnutt could later work in a state normal school because such facilities were coming into existence in the South in the 1870s, as black schools took on the conscious task of teacher training and as states began to support the training of blacks to teach in a separate black public school system. The Hampton Normal and Agricultural Institute, scene of Washington's training, was founded nine years before the normal school Chesnutt led; Tuskegee was established as a normal school for colored teachers in 1881.[4]

The new network of black educational establishments composed of the town elementary school, its more poorly endowed imitation in country districts, and the normal school designed to prepare black teachers framed the space of Chesnutt's early life; and being set in this social structure gave Chesnutt more than a setting. Being placed as he was gave Chesnutt access to cultural knowledges he would otherwise scarcely have had. We need to remember that seventy percent of Southern blacks were still illiterate in the year Chesnutt became a school principal, and that the great majority of the remainder lacked the higher education offered blacks in North Carolina almost exclusively at the Fayetteville Normal School.[5] Having access to education in its most highly elaborated forms gave Chesnutt, in turn, a status he would otherwise have lacked. The prize pupil Chesnutt was by age thirteen a teacher and by age twenty-two a principal in a culture in which educators formed the major leadership cadre, when—uneducated—he might have expected a life in tenant farming or domestic service. And being placed there meant being introduced into a different cultural ethos as well.

It is obvious very early on that having the educational advantages he had made Chesnutt experience himself as different from other kinds of Southern blacks. Writing in his journal while teaching in a country school, Chesnutt says of the rural blacks of this district: "Uneducated people, are the most bigoted, superstitious, hardest-headed people in the world! . . . These people don't know words enough for a fellow to carry on a conversation with them. He must reduce his phraseology several degrees lower than that of the first reader."[6] *Words* here means the correctly elaborated standard English embodied in writing and learned in school. (Robert Harris's philosophy of education scheduled "an exercise in articulation at every recitation" in an effort to replace his students' southern black speech with the English of writing, "so different is their language from that of the books.")[7] In Chesnutt's comment "words" in his teacher's sense, the possession or nonpossession of an educated language, form the basis for a social estrangement felt as absolute, and the instrument of literacy in school—the graded spelling book—yields the scheme of hierarchy that establishes others as "beneath." But more than language—or something else travelling together with language—supplies the basis for the profound self-differentiation Chesnutt expresses here. Recoiling from these foreign-seeming neighbors, Chesnutt threw himself into the project of reading Byron and Cowper and teaching himself Latin and history in his spare time.[8] In doing so Chesnutt set himself different tasks from his neighbors, tasks a teacher might have set him. (Chesnutt's project in leisure is always to put himself through a yet more rigorous school). But in doing so he took an approach to self-fashioning that set him apart even more decisively.

Chesnutt, here as always, is one of American culture's most compulsive self-improvers. With little external support, Chesnutt in Fayetteville in his rare leisure taught himself Latin, music, history, German, and French, and was never without a plan systematically to master some appointed field. (His plan for the summer of 1879 was to give "one hour daily to Latin, one to German, one to French, and one to literary composition," to teach himself shorthand, and to work one hour in the garden. "Miscellaneous reading and tending to the baby will occupy the remainder of my time," he adds with characteristic forethought.)[9] Chesnutt's schemes of self-education—in effect a plan to give himself the liberal arts college education not available to blacks or whites in Fayetteville—are in one sense highly idiosyncratic; but at their core they display an outlook with clear cultural connections. Chesnutt organizes his life around the idea that the self exists to *make* something of itself. He presumes that the self's project is, through a discipline self-designed and self-imposed, to appropriate rari-

fied knowledges to itself; and he presumes that the self's goal is
through this acquisition to advance itself toward a worldly career
that will carry the meaning of achievement and success. In this he
perfectly exemplifies the ethos that marks the most achievement-
oriented segment of Northern white culture of his time, the new
professional class of the postbellum decades.[10] The culture of professionalism forms Chesnutt's mental world as early as his early
teens. This ethos (not letters alone) is what makes him see blacks
of traditional agrarian culture as denizens of an *other* world. And
if we ask where Chesnutt encountered this ethos, the answer is in
school and in the spirit of the teaching corps.

The point here is that no one comes to authorship out of nowhere. Writers can only ever emerge into authorship by working
from within from some particular situation, with the specific obstructions and advantages that situation contains. In black social
history in the post–Civil War generation, the dominant social
situations—illiteracy, rural poverty, entrapment in tenancy and
mortgage lien dependencies, the economic need to command children as workers—formed virtually decisive obstacles to individual
writerly aspiration (if not to traditional communal oral expression). But there was more than one black social situation in the
South during Reconstruction, and other situations made other
projects thinkable. What we see behind Chesnutt is an early stage
in the emergence of a black professional class in the post–Civil
War decades. This new class—what W.E.B. Du Bois later called
the "talented tenth"[11]—was largely formed in the new black normal schools and colleges of the postbellum period, and formed
there in a double sense. Such schools are where black members
of educated professions (teachers especially) got their education
proper. And these schools were the scenes of their resocialization,
their reacculturation into a Northern, bourgeois-based culture of
self-discipline and high-achieverism that molded their ambitions
and profoundly differentiated them from other groups. Chesnutt's
ambition for a literary career is by no means a standard issue of
such schools. But he won the preconditions for his ambition—
especially his mastery of written English and his ability strenuously to organize himself toward future achievement—through

the schooling in which he was so centrally enmeshed. In this sense
we could say that black literary authorship as a professional aspiration found the condition of its possibility in the emergence of the
black higher education system of the post–Civil War years.

I have been suggesting how a certain background supplied a
ground of authorship for Chesnutt, yielded the cultural resources
that make that career imaginable in a certain form. But this background might now be particularized somewhat further; for the
postbellum black education system was itself subdivided in a way
that had an intimate bearing on Chesnutt's case. Chesnutt's choice
of subjects in his campaign for self-improvement—his intense devotion to languages especially—is in historical context a deeply
loaded gesture. It says where he stands in the curriculum conflict
that polarized black education at this time and that focussed far-
reaching ideological antagonisms.

The Hampton Institute, its offspring the Tuskegee Institute, and
the many imitators they spawned were programmatically devoted
to a training in practical labor skills called industrial education.
But it is not always remembered that the Hampton-Tuskegee-style
schools embraced this model of education in conscious rejection of
the normal Northern model of higher education, the so-called classical curriculum. General Samuel Chapman Armstrong, Hampton's strong-willed and influential founder, excluded classical
studies from the Hampton curriculum as a potential breeder of
"vanity."[12] Booker T. Washington, Armstrong's protege and the
major disseminator of Armstrong's educational plan, displays a virtually phobic hostility toward what he calls "Greek and Latin
learning" or "mere book education" in his autobiography.[13] The
studiously toneless prose of *Up from Slavery* breaks into sardonic
mockery whenever it envisions a Southern black being educated
on that rival plan. Washington writes of his first tour through the
black belt of Alabama:

> One of the saddest things I saw during the month of travel was a
> young man, who had attended some high school, sitting down in a
> one-room cabin with grease on his clothing and filth all around

him, and weeds in the yard and garden, engaged in studying a French grammar.

Or again, of his first Tuskegee students:

> I soon learned that most of them had the merest smattering of the high-sounding things that they had studied. While they could locate the Desert of Sahara or the capital of China on an artificial globe, I found that the girls could not locate the proper places for the knives and forks on an actual dinner-table, or the places where the bread and meat should be set.[14]

The now-standard indictment of Armstrong and Washington's trade-oriented education is that it made black schooling an instrument of active accommodation to a social system becoming more harshly discriminatory after the end of Reconstruction. This curriculum accepted that the social future of Southern blacks would be in the low-status jobs reserved for them in the Southern racial-economic system and designed education as training *for* and *into* these disadvantaged positions.[15] (The education idealized in the second passage cited may not help the young woman become a diplomat, but would make her an admirable maid.) And notoriously, Washington and his followers meant their scheme of education to teach its subjects to seek limited advancements at the level of their work and not challenge their disenfranchisement in the realm of political rights.

But while these charges are grave and well-founded, we need to remember that the proponents of black industrial education had other social intentions than the creation of mass acquiescence. The evil of a more bookish or intellectual model of education to this party is partly that it fails to give pupils the practical skills their actual life will require of them, but even more that it makes them outwardly mobile, orients them up and away from a mass black life that must then remain as culturally impoverished as ever. When a vice principal who traced former Hampton students into their later lives concludes in 1885 "that very frequently the dull

plodder at Hampton is the real leader of his people toward better
things, while the bright scholar who was our delight at school,
because of his mental acuteness, either yields to temptation or
leaves school work for the more tempting offers of clerkships or
political appointments," his anti-intellectualism and antipolitical-
ism are palpable, but so is his sense that intelligence cultivated on
certain terms generates the will to advance oneself rather than to
stay back and serve one's people.[16] Washington concludes of the
products of a nonindustrial education he observed in Washington,
D.C., that they "had more money, were better dressed, wore the
latest style of all manner of clothing, and in some cases were more
brilliant mentally" than Hampton graduates, but that "having
lived for a number of years in the midst of comfortable surroundings, they were not as much inclined as the Hampton students to
go into the country districts of the South, where there was little of
comfort, to take up work for our people."[17] Washington assumes
that the classical curriculum leads to class differentiation, to the
immurement of educated blacks in a separate social world of
articulateness, prosperity, "selfish success," and conspicuous consumption, while industrial education prevents the social estrangement of the educated, makes them put their higher education to
the service of bringing basic education to the knowledge-deprived
masses.

Clearly, the industrial curriculum fashioned in the 1870s and
1880s embodied not a teaching plan alone but a proposed answer
through teaching to fundamental questions of black social history:
what social places blacks should claim; what economic advances
might be worth their forfeiture of newly lost political rights; and
how a base of withheld knowledges and skills could be built up
for a population with limited means of access to such cultural resources. But all of these social questions received other answers
than the ones Washington gave; and a rival vision of black American life found its symbolic focus in a rival curriculum. From the
first, many black schools and colleges adopted the classical liberal
arts curriculum familiar from Northern schools. From an early
date this educational model had its articulate defenders—for instance the educator Richard Wright, who became the principal of

the Augusta, Georgia, Colored High School (the only public high school for blacks in Georgia) in the same year that Chesnutt became principal in Fayetteville.[18] And when, at the time of the institutionalization of segregation and legal repeal of black civil rights, opposition emerged to Washington's accommodationism, it seized this alternative curriculum as its rallying point. W. E. B. Du Bois's *The Souls of Black Folk* is in a fundamental, not incidental way an appeal for the classical curriculum to supplant industrial schooling in black higher education. For Du Bois, Southern blacks need to claim civic recognition of their humanity, not acquiesce in their loss of rights; need to be able to aspire as college-educated Northerners aspire, not be delivered over to servile and inferior careers; need to learn to form a fully adequate idea of their potential humanity, not be schooled into an image of self-deficiency. And to Du Bois the only path of attainment to this "higher individualism"[19] is through acquisition of "the higher culture" embodied in the liberal arts curriculum—so that to accept a different curriculum is to accept the social reproduction of blacks into an inferior humanity.

Through the process sketched here, in the late nineteenth-century South what began as pedagogical differences between two programs of black instruction came to incarnate differences in social and moral philosophy of the gravest sort. But it might be noted in the context of this chapter that *as* they projected different black social futures these schoolings also yielded different potential literary preparations. Booker T. Washington disliked literature in the high-cultural or liberal arts sense. In *Up from Slavery* he boasts: "fiction I little care for. Frequently I have to almost force myself to read a novel that is on everyone's lips."[20] And the widely-copied Tuskegee plan of instruction implements a consistent antiliterary prejudice. When Washington says in his Atlanta Exposition speech of 1895 that "no race can prosper till it learns that there is as much dignity in tilling a field as in writing a poem,"[21] he means that aspirations like literary ones need to be disparaged for blacks: that they must be taught to embrace the manual labor of "the bottom of life" *and not* the mindwork of the higher stations. What such preachments would mean in practice can be seen in the curriculum adopted in 1931 by the Spencer High School of Columbus, Georgia. This black school (not uncharacteristically) chose to eliminate "traditional subjects which have no value for hand-minded boys and girls," and so taught English in the form in which a future bricklayer might require it, English comprised of "its use by contractors in contracts, specifications, and business letters."[22] The deprivation such schooling would have created for a student without other resources—a deprivation both of verbal command and of the chance to discover writing as a form of plea-sure and power—is all too clear. By contrast, within the classical curriculum, literary study was emphasized and valued. When Du Bois wants to image a "higher culture" able to transport its pos-sessors beyond the false consciousness of segregated society, he reaches at once toward literary examples: "I sit with Shakespeare and he winces not. Across the color line I move arm in arm with Balzac and Dumas."[23] A student educated in accord with this prejudice would have a wholly different relation to writing as an object or knowledge, desire, and emulation.

My point is that if Chesnutt's authorship was enabled by his involvement in the new black educational institutions of his time, it is no less important that he was affiliated with a certain version of such schools. By chance of birth, the school the young Chesnutt happened to have available in his town adhered to the classical curriculum. Robert Harris implemented the upper levels of that curriculum when he established his normal school, in which he also founded a literary society.[24] Through his participation in Har-ris's schemes, Chesnutt was initiated through the classical, not in-dustrial model: the youth desperately driving himself to master Byron, Cowper, Latin and French has identified the liberal arts as the knowledge he needs and craves. (Chesnutt did not learn to make bricks.) And through the particular form of his schooling, Chesnutt won the education available to a Southern black richest in literary training and most conducive to literary ambition.

We can think of Chesnutt's life as wholly personal, but in the personal form of his life Chesnutt realized a social scheme of iden-tity formation particular to (and contested in) his time. As Wash-ington could have predicted, having filled his head with book learning Chesnutt was not content to stay in the rural black South. After champing at the bit in his normal school, Chesnutt headed north in 1883, settling first in New York, then Cleveland. As Washington would have guessed of someone so educated, Chesnutt in his adult life used his education to the end of self-advancement, and specifically to seize a professional position in a white, urban world. The one-time teacher of Fayetteville trained as a lawyer, passing the Ohio bar examination with the highest grade in the state in 1887, then—combining this training with an earlier skill self-taught—thrived as a legal stenographer of national reputation. In embracing a professional status, Chesnutt established himself in just the sort of class position Washington saw liberal education as breeding. In Cleveland, Chesnutt became the ultimate bourgeois, surrounding himself with every marker of upper-middle-class identity: a house in the best neighborhood, dressmakers for his wife and daughters, Ivy League and Seven Sisters colleges for his children, elaborate plans for "summering" out of the city. *Concomitant with* this social position, in the life Chesnutt established for himself he adopted the racial politics allied with a certain form of education. "I do not believe in a tame or . . . patient submission," Chesnutt wrote Washington; "I am squarely opposed to any restriction of the franchise in the South on any basis now proposed."[25] *And* Chesnutt as opposed to Washington read devoutly, cared for fiction greatly, and considered writing it an elevated human goal.

These features of Chesnutt's biography are separable in theory but not as he lived them. Together they show the shape in which he sought to realize his life; and in each of them—or precisely in their conjunction—Chesnutt shows his life's indebtedness to a certain scheme of Southern acculturation. Chesnutt had what Du Bois later called the "education that encourages aspiration."[26] In that institutional setting and through his extraordinarily intense identification with its program, Chesnutt formed an idea of selfhood strongly centered on mental achievement and corresponding social success. Authorship was not the only goal of Chesnutt's life. But Chesnutt always located writing among the highest human attainments. And this highly personal self-thinking has its origin in a certain cultural situation.

III

In the late 1870s and early 1880s Charles Chesnutt is compulsively engaged in preparing himself for some great thing he is to become. In his schemes of study we see him arming himself for a future work that will realize his special abilities and represent his achievement, but the particular form of his calling remains vague. At a certain point around 1880, Chesnutt begins to think of authorship as the possible form of his *Beruf.* The journal Chesnutt kept at this time is one of the great private records of the growth of the self-made man. It is also a great document of American culture-hunger, and of the ironies exposed when a colored man tries to realize an apparently universal "human" ideal of self-culture in a society that discriminates among men in racial terms: this is where we can learn about Chesnutt's exclusion from the society of those comparably cultivated in Fayetteville on account of his color, and his difficulties getting tutors to teach liberal arts to a pupil whose color might lose them white trade. This journal has the further interest that it lets us watch Chesnutt in the act of formulating the idea of a literary career.

The journal in the early 1880s shows Chesnutt the soon-to-be-promoted principal looking for a way up and out. Just back from his first trip to scout out the employment possibilities of a Northern city, Chesnutt writes with a whetted appetite for worldly success but also a sharpened consciousness of his lack of resources to attain the successes he has seen. Literature enters Chesnutt's ambition as a solution to the problem of advancement without capital:

> I want fame; I want money; I want to raise my children in a different rank of life from that I sprang from. In my present vocation, I would never accumulate a competency, with all the economy and prudence, and parsimony in the world. In law or medicine, I would be compelled to wait half a life-time to accomplish anything. But literature pays—the successful. . . . It is the only thing I can do without capital, under my present circumstances, except teach. . . . I shall strike for an entering wedge in the literary world.[27]

For a writer from Chesnutt's situation, authorship is not conceivable as an unconditioned or disinterested desire. Coming from the position he does, Chesnutt needs other things more deeply than he needs writing. As a black man in nineteenth-century North Carolina, Chesnutt needs out: in his case unlike Jewett's, for a country-bred author to stay home would mean for him to stay in the stigmatized positions a discriminatory society reserves for his race. As someone bred into a certain culture of aspiration, Chesnutt's other fundamental need is a profession, attainment to a career of a certain status and the marks of success that will testify to that status. (In later life Chesnutt would only write when he was sure it would not reduce his professionalistic standard of living.) *Writing* enters Chesnutt's thought here as a career through which he could achieve such mobility and attain such success. Interchangeable with other careers—law, medicine—in its social attractions, it is distinguished from them principally in the lower entry requirements that it sets for aspirants.

When their works are sitting parallel-fashion on the shelf, it is natural for us to think that writers are all writers in the same sense of the word. But writers practice on the different understandings of authorship that they have found thinkable in their different cultural situations. For Chesnutt, the wish to write is never separable from the will to a certain sort of social mobility. We can see him building other strands into his definition of authorship in a second notebook entry of this same month, which I must quote at length:

> Judge Tourgee has sold the "Fool's Errand," I understand, for $20,000. I suppose he had already received a large royalty on the sale of the first few editions. The work has gained an astonishing degree of popularity, and is to be translated into the French.
>
> Now, Judge Tourgee's book is about the south,—the manners, customs, modes of thought, etc., which are prevalent in this section of the country. Judge Tourgee is a Northern man, who has lived at the South since the war, until recently. He knows a great deal about the politics, history, and laws of the South. He is a close observer of men and things, and has exercised this faculty of observation upon

the character of the Southern people. Nearly all his stories are more or less about colored people, and this very feature is one source of their popularity. There is something romantic, to the Northern mind, about the southern Negro, as commonplace and vulgar as he seems to us who come into contact with him every day. And there is a romantic side to the history of this people. Men are always more ready to extend their sympathy to those at a distance, than to the suffering ones in their midst. . . . And [the people of the North] see in the Colored people a race, but recently emancipated from a cruel bondage; struggling for education, for a higher social and moral life, against wealth, intelligence, and race prejudice, which are all united to keep them down. And they hear the cry of the oppressed and struggling ones, and extend a hand to help them; they lend a willing ear to all that is spoken or written concerning their character, habits, etc. And if Judge Tourgee, with his necessarily limited intercourse with colored people, and with his limited stay in the South, can write such interesting descriptions, such vivid pictures of Southern life and character as to make himself rich and famous, why could not a colored man, who has lived among colored people all his life; who is familiar with their habits, their ruling passions, their prejudices, their whole moral and social condition; their public and private ambitions; their religious tendencies and habits;—why could not a colored man who knew all this and who, besides, had possessed such opportunities for observation and conversation with the better class of white men in the south, as to understand their mode of thinking; . . . why could not such a man, if he possessed the same ability, write a far better book about the South than Judge Tourgee or Mrs. Stowe has written? Answer who can! But the man is yet to make his appearance; and if I can't be the man I shall be the first to rejoice at his debut, and give God speed! to his work.[28]

Having identified writing as a worldly work, Chesnutt here seizes a possible subject for his work: he will write of the postwar black South, he will establish himself as a writer by exploiting his knowledge of "colored life." But this self-definition too is highly mediated. Chesnutt discovers the life around him as a literary subject not by living near it but by seeing it *made* a subject in a literary work. Albion Tourgée's novel of Reconstruction-era North Carolina, *A Fool's Errand* (1879), identifies his own lived world to Chesnutt as potential *materia poetica*. But it is Tourgée's success, not his literary treatment alone, that qualifies his "stories . . . more or less about colored people" for emulation. Chesnutt finds a subject by recognizing a prior literary modelling of that subject. In that model he grasps that writing of that subject could make one "rich and famous": Tourgée's celebrity royalties are the first referent of Chesnutt's discussion. And in Tourgée's rise to wealth and fame Chesnutt grasps what makes this subject yield such rewards. Chesnutt sees the literary matter of Southern black life as speaking to a certain *interest,* the interest of "the northern mind" in Southern blacks' historical situation. The interest so located creates a literary market—makes "people of the North" inclined to buy Tourgée's fictional history. Accordingly, producing *for* that market—reproducing local black life in literature for those "at a distance"—appears to Chesnutt as a possible path to a requisite personal success.

The chief fact that lies behind this passage is one we have encountered in previous chapters: between 1860 and 1900 the instruments of literary production were not evenly distributed in the United States but profoundly and decisively centered. In Chesnutt's time the journals and publishing houses that could win paying publics and prestige for literary authors were established not in the South but in the North, particularly in Boston and New York. To the extent that Chesnutt needs writing to yield fame and fortune, he makes the contemporary mechanisms of literary production become fundamental considerations in his authorial program. As a result Chesnutt's ambitions insert writing into a precisely localized circuit of institutional relations: writing as he conceives it means finding a form within the set of forms active in the Northern literary economy, and means writing *toward* that economy as the hoped-for site of his success.

These two entries show enduring features in Chesnutt's personal construction of the literary career. But a third passage from Chesnutt's 1880 journal shows quite another side of his literary

self-conception. Two weeks after the Tourgée entry Chesnutt writes
in a mood of sublime self-dedication:

> I think I must write a book. I am almost afraid to undertake a book
> so early and with so little experience in composition. But it has been
> my cherished dream, and I feel an influence that I cannot resist
> calling me to the task. Besides, I do not know but I am as well
> prepared as some successful writers. A fair knowledge of the clas-
> sics, speaking acquaintance with the modern languages, an intimate
> friendship with literature, etc.; seven years experience in the school
> room, two of married life, and a habit of studying character have I
> think, left me not entirely unprepared to write even a book.
>
> Fifteen years of life in the South, in one of the most eventful eras
> of its history; among a people whose life is rich in the elements of
> romance; under conditions calculated to stir one's soul to the very
> depths;—I think there is here a fund of experience, a supply of
> material, which a skillful pen could work up with tremendous ef-
> fect. Besides, if I do write, I shall write for a purpose, a high, holy
> purpose, and this will inspire me to greater effort. The object of my
> writings would be not so much the elevation of the Colored people
> as the elevation of the Whites,—for I consider the unjust spirit of
> caste which is so insidious as to pervade a whole nation, and so
> powerful as to subject a whole race and all connected with it to
> scorn and social ostracism—I consider this a barrier to the moral
> progress of the American people; and I would be one of the first to
> head a determined, organized crusade against it. Not a fierce indis-
> criminate onslaught; not an appeal to force, for this is something
> that force can but slightly affect; but a moral revolution which must
> be brought about in a different manner. . . . The subtle almost in-
> definable feeling of repulsion toward the negro, which is common
> to most Americans . . . cannot be stormed and taken by assault; the
> garrison will not capitulate; so their position must be mined; and
> we will find ourselves in their midst before they think it.
>
> This work is of a twofold character. The negro's part is to prepare
> himself for social recognition and equality; and it is the province of
> literature to open the way for him to get it—to accustom the public
> mind to the idea; and while amusing them to lead people out, im-

perceptibly, unconsciously, step by step to the desired state of feeling. If I can do anything to further this work, and can see any
likelihood of obtaining success in it, I would gladly devote my life
to the work.[29]

Washington was wrong to think that liberally educated black
professionals were self-interested only. The incipient black professional class of this time differed from its white social cognate in its
inevitable heavy consciousness of its race's social plight and in its
linking of individual achievement with duty toward its race. Here
this group's racial service ideal surfaces in Chesnutt and finds authorship as a means to its ends; and when Chesnutt adds this element to his literary self-conception, it changes the way other
elements behave. Chesnutt here seizes the idea that if the forms of
literary expression must be found in a dominant culture, they can
still be used in the interest of subordinated peoples. He grasps that
if writing must be directed to Northern white audiences, it can
nevertheless aim to further black causes *with* those audiences—can
make itself a means to enter the minds and remodel the mental habits of white readers as they read. On his way to writing every writer
must first build from the available cultural materials a practice-
governing idea of what writing *is* and *does,* and this is the idea
Chesnutt constructs: that by mastering the literary conventions in
which a distant culture images Southern racial life, a black author
can make himself a personal success, while also helping a society
prejudiced against people like him to change its mind.

IV

Chesnutt did not fulfill the resolutions of his diaries in 1880. Writing in a different sense of the word—stenography—gave him his
way upward in his twenties. But Chesnutt continued to be afflicted
with literary ambition. And when he returned to this career in his
spare time in the late 1880s, he approached it through the route
his journals had worked out.

   At that time, Chesnutt found his way to writing not through the
Tourgéean social novel but through another form that emerged to

literary life in the intervening years. Nineteenth-century regional
fiction had always had an active Southern department. Mark
Twain, George Washington Cable, Mary Noailles Murfree, and
Constance Fenimore Woolson had all written widely read Southern fictions by the early 1880s. But in this decade a new variant of
the Southern local color story appeared in print. Joel Chandler
Harris's folktale volume *Uncle Remus: His Songs and His Sayings*
(1881) and Thomas Nelson Page's old plantation tale "Marse
Chan" (*The Century Magazine*, 1884) established a new formula for
the literary production of Southernness, in which a white auditor
solicits tales from an old black retainer left over from slavery days.
The consolidation of this literary genre in the works of Harris and
Page formed the immediate occasion for Chesnutt's literary emergence. The first considerable stories that Chesnutt wrote and the
first of his work to attract more than transient attention—"The
Goophered Grapevine" and "Po' Sandy," collected in *The Conjure
Woman* in 1899 but first printed in 1887–88—were written with
Harris's and Page's precedents clearly in mind. Chesnutt became
an author *in this form,* then; and if we want to know what Chesnutt does with literary writing we must first ask what he does with
this form.

Chesnutt's conjure tales are in one sense remarkable for their
massive conventionality. Brilliantly inventive in their conceits and
suave in the manner of their telling, in their fictional structures
these early tales stick close to the most formulaic features of their
genre: the white speaker's prologue; the handing over of the
speaking function to an old black uncle; the black folktale told in
heavy dialect. One difference of Chesnutt's practice is that without
in any sense exploding the artifice of this kind of tale, Chesnutt
lightly underlines the fact of its artificiality. Chesnutt stays so close
to generic conventions that they inevitably become revealed,
though without comment or overt parody, as conventions: when,
in the dozen conjure stories Chesnutt eventually wrote, Uncle Julius always shows up at an opportune moment *yet again,* with *yet
another* story to tell in which someone *yet again* seeks out "the
cunjuh wom'n up tuh deh Lumberton road" who *yet again* (for a
price) "wukd huh roots," we learn to recognize the set moves of a

certain formal protocol. The air of slight stiltedness or lightly indicated artificiality that Chesnutt produces for this form is also
conveyed through his stories' half-exposed pastoralism, their
manufacture of a version of history charmingly, even delightfully,
ahistorical—as in the conceit that a quite bucolic grape industry,
not the nonbucolic tobacco or textile industries of 1880s history,
represents a principal form of North Carolina's postwar economic
development. (Chesnutt's stories let us in on the joke of regionalism's "realism" if we recognize such fancies as fancies; if we do
not, they pass this genre's pastoral fictions on us with straight
face.)

   But if Chesnutt embraces the unrealities of this form, he also
achieves an unusual precision of historical identification for the
parties to the regionalist transaction. The John of the conjure stories is thus the thousandth incarnation of the well-spoken frame
narrator who comes to a region from afar, a fictional brother—if
not formulaic substitute—for the white traveller of Page's "Marse
Chan," the Cumberland vacationer of Murfree's "Dancin' Party at
Harrison's Cove," the city girls on retreat in Jewett's *Deephaven,*
and so on. But Chesnutt's rendering of this wholly stock figure is,
by the standards of this genre, unusually rich in social markers.
John begins "The Goophered Grapevine":

> Some years ago my wife was in poor health, and our family doctor,
> in whose skill and honesty I had implicit confidence, advised a
> change of climate. I shared, from an unprofessional standpoint, his
> opinion that the raw winds, the chill rains, and the violent changes
> of temperature that characterized the winters in the region of the
> Great Lakes tended to aggravate my wife's difficulty, and would un-
> doubtedly shorten her life if she remained exposed to them. The
> doctor's advice was that we seek, not a temporary place of sojourn,
> but a permanent residence, in a warmer and more equable climate.
> I was engaged at the time in grape-culture in Northern Ohio, and as
> I liked the business and had given it much study, I decided to look
> for some locality suitable for carrying it on. I thought of sunny
> France, of sleepy Spain, of Southern California, but there were ob-
> jections to them all. It occurred to me that I might find what I

wanted in our own Southern States. It was a sufficient time after
the war for conditions in the South to have become somewhat settled; and I was enough of a pioneer to start a new industry, if I could
not find a place where grape-culture had been tried. I wrote to a
cousin who had gone into the turpentine business in central North
Carolina. He assured me, in response to my inquiries, that no better
place could be found in the South than the State and neighborhood
where he lived; the climate was perfect for health, and, in conjunction with the soil, ideal for grape-culture; labor was cheap, and land
could be bought for a mere song.[30]

Every time he opens his mouth, this man says where he comes
from in the America of his time. He is Northern, of course. But his
Latinate diction and measured speech rhythms also mark him as
of the educated class; his wife's health marks him as of the class
in which women are leisured and inclined to neurasthenia; his
deference to doctors ties him to the social formation in which
medicine has become a province of certified professionals and
nonprofessionals have been made into amateurs; his thoughts of
Spain, France, and California link him to the class that practices
international and domestic tourism; his history in the grape business says that he is used to owning the means of production (in
Ohio he must have known Mr. Welch and Mr. Smucker); his wish
to found industries where land and labor are cheap shows him of
the class that initiates economic development in underdeveloped
zones. All of these traits identify John as of the upper middle class
stabilized in the North in the 1850s and after—a class which, as
Chesnutt shows, is defined not by one or two traits but by a whole
range of dispositions conformed together. By marking him as it
does, Chesnutt's tale expresses its sense of where the contemporary incursion on regional cultures is coming from. It makes clear
that the outside world is impinging on the local not through mere
individual visits or the march of a generalized "modernity" but
through a concrete social process, through a certain social group's
pursuit of its particular investment and recreational interests.

Uncle Julius, the black vernacular speaker of Chesnutt's tales, is as conventional a figure as John, and his conventionality too is emphasized, not disguised: witness his minimal departure in name from Harris's Uncle Remus. But without realizing Julius out of his formulaic origin, Chesnutt is careful to link him too to a real contemporary culture—in this case the unmodernized black folk culture to be found in country districts. Here again Chesnutt takes pains to render the whole form of a social "world." Julius's is a world with a different verbal form: his speech is regionally accented, not delocalized; his is the language of speaking, not (like John's) of speech imitating writing. (Julius's words are often unintelligible when read but intelligible enough when mentally voiced.) Julius's world has its own differently constructed medical system, based on "cha'ms" and conjure women, not rest cures and male professionals. It has its own organization of religion, a voodoo-derived religion of "ha'nts" and spirit management most unlike John's decorous but despiritualized Christianity. It has its own economy, conducted through face-to-face exchanges of goods and services, not abstract market relations. It has its own different sense of space: in Julius's world people belong somewhere and stay there instead of moving around; places and things are not abstractly interchangeable (as Spain and California are for John) but wholly distinct, distinguished by the lived histories associated with them—so the swamp that to John is just more land to develop is to Julius a place in particular to be honored as such, the place where Mahaly was buried; the place where the branch creek crosses the short road is the place where Chloe drowned herself; and so on. And Julius's world has its own different mechanism of cultural self-maintenance: the telling of stories. Storytelling as *The Conjure Woman* presents it marks a distinction between America's local and postlocal societies: Julius knows a thousand stories, John (apparently) none. In a culture like Julius's, Chesnutt brilliantly suggests, tale-telling is not mere pastime but the means by which a sense of the world is stored and transmitted. When Julius wants John to realize what something around him means, he always tells him the whole story: the meaning is, as it were, lodged in the tale, which must be orally recollected for the meaning to be made present again. (When John's wife Anne asks "'And why does Chloe's haunt walk?'" in "Hot-Foot Hannibal," Julius replies: "'It's all in de tale, ma'm, it's all in de tale.'" [203].)

In Jewett the relations between an outlander and the native of an herbal, magical, storytelling, place-specific world are friendly, indeed hospitable. But one of Chesnutt's distinctions among local colorists is that he understands the parties to the regionalist dialogue to be antagonists, not friends. Once he has set up his juxtaposition of these two cultural formations, Chesnutt unfolds a contest between them, a contest of domination and indigenous resistance played out on several planes.

Within Julius's tales, slavery is the scene of this contention. The former white masters and their black slaves are the contending parties here, and the slaves' art of "cunjuh" forms the heart of the struggle between them. Always the object of special interest to fictional historians of African-American folk culture (Chesnutt's history of conjure has George Washington Cable's *The Grandissimes* behind it and Zora Neale Hurston's *Mules and Men* ahead of it), conjure is understood in *The Conjure Woman* at once as a magical art for the management of life forces and a quite practical social institution, the means for blacks to carry forward courtships, pay back injuries, and so on. But Chesnutt also shows that when this African-derived system gets enclosed within the system of American slavery it takes on a further function, as a recourse for the oppressed. There is no such thing as total domination in Chesnutt. When one group is subjugated by another its own cultural institutions get carried into subjugation with it, and institutions that were once just facts of its life are remade into forms for possible resistance. So conjure, part of the religion of the slaves before slavery, survives into slavery as a power slaves can resort to against the domination of their masters. And in Julius's tales this power works: by magically making their master the object of his own harsh work discipline, the slaves of "Mars Jeems's Nightmare" school him out of his cult of infinite productivity; through conjure's metamorphic powers the mother and child in "Sis' Becky's Pickaninny" overcome the slaveholder's power to break family bonds. But conjure's resistance, if it is never impotent, is never omnipotent either; and Chesnutt's tales are at their most moving in charting the limits of such power.

"Po' Sandy" provides an example here. The slave Sandy's story is a parabolic revelation of what slavery means. Sandy is such a good worker that all his master's children want to have his services. Since this father is generous he divides up Sandy's time, sending him off each month to work for a different child. The point here, as always wholly unstated, is that in slavery the more capable one is, the more others desire to own his labor; and that to be a slave means to be at someone else's disposal, literally not to be able to be where one wishes to be.[31] When he reaches the limit of his ability to tolerate such domination, gets "monst'us ti'ed er dish yer gwine roun' so much," Sandy asserts his hunger to regain control of his own location—"I wisht I wuz a tree, er a stump, er a rock, er sump'n w'at could stay on de plantation fer a w'ile" (45); and with these words conjure magically reveals itself as a way out. Sandy's wife turns out to be a semiretired conjure woman, and through her potent art she changes Sandy, rescues him from the hardships of the human order by turning him into a tree. But the master owns Sandy the tree as surely as he owned Sandy the man, and when he needs lumber on a day when Sandy's wife has been sent to work elsewhere, he has the tree felled and milled to his ends. (The milling of Sandy is one of American literature's great images of the violence of manufacture.) The slave's imaginative recourse itself turns out to be at the master's disposal; so that the same story that reveals the power of residual cultural forms like conjure also plots that power's final limit, its inability to change the fact of domination within which it acts.

In content the conjure stories have antebellum slavery as their historical referent. But at the level of their telling they gauge dominances and resistances in another social situation, the new economic order of the postbellum South. Julius's stories are told on the site of impending development. Julius has what John calls a "predial rather than a proprietary" attitude toward "my tract of land and the things that were on it" (65).[32] Together with his other different cultural understandings, he has a different understanding of property, based not on the alienable ownership of buying and

selling but on possession through personal contiguity and association, and aimed not toward maximized return on investment but
the maintenance of traditional uses. In this, Julius is linked to the
historical populations of blacks who stayed on their former plan-
tations after slavery but strove to work them to their own interests
and in their own ways, according to the precapitalist ethic of their
distinctive group culture.[33] John represents the incursion, upon
such postemancipation black folk economies, of another form of
domination based in another alien economics. He has come South
to acquire land and labor "cheap" because not exploited for maximized profit and to manage it for such profit, sending his product
to a national market by a newly built rail link (R. J. Reynolds
might be his real-life prototype); and he represents the threatened
expropriation of the possible economic resources of postwar Southern blacks for a Northern-style capitalist mode of production.[34]

    In *The Conjure Woman* Julius always appears at the point where
this new order impinges on his more traditional interests. And in
the face of this new domination, he too is not without resources.
The residual culture of blacks in slavery has endowed him with his
own cultural possession—stories—that can be redeployed as a
means to cultural self-defense. By telling stories of "slabery days"
Julius exerts his own conjurelike power, and here again this power
works. Through the action of storytelling Julius persuades his
hearers to curtail their development plans and so protects his residual uses of their land. By telling "Po' Sandy," Julius talks John
out of making the old schoolhouse over into a new kitchen, and
so preserves it as a place for his church to meet. By telling "Mars
Jeems's Nightmare," he talks a new master out of a new cult of
efficiency and productivity, and gets his shiftless relative rehired.
By telling "The Gray Wolf's Ha'nt," he persuades John to leave the
swamp undeveloped for agribusiness purposes, and so protects his
own "monopoly" (194) in the honey tree located there. But if Julius and his mode of enchantment exert real power, that power too
has clear limits. Every time he wins a concession from a new property order, Julius pays tribute to the fact that that order can't not
be dealt with. Julius wins local advantages through storytelling

while conceding that his situation as a whole is under someone else's control.

Chesnutt's fables describe the asymmetrical power struggles of antebellum blacks against antebellum slavery. They describe the similarly asymmetrical struggles of postwar blacks against New South economic history. But these fables also engage a third historical situation, in which their author is much more nearly involved. Within *The Conjure Woman,* John and Anne may represent a certain mode of economics but they function primarily as an audience (what they do in the book is listen to stories); and their life as an audience is defined with the same social precision as the rest of their attributes. John and Anne listen to Julius's tales but they are more used to reading: this couple is found reading in several stories before better entertainment comes along. Unlike Julius, Anne and John come from a world where stories are assumed to be written by other people and circulated in print, not collectively known and shared. Their reading, in turn, is set in a larger ethos that ranges such entertainment under the values of high culture, respectable privacy, and decorous self-control. Reading has these affiliations (for instance) in John's opening to "The Conjurer's Revenge":

> [Sunday] afternoons we spent at home, for the most part, occupying ourselves with the newspapers and magazines, and the contents of a fairly good library. We had a piano in the house, on which my wife played with skill and feeling. I possessed a passable baritone voice, and could accompany myself indifferently well when my wife was not by to assist me. [103]

All of these traits link Julius's audience with a particularized historical audience of Chesnutt's time that shared John and Anne's other marks as well: their wealth; their leisure; their disposition toward vacation travel; their attraction to undeveloped places. These hearers figure the class of readers addressed in the high-cultural literary journals of the post–Civil War decades. They embody the suggestion that the same socially assertive contemporary

class that manifests itself in the economic realm in capitalistic development reappears in the cultural sphere as the public with "cultured" tastes.

Through these identifications Chesnutt puts his own audience
at issue in his work and makes his fables figure a negotiation with
a dominant literary culture. The periodicals that produced "high"
literary writing toward a leisure-class public in the later nineteenth
century, we have many times noted, were the chief cultural vehicles for American regional fiction. Genteel hearers form the
frame for Chesnutt's conjure tales because Chesnutt knows that
readers like these in their entertainment habits and social interests
frame the scene of reception for stories like his own. (By the time
of the conjure stories Chesnutt knows the social composition of
"readers to the North" much more precisely than he did in his
1880 journal entries.) Faced with an audience so composed, Chesnutt was by no means wholly disadvantaged. This public's hunger
for the colorful ways of "different" local cultures made Chesnutt's
knowledge of Southern black voices and folktales into a market-
able asset. In this situation Chesnutt too was able to activate a
black vernacular heritage as a force in aid of his interests. And
Chesnutt's conjure at a third remove, like Julius's, produced real
results. By retelling these stories, by resynthesizing black oral culture within the written forms of a high-cultural genre, Chesnutt
was able to make something of himself. When "The Goophered
Grapevine" and "Po' Sandy" were accepted in the *Atlantic,* this
literary nobody was able to establish himself as an author in the
cultural site that carried the greatest degree of prestige.[35]

But the bleak wisdom of the conjure stories is that conjure exercises power only within situations that set limits to its power—a
moral Chesnutt clearly applies to himself. Julius masters John and
Anne's attention through his stories, and his hearers give him economic advantage and an improved position as a reward for his
work. But Julius is not only a winner in this exchange: his audience gets, if it also gives, through the transaction of storytelling.
These hearers are often bored. The way of life they have organized
for themselves makes things both scrupulously refined and—as
John confesses at the end of his inventory of reading materials and

musical accomplishments—"a little dull." At times this boredom
mounts to the pitch of crisis: in "Sis' Becky's Pickaninny," Anne
has fallen into a *tedium vitae* suggestive of the sickness unto death.
It is against the background of this deep experiential deprivation
that Anne turns to Julius for entertainment—"a story would be a
godsend today" (167), says this wife almost terminally bored; and
when he tells his stories she recovers "delightful animation" (159).
This is her gain. By entering into Julius's stories, this person devi-
talized by her own cultural refinements can imaginatively possess
the more amusing, or pathetic, or tragic, in short the more fully
animated life of blacks in slavery, and thereby reclaim a life force
she has forfeited. In exchange for this gain Anne makes conces-
sions to Julius, but he has purchased them at a price. *He has put
his peoples' life at someone else's disposal. He has served one group's life
up as the stuff of another group's entertainment.*
   In this description of Anne's "interest" (40)—the word echoes
Mars Dugal' McAdoo's "monst'us good intrus" (18) and describes
both her attention and her profit—Chesnutt images the social organization of reading that his own works would go forth to meet.
Reading as late nineteenth-century high-literary culture organizes
this practice is strongly conjoined with experiential acquisitiveness, a disposition with two parts: a habit of assuming that others
are more fully alive than oneself and a presumption that there is
no reason not to appropriate that life for oneself. This theory of
reading is written all over the high-cultural international authors
of this time—I think of Henry James, with his horde of characters
too old or ill or inhibited to live all they can who nevertheless
contrive to have their lost life or "super-sensual hour"[36] by consuming the spectacle of another's. (In 1883 James defines "entertainment" to mean "that we have been living at the expense of
someone else"[37]—Anne's economy exactly.) These are also the
assumptions that nineteenth-century regionalist fiction plays to,
which is no doubt why this genre served the interests of its public
so well—regionalism being definable as the literature that posits
that someone else's way of living and talking is more "colorful"
than one's own (culturally superior) way, in other words, that a
primary vitality absent from the refined is present in the backward,

and that this other life can be annexed for the cultivated class's leisured recreation, made pleasurably inhabitable in print. (What does the characterless or colorless narrator of *The Country of the Pointed Firs* do but enter into and *take in* the more strongly felt loves and griefs of Dunnet Landing folk—then export them for the consumption of distant readers?) When Chesnutt figures this culturally structured way of reading in *The Conjure Woman,* I take it he is casting up the whole meaning of his work's situation. The exchange between Julius and Anne embodies his dark surmise that the audience that welcomed his stories and validated his literary status did so in exchange for the chance he gave it to appreciate (and appropriate) the intensities of black cultural life. The exchange suggests his rueful recognition that he could win his place *in* authorship on the condition of playing to habits of vicarious consumption and sympathetic expropriation unmodified *by* his authorship—that the structure of social and literary interests that established regionalism as a genre for the elite both made a place for him as a writer in elite culture and constrained his work to serve the imaginative agenda of that culture, the agenda not of dismantling prejudice but of feeding an appetite for consumable otherness.

After the publication of the first conjure tales, Chesnutt found out much more directly how much the literary-cultural situation that made a place for him in letters bounded the scope of that place. It is not easy to tell from the *Conjure Woman* stories how ambivalent Chesnutt felt toward this genre of writing. But his letters make clear that he saw the Joel Chandler Harris–Thomas Nelson Page formula as a deeply distortionary representation enforced by organs of dominant-cultural expression. In 1890 he writes to George Washington Cable:

> I notice that all of the many Negroes (excepting your own) whose virtues have been given to the world in the magazine press recently, have been blacks, full-blooded, and their chief virtues have been their dog-like fidelity to their old master. . . . Such characters exist. . . . But I can't write about those people, or rather I won't write about them.[38]

Chesnutt mastered this genre sufficiently to get his works placed in highly visible periodicals. (A third Julius story, the superb "Dave's Neckliss," appeared in the *Atlantic* in 1889, and a fourth, "The Conjurer's Revenge," in the *Overland Monthly* in the same year.) But after this initial success he determined to separate his work from this form: "I think I have about used up the old Negro who serves as mouthpiece," he wrote in September 1889, "and I shall drop him in future stories, as well as much of the dialect."[39]

He turned, at this point, to a new project, eventually printed as *The House behind the Cedars* but known through many drafts as *Rena Walden*. In it Chesnutt takes a new subject: not "blacks full-blooded" but Southern mulatto culture, specifically the plight of "black" men and women with white fathers who identify with the values of an elite white civilization but are shut out of it because of their racial "taint." The matter of mulatto high culture is obviously much closer to Chesnutt's heart than Julius's form of black life. (Chesnutt's rural schoolteacher journals should remind us that this vernacular author felt no closer to illiterate rural folk culture than his high-cultural readers did.) The story of Rena Walden and her brother lets Chesnutt write about cross-racial children and old order free Negroes. It lets him write about the literary affiliations that mixed racial origin might bring: the primal scene for the Walden children is set at the bookcase that stands for their absent white father, the place where they read his literary classics and hear the "blood of white fathers . . . [cry] out for its own."[40] This story lets Chesnutt write about the formation, through such reading, of professionally oriented black aspiration: Rena Walden becomes a highly certified teacher, and her brother passes for white and becomes a successful lawyer. And in this story Chesnutt describes the miserable double legacy he knew to derive from this origin: simultaneous exclusion from the culture of one's desires and estrangement from the culture of one's racial designation.

In embracing this new subject Chesnutt proposed a new work for himself as a writer. He strove to be the historian of an unrecorded phase of black experience, and so to bring the variegations of American racial life to public acknowledgement. And Chesnutt clearly wished to found his literary identity on this mission. In

1891 he proposed *Rena Walden and Other Stories* as the title of his first projected book, choosing this project, not the conjure stories, to establish him in his "debut."[41] But when Chesnutt converted to this other project he found his literary welcome significantly changed. When he submitted *Rena Walden* to *The Century Magazine* in 1890, it was rejected on the grounds that its lack of humor and "mellowness" made its characters (in the editor Richard Watson Gilder's word) *"uninteresting."*[42] (White readers would derive little "interest," Gilder apparently thought, from hearing about blacks just like themselves in cultivation who had been victimized by their white sires.) Another revision was turned back by Houghton, Mifflin, the parent house of the *Atlantic Monthly,* in late 1891. Chesnutt revised the work again in 1894, again without getting it placed. He revised it again in the late 1890s only to have it set aside yet again.

The years of the *Rena Walden* project are a crucial time in Chesnutt's literary career. This is the time when he could have been pressing on from a lucky early success to consolidate his status as a writer and extend his literary powers: in James's career, Chesnutt's 1887–99 would correspond to the time between the first international stories (1871) and *The Portrait of a Lady* (1881); in Howells's, to the period from the light first novel *Their Wedding Journey* (1871) to the self-consciously major *A Modern Instance* (1882). But for Chesnutt this is a time of literary blockage—not because he lacked projects or the will to make them public but because the organs of official literary culture refused those projects public life. Toward the end of the 1890s Chesnutt's literary prospects improved somewhat. The new editor of the *Atlantic,* North Carolinian Walter Hines Page, took an interest in Chesnutt. He offered to read through Chesnutt's output to see if a book could be found in it. With high hopes Chesnutt sent in his collected works. Page wrote him "that your stories are undergoing a rather unusual experience here; because they are being read, I believe, by our whole staff of readers." In December 1897 he told Chesnutt: "I hope to have in a very little while definite word to send you." But when the definite word came—in March 1898—it was that Houghton, Mifflin did not see a publishable book among Chesnutt's stories; unless, an appended paragraph added, Chesnutt "had enough 'cunjure stories' to make a book: . . . If you could produce five or six more like these, I think I am safe in making you a double promise—first, of magazine publication [in the *Atlantic*], and then the collection I think would make a successful book."[43] The good soldier of letters, Chesnutt in 1898 sat down and wrote six more stories in this vein to order, which—selected by his editor and rejoined with stories now ten years old—made up Chesnutt's first volume.[44]

"I wish to write a book," Chesnutt had written in 1880. Almost twenty years later he had his wish. But by the time the half-created, half-commanded *The Conjure Woman* was published, Chesnutt had learned the terms set for his debut. He knew that he could win access to the ranks of authors on the condition that he do one kind of literary work and not another: on the condition that he reembrace a genre he had grown out of and write the fiction of black life—local color fiction—that his audience was interested to hear.

Afterword

There was literary life for Chesnutt on the other side of this debut. With the success of *The Conjure Woman*, Chesnutt was able to get other works printed, and he at last made the career move he had long contemplated. Having first assured himself of financial security by measuring his savings, Chesnutt stepped away from his business career in September 1899 and set up as a writer full-time.[45] His work of the prolific years 1899–1901—which deserves full consideration on another occasion—takes up the subject he had found blocked in the nineties: the last revision of *Rena Walden*, renamed *The House behind the Cedars*, was published then; so was Chesnutt's book of parables of the "light" black bourgeoisie and its estranged kinship with lower-class black life, *The Wife of His Youth and Other Stories;* so was Chesnutt's study of black professionalism and its self-deceptions before a South becoming rabidly segregationist, *The Marrow of Tradition*. It is wrong to think that Chesnutt's long-enforced constraint within regionalist formulas set absolute limits to his creativity. But Chesnutt's history of access took its toll.

After two prolific years he aborted his literary career and returned to business, a turn that can be explained in several ways. Chesnutt was stung by the relatively cool reception of *The Marrow of Tradition,* his novel of officially sanctioned racism and physical and psychological racial violence centered on the Wilmington riots of 1899—a North Carolina "local" story his public was not eager to hear. After witnessing his most ambitious work's relatively small sale, he wrote to Houghton, Mifflin: "I am beginning to suspect that the public as a rule does not care for books in which the principal characters are colored people, or written with a striking sympathy with that race as contrasted with the white race."[46] Also, although Chesnutt wanted very badly to be a writer, it is only fair to admit that he wanted other things more. His 1899 toting-up of his savings makes clear that Chesnutt needed to be able to live securely in the style of success before he would risk himself to writing; and when this career showed itself unprofitable, he reverted to surer ways to wealth. In this sense the peculiar worldly requirements Chesnutt had placed on authorship from the beginning helped make this career unviable in the long run.

But the unsustainedness that is the decisive fact of Chesnutt's literary career has an inevitable relation to his literary beginning. For at the time when Chesnutt was learning what this work would mean in practice, his literary situation taught him to be wary of this venture: taught him that the literary door would be open to a black author to the extent that he helped maintain preferred fictions of racial life.

NOTES

INTRODUCTION

1. Theodore Dreiser, *Newspaper Days* (1931; New York: Beekman, 1974), pp. 2–3. The incident described in this paragraph is narrated in the first chapter of *Newspaper Days*. For further information on Dreiser's early career see also his memoir *Dawn* and Richard Lingeman, *Theodore Dreiser: At the Gates of the City, 1871–1907* (New York: G. P. Putnam's Sons, 1986).

2. *Ainslee's Magazine* 1 (July 1898): 573. The same issue of *Ainslee's* ran an article by Dreiser entitled "The Making of Small Arms."

3. Quoted in Stanley Kramer, *A History of Stone and Kimball and Herbert S. Stone and Co. with a Bibliography of Their Publications, 1893–1905* (Chicago: Norman W. Forgue, 1940), p. 3.

4. Ibid., p. 44.

5. This passage, from the *Dziennik Chicagoski* [*Chicago Polish Daily*], is quoted in Arthur Leonard Waldo, "Polish-American Theatre," in *Ethnic Theatre in the United States*, ed. Maxine Schwartz Seller (Westport, Conn.: Greenwood Press, 1983), pp. 392–93. Waldo discusses Zahajkiewicz's career on pp. 391–92.

6. Kramer, *History of Stone and Kimball*, p. 39.

7. Two later Herbert Stone creations would specify this publisher's intended audience if it were in doubt: *How to Play Golf* was published the year before *The Awakening*, and Stone subsequently edited the interior decorating fastasia *The House Beautiful*.

8. For a major contribution both to the theory of audiences in general and to the history of the late nineteenth-century American mass-market audience in particular, see Richard Ohmann, "Where Did Mass Culture Come From? The Case of Magazines," *Politics of Letters* (Middletown, Conn.: Wesleyan University Press, 1987), pp. 135–51.

9. Kramer, *History of Stone and Kimball*, p. 44.

10. Michael Warner, *The Letters of the Republic: Publication and the Public Sphere in Eighteenth-Century America* (Cambridge: Harvard University Press, 1990), p. 5. Warner's remark refers to print, not to the much more variously deployed medium of writing, but his important argument bears generalization, I think, to this more inclusive form.

CHAPTER ONE

1. John Locke's *Some Thoughts Concerning Education* (1693) turns on a critique of whipping; on the centrality of Locke's educational theories to eighteenth-century American political thought, see Jay Fliegelman, *Prodi-*

gals and Pilgrims: The American Revolution against Patriarchal Authority, 1750–1800 (Cambridge: Cambridge University Press, 1982). The Supreme Court ruling in *Ingraham* v. *Wright* and the general history of school controversy over corporal correction are considered by various authors in Irwin A. Hyman and James H. Wise, eds., *Corporal Punishment in American Education* (Philadelphia: Temple University Press, 1979).

2. See Theodore Dwight Weld, *American Slavery as It Is: Testimony of a Thousand Witnesses* (1839; New York: Arno Press, 1968), esp. pp. 62–72; Frederick Douglass, *Narrative of the Life of Frederick Douglass* (1845; New York: New American Library, 1968), pp. 24–26; and, for other examples of whipping as initiation scene, see the William Wells Brown and Solomon Northrup narratives reprinted in Gilbert Osofsky, ed., *Puttin' on Ole Massa* (New York: Harper and Row, 1969), pp. 180–82, 242–43, and Linda Brent, *Incidents in the Life of a Slave Girl* (1861; New York: Harcourt Brace Jovanovich, 1973), pp. 11–12.

3. The fullest history I know of antiflogging reform in this context is Harold D. Langley, *Social Reform in the United States Navy, 1798–1862* (Urbana: University of Illinois Press, 1967), pp. 131–209; see also Major Leo F. S. Horan, "Flogging in the United States Navy: Unfamiliar Facts Regarding Its Origin and Abolition," *United States Naval Institute Proceedings* 76 (1950): 969–75, and for a splendid discussion centered on Herman Melville, Michael Paul Rogin, *Subversive Genealogy: The Politics and Art of Herman Melville* (New York: Alfred A. Knopf, 1983), pp. 90–96.

4. Elizabeth Palmer Peabody, *Record of a School,* 2nd ed. (Boston: Russell, Shattuck, and Co., 1836), pp. 23–25.

5. Bernard Wishy, *The Child and the Republic* (Philadelphia: University of Pennsylvania Press, 1968), pp. 45–46. The text involved is an 1844 issue of *Mother's Assistant.*

6. For Michel Foucault's reading of this historical transformation, see his *Discipline and Punish,* trans. Alan Sheridan (New York: Pantheon Books, 1977). His reading of nineteenth-century disciplinary humanitarianism will be found on pp. 73–82.

7. Earlier discussions of this subject that I have found helpful include, from the side of intellectual history of family life, Wishy, *The Child and the Republic,* chaps. 1–7, and, from the side of social history, Mary P. Ryan, *Cradle of the Middle Class: The Family in Oneida County, New York, 1790–1865* (Cambridge: Cambridge University Press, 1981), chaps. 2 and 4.

8. On the disindividualization of power in the modern surveillance scenario, see Foucault, *Discipline and Punish,* pp. 200–202.

9. Horace Bushnell, *Christian Nurture,* ed. Luther A. Weigle (1847; New Haven: Yale University Press, 1966), p. 17.

10. Ibid., pp. 278–79; Catherine E. Beecher, *A Treatise on Domestic Economy,* rev. ed. (Boston: T. H. Webb and Co., 1842), p. 228.

11. Bushnell, *Christian Nurture,* p. 40.

12. Ibid., p. 86; Mrs. Horace [Mary Peabody] Mann, *Moral Culture of Infancy* (Boston: T. O. H. P. Burnham, 1863), p. 169. The preface to this volume makes clear that Mrs. Mann's letters were written in 1841 but withheld from publication because the children she discussed could be easily identified.

13. Lyman Cobb, *The Evil Tendencies of Corporal Punishment as a Means of Moral Discipline in Families and Schools Examined and Discussed* (New York: Mark H. Newman and Co., 1847), p. 104.

14. Lydia Sigourney, *Letters to Mothers* (New York: Harper and Brothers, 1839), p. 128. This configuration is the subject of Melville's *Pierre,* which makes overt the eroticism and the moral fabrication this transaction involves; but note that they are already *all but* overt in Sigourney's orthodox account.

15. Bushnell, *Christian Nurture,* p. 21.

16. Quoted in Ryan, *Cradle of the Middle Class,* p. 160; Cobb, *Corporal Punishment,* p. 104.

17. Bushnell, *Christian Nurture,* p. 12.

18. Ibid., p. 44.

19. Mann, *Moral Culture of Infancy,* pp. 161, 180. Mrs. Mann's addition—"self-reproach, reflected from the mother-confessor"—will remind us that this corrective consciousness, though inward in its felt action, is manufactured "in" the self by, and works in the service of, an agent outside the self.

20. Ryan's *Cradle of the Middle Class* is the book that achieves the greatest specificity of social description of this transformation. See also Ann Douglas, *The Feminization of American Culture* (New York: Alfred A. Knopf, 1977), pp. 44–79, and Nancy F. Cott, *The Bonds of Womanhood* (New Haven: Yale University Press, 1977). In her preface to *The Mother's Book* (Boston: Carter and Hendee, 1831), Lydia Maria Child directs her advice to "the middling class in our own country" (p. v).

21. Sigourney, *Letters to Mothers,* pp. 85–86.

22. My phrasing here means to invoke the work of Jacques Donzelot, since what I am documenting is the American version of the process he describes in which a historically new concern for the welfare of the child produces at once a new closing in on itself of the bourgeois family *and* the erection of a new array of public regulatory institutions with family life as their site of surveillance. See Jacques Donzelot, *The Policing of Families,* trans. Robert Hurley (New York: Pantheon Books, 1979). On the nineteenth-century school reform movement, see in particular Jonathan Messerli, *Horace Mann: A Biography* (New York: Alfred A. Knopf, 1972), pp. 251–79, 309–48, 401–24, and Stanley K. Schultz, *The Culture Factory: Boston Public Schools, 1789–1860* (New York: Oxford University Press, 1973), esp. pp. 125–53.

23. See Schultz, *Culture Factory,* p. 300. On the establishment of school

as the social base for childhood, see Ryan, *Cradle of the Middle Class*, pp. 162–65.

24. Horace Mann, "Reply to the 'Remarks' of Thirty-One Boston Schoolmasters on the Seventh Annual Report," printed with the other materials of the 1844 controversy in *The Common School Controversy* (Boston: J. N. Bradley and Co., 1844), p. 135; "Annual Report for 1845," *Life and Works of Horace Mann*, 5 vols. (Boston: Lee and Shepard, 1891), 4:26. Mann's anticorporal argument is outlined in these writings and in the seventh annual report (1843), among other places.

25. The schoolmasters' "Remarks on the Seventh Annual Report of the Hon. Horace Mann, Secretary of the Massachusetts Board of Education" is included in *The Common School Controversy;* for cultural markers of the schoolmasters' position see, for instance, their defensive comments about *"breaking* the will" (p. 130), a socialization practice associated with unliberalized American Protestantism, and their patently patriarchal comment that "the subjection of the governed to the will of one man, in such a way that the expression of his will must be the final decision of every question, is the only government that will answer in school or in family" (p. 131). For the cultural history of the breaking of the will, see Philip Greven, *The Protestant Temperament: Patterns of Child-Rearing, Religious Experience and the Self in Early America* (New York: Alfred A. Knopf, 1977), pp. 32–43. On the patriarchal family and its displacement in the early nineteenth century, see especially Ryan, *Cradle of the Middle Class.* Messerli gives useful background for Mann's confrontation with the thirty-one schoolmasters in *Horace Mann,* pp. 412–21.

26. "Remarks," pp. 128, 121.

27. Mann, "Reply to the 'Remarks,'" pp. 130–35, 136. The figuring of the school as second mother or home away from home is a persistent trope in school-reform writing. Mary Peabody Mann's encomium to the ideal mother rather surprisingly ends by saying that "such a mother should every teacher be, especially of young children." Earlier in the book she makes the (female) teacher the literal re-creator of maternal presence in the educational realm: "As the germ of maternal sentiment is in all women, relations may be established between teacher and child that may take the place of the natural one, so far as to answer all the purposes required" (Peabody Mann, *Moral Culture of Infancy,* pp. 170, 116). The conjunction of the public school's insertion of itself *in loco parentis* with the immigration waves of the 1840s is well considered in Schultz, *Culture Factory,* pp. 209–309.

28. Donzelot notes how child-centered legislation in France strategically "sought to reduce the sociopolitical capacity of [the laboring classes] by breaking the initiatory ties that existed between children and adults" (*Donzelot, Policing of Families,* p. 79). But students of American develop-

ments must be struck by the date Donzelot gives for the French compulsory education law: 1881, or thirty years after the Boston ordinance.

29. See Hyman and Wise, eds. *Corporal Punishment in American Education,* pp. 70–71.

30. We would be able to read Hawthorne's seventeenth-century disciplinary fantasy in its nineteenth-century context if we remembered the lively discussion, in Hawthorne's time, of the inappropriateness of punishments by public shaming. In her preface to *Record of a School,* Peabody writes very fervently about children's rights to privacy in school punishment, a point on which she dissents from Bronson Alcott. Child advises mothers this way: "Punishments which make a child ashamed should be avoided. . . . It is a very bad plan for children to be brought into a room before strangers with a foolscap, or some bad name, fastened upon them" (Child, *The Mother's Book,* pp. 37–38). I find it striking that in "Main Street," the last work Hawthorne wrote before *The Scarlet Letter,* Puritan punishment appears in the more classically controversial form of whipping—Hawthorne's whipping scene here resembling the great 1840s accounts in Douglass's *Narrative* and Richard Henry Dana's *Two Years before the Mast* to an extraordinary extent.

31. Nathaniel Hawthorne, *The Scarlet Letter,* vol. 1 of the Centenary Edition of the Works of Nathaniel Hawthorne (Columbus: Ohio State University Press, 1962–), p. 140.

32. Edgar Allan Poe, "The Tell-Tale Heart," *Complete Tales and Poems of Edgar Allan Poe,* ed. Hervey Allen (New York: Modern Library, 1938), p. 306.

33. Foucault, *Discipline and Punish,* p. 75.

34. Poe, "The Imp of the Perverse," *Complete Tales,* p. 281. The hurting of cats, the perversion of the narrator of "The Black Cat," is a widespread topos of infantile bad behavior in the literature of discipline through love. In Catharine Sedgwick's *Home* (1835; Boston: James Munroe and Co., 1846), the model disciplinary incident turns on a boy's tormenting of his sister's kitten; Harriet Beecher Stowe makes the stoning of kittens the occasion for Mrs. Bird's exemplary discipline in *Uncle Tom's Cabin; or, Life among the Lowly* (1852; New York: Penguin, 1981), p. 143.

35. Sedgwick, *Home,* p. 27; Peabody, *Kindergarten Guide* (Boston: T. O. H. P. Burnham, 1863), p. 22.

36. See Susan Warner, *The Wide, Wide World,* 2 vols. (1850; New York: G. P. Putnam and Co., 1856), 1:193; numbers after subsequent quotations from the novel refer to pages in this text.

37. My understanding of what might be called motivation by reunion has been helped by Nancy Schnog's "Inside the Sentimental: The Psychological Work of *The Wide, Wide World,*" *Genders* 4 (1989):11–25.

38. Jane Tompkins, *Sensational Designs: The Cultural Work of American*

Fiction, 1790–1860 (New York: Oxford University Press, 1985), p. 156. The social undifferentiatedness of the context Tompkins proposes is evident throughout her otherwise useful chapter on Warner, "The Other American Renaissance": revivalism thus has "'terrific universality'" (p. 149; the undisowned phrase is Perry Miller's); evangelical thought "pervaded people's perceptions" (p. 156), informed "how people in the antebellum era thought" (p. 158), and so on. For a striking reading of the function of evangelicalism in the emergence of the middle class in the nineteenth-century, see Ryan, *Cradle of the Middle Class,* chaps. 2 and 3.

39. See Forrest Wilson, *Crusader in Crinoline: The Life of Harriet Beecher Stowe* (Philadeplhia: J. B. Lippincott, 1941), p. 256.

40. Stowe, *Uncle Tom's Cabin,* p. 326; numbers in parentheses refer to pages in the Penguin edition cited in n. 34.

41. For historical antecedents to Stowe's meditation on this problem of slave society see Greven, *Protestant Temperament,* p. 277.

42. Cobb, *Corporal Punishment,* p. 108. Emotional blackmail was the disciplinary sanction that Locke proposed in place of whipping: for the father to *"caress and commend* [his children] *when they do well;* [and] *shew a cold and neglectful Countenance to them upon doing ill; . . .* will of it self work more than Threats or Blows" (*Some Thoughts Concerning Education, The Educational Writings of John Locke,* ed. James L. Axtell [Cambridge: Cambridge University Press, 1968], p. 153.)

43. Topsy is the classic literary exemplification of Foucault's remark on discipline by interiority: "The man described for us, whom we are invited to free, is already in himself the effect of a subjection more profound than himself. A 'soul' inhabits him and brings him to existence, which is itself a factor in the mastery that power exercises over the body" (Foucault, *Discipline and Punish,* p. 30). When Eva touches Topsy, it is "soul" her love produces: "Yes, in that moment, a ray of real belief, a ray of heavenly love, had penetrated the darkness of her heathen soul!" (410).

44. *Mother's Magazine* quoted in Ryan, *Cradle of the Middle Class,* p. 159; Mann, "Reply to the 'Remarks,'" p. 147; Cobb, *Corporal Punishment,* p. 104.

45. The most resonant statement of this position is in D. A. Miller, *The Novel and the Police* (Berkeley: University of California Press, 1989), pp. 1–32. For a development of this case using American examples, see Mark Seltzer, *Henry James and the Art of Power* (Ithaca, N.Y.: Cornell University Press, 1984).

46. On Sedgwick's educational involvements see Kathryn Kish Sklar, *Catherine Beecher: A Study in American Domesticity* (New Haven, Conn.: Yale University Press, 1973), pp. 176–77. Mary Kelley fills in the social background of the popular women writers of this time (Sedgwick among them) in the second chapter of her *Private Woman, Public Stage: Literary Domesticity in Nineteenth-Century America* (New York: Oxford University

Press, 1984); but where Kelley stresses their links to what she calls old elites, I would stress their grounding in the new middle class's tutelary offices—a grounding evident in their writing of novels and domestic manuals, novels and cookbooks, novels and children's readers, and so on. (Eventual author of *House and Home Papers* and coauthor of *The American Woman's Home*, Stowe's last work before *Uncle Tom* was the religio-domestic disciplinary tract, *Earthly Care a Heavenly Discipline.*) The other source-book on the popular writers of nineteenth-century domesticity is Nina Baym, *Woman's Fiction* (Ithaca, N.Y.: Cornell University Press, 1978).

47. See Messerli, *Horace Mann*, p. 425. We would not have trouble seeing Hawthorne as a domestic author if we restored his homey essays, or his children's writings, or even "The Gentle Boy," to centrality in his canon.

48. See James L. Hart, *The Popular Book: A History of America's Literary Taste* (New York: Oxford University Press, 1950), chaps. 6 and 7; Kelley, *Private Woman, Public Stage*, pp. 3–27; and Susan Geary, "The Domestic Novel as Commercial Commodity: Making a Best Seller in the 1850s," *Papers of the Bibliographical Society of America* 70 (1976):365–93.

49. See Baym, *Novels, Readers, and Reviewers: Responses to Fiction in Antebellum America* (Ithaca, N.Y.: Cornell University Press, 1984), pp. 47–54. Douglas insists on the bond between reading and middle-class domestic privacy in *Feminization*, pp. 61–62.

50. This phrase is cited from an 1858 book review in Baym, *Novels, Readers, and Reviewers*, p. 49.

51. I discuss these developments in later chapters, especially chapter 5.

52. Miller develops another answer to this question in his "Discipline in Different Voices: Bureaucracy, Police, Family, and *Bleak House*," *Representations*, no. 1 (1983):59–89, esp. pp. 72–78: this essay is now re-printed in *The Novel and the Police*, pp. 58–106.

53. See Baym, *Novels, Readers, and Reviewers*, pp. 40–42, 54–55.

54. I have in mind Henry Nash Smith, "The Scribbling Women and the Cosmic Success Story," *Critical Inquiry* 1 (1974):47–70; Baym, *Woman's Fiction*, pp. 11–50; Kelley, *Private Woman, Public Stage*; Tompkins, "The Other American Renaissance"; and Joanne Dobson, "The Hidden Hand: Subversion of Cultural Ideology in Three Mid-Nineteenth-Century Women's Novels," *American Quarterly* 38 (1986):223–42.

CHAPTER TWO

1. Hawthorne, letter to E. P. Whipple, 2 May 1852, *The Letters, 1843–1853*, Centenary Edition, 14:536.

2. Hawthorne, *The Blithedale Romance*, Centenary Edition, 3:5; all subsequent quotations from *The Blithedale Romance* are taken from this volume and are followed by page numbers in parentheses.

3. On the American history of mesmerism, see Robert C. Fuller, *Mesmerism and the American Cure of Souls* (Philadelphia: University of Pennsylvania Press, 1982), esp. pp. 16–47. Puysegur and the concept of a clairvoyance yielding "lucity" are discussed on pp. 10–11.

4. See Gillian Brown, "The Empire of Agoraphobia," *Representations*, no. 20 (Fall 1987): 134–57. For another discussion of the cultural history of privacy and of the highly charged bounding-off of public and private space in the antebellum decades, see Karen Haltunnen, *Confidence Men and Painted Women: A Study of Middle-Class Culture in America, 1830–1870* (New Haven, Conn.: Yale University Press, 1982), esp. pp. 102–12.

5. Lois W. Banner discusses the cultural authority of what she calls "the steel-engraving lady" in her *American Beauty* (New York: Alfred A. Knopf, 1983), pp. 45–65.

6. Stowe, *Uncle Tom's Cabin*, p. 333.

7. To be fully understood, the quite spectacular emergence of women into public artistic celebrity around 1850 would have to be grasped together with the much more heavily obstructed movement of women into other forms of public life at the same time. Priscilla is partly defined in opposition to Zenobia, who contemplates a countercareer as a feminist political orator. Zenobia's historical correlatives are the women who asserted themselves as speakers in the antislavery and women's rights causes in the late 1830s and 1840s, who found their ways barred by the still strongly enforced social insistence that women not speak in public before mixed male-female audiences. Lillian O'Connor's useful volume, *Pioneer Women Orators* (New York: Columbia University Press, 1954), reminds us that women were enrolled as students at the coeducational Oberlin College, but were not allowed to perform the public-speaking exercises in oratory classes; and that many women publicly prominent in education had male spokesmen read their messages aloud when called on to speak in mixed company (pp. 22–40). Calvin Stowe read Harriet Beecher Stowe's responses to the crowds she drew on her English tour (see Wilson, *Crusader in Crinoline*, p. 349).

8. Banner discusses Fanny Elssler's tour in *American Beauty*, pp. 63–64. On Jenny Lind's American concert tour, see P. T. Barnum, *Struggles and Triumphs* (1869; New York: Penguin American Library, 1981), esp. chaps. 17–19, and Neil Harris, *Humbug: The Art of P. T. Barnum* (Chicago: University of Chicago Press, 1973), pp. 111–42.

9. The most comprehensive treatment of 1850s literary promotion and the expansion of the American book market is Geary, "The Domestic Novel as a Commercial Commodity." See also the discussion of publication and promotion in Kelley, *Private Woman, Public Stage*, pp. 3–27.

10. See *Ruth Hall and Other Writings by Fanny Fern*, ed. Joyce W. Warren (New Brunswick, N.J.: Rutgers University Press, 1986), p. 176; Kelley, *Private Woman, Public Stage*, p. 3; Wilson, *Crusader in Crinoline*, pp. 291,

344–86. Stowe was assured of an English "reception as enthusiastic as that of Jenny Lind" (ibid., p. 334). An important related discussion of "the modelling of a highly visible identity under . . . new circumstances of conspicuous performance" (p. 164) is Philip Fisher's "Appearing and Disappearing in Public: Social Space in Late-Nineteenth-Century Literature and Culture," in *Reconstructing American Literary History,* ed. Sacvan Bercovitch (Cambridge, Mass.: Harvard University Press, 1986), pp. 155–88. Fisher, however, locates in the 1890s the developments I see beginning in the late 1840s.

11. Catharine and Harry Sedgwick's comments are cited in Kelley, *Private Woman, Public Stage,* pp. 129–30. Kelley's discussion of female literary pseudonyms, pp. 124–37, is a crucial contribution to the historical meaning of women's veiling in the mid-nineteenth century.

12. See Kelley, *Private Woman, Public Stage,* p. 158. Barnum's Jenny Lind chapters make clear that she profited from her performance career quite as much as he did.

13. Barnum, *Struggles and Triumphs,* p. 173. On Bonner, see Kelley, *Private Woman, Public Stage,* pp. 3–6, 21–24, 161–63. Kelley's evidence suggests how much generosity such a manager might be capable of, and what benefits a woman might gain through her dealings with him, facts that must not be underrated. (In *Ruth Hall,* Ruth thinks of her manager as a real brother, unlike her miserable actual brother, Hyacinth.) But it is a tendency of Kelley's argument to slip over the market relation that a bond *to* a publicist-promoter necessarily involved: Kelley thus treats this bond as background or introductory information instead of as a relation that helps *constitute* the female literary "success."

14. In the same vein Barnum calls Lind's tour "an enterprise never before or since equalled in managerial annals" and gloats: "I had marked the 'divine Jenny' as a sure card" (Barnum, *Struggles and Triumphs,* pp. 170–72).

15. Cited in Geary, "The Domestic Novel as Commercial Commodity," pp. 378, 382.

16. Ibid., p. 383; see also ibid., pp. 383–89.

17. On actor and spectator in nineteenth-century European culture see for instance Richard Sennett's discussion of Pagliaccian virtuosity and the new etiquette of audience silence in *The Fall of Public Man* (New York: Alfred A. Knopf, 1977), pp. 195–218.

18. Hawthorne, *The American Notebooks,* Centenary Edition, 8:169.

19. See Barnum, *Struggles and Triumphs,* pp. 213–14.

20. Cited in Wilson, *Crusader in Crinoline,* p. 345.

21. N. P. Willis, *Memoranda of the Life of Jenny Lind* (Philadelphia: Robert E. Peterson, 1851), pp. 163, 166, 159. Willis's reverie continues, in a locution truly astonishing: "To see such a heaven as her heart untenanted, one longs to write its advertisement of 'To Let'" (p. 160). Readers of the

Willis *Memoranda* will be struck by the close analogies to Priscilla in Lind's "white garb of purity" (p. 132), her pallid and "insensuous" appearance (pp. 140–41), her upbringing as a "poor and plain little girl" locked "in a little room" (p. 5), and so on.

22. Willis, *Memoranda,* pp. 163–65. "Your uninvited presence here is an intrusion," Lind tells the invaders of what *Blithedale* calls her "private withdrawing room" (110–11); but the celebrity privacy that brands public entrance as intrusion in fact invites just such intrusion, as Willis virtually says.

23. See Geary, "The Domestic Novel as Commercial Commodity," pp. 388–89. As Geary notes, the really fascinating question this publicity raises—whether Fern wrote up her life in the knowledge that it would be marketed in this way—is impossible now to answer.

24. Rolls-Royce ran this advertisement in the April 1988 issue of *Gourmet* magazine.

25. Does my phrasing sufficiently suggest that I see *Blithedale* as prophetically describing the "living room" of the modern private home, focussed on the sound system, television, and VCR? That the average American watches television seven or more hours a day *in* such enclosures is the social fact *Blithedale* helps to foresee. On the American tradition of opposition to privacy as a spatial and social construct, see Dolores Hayden, *The Grand Domestic Revolution: A History of Feminist Designs of American Homes, Neighborhoods, and Cities* (Cambridge, Mass.: MIT Press, 1981).

26. My understanding that mass-cultural instruments can build social groups into markets because they also meet those groups' socially created needs has been influenced by Ohmann, "Where Did Mass Culture Come From?" Like Fisher, Ohmann focusses these developments in the 1890s.

27. Hawthorne, *The Scarlet Letter,* p. 4. Further evidence that the issue of Hawthorne's writing around 1850 is the issue of enlarged publicity would be found in the 1851 preface to *Twice-Told Tales* and in his other novels of 1850–52, both of which open with a crisis of public exposure: Hester's exposure on the Puritan scaffold in *The Scarlet Letter* and the "going visible" that accompanies Hepzibah's opening of her shop in *The House of the Seven Gables.* On the promotion or public creation of Hawthorne in the 1850s and after, see my *The School of Hawthorne* (New York: Oxford University Press, 1986), pp. 48–66.

28. The following passage exemplifies Melville's struggle to describe "life" and its alienation in contemporary writing:

Pierre is young; heaven gave him the divinest, freshest form of a man; put light into his eye, and fire into his blood, and brawn into his arm, and a joyous, jubilant, overflowing, upbubbling, universal life in him everywhere. Now look around in that most miserable room, and at that most miserable of all the pursuits of a man, and say if here be the place, and this be the trade, that God intended him for. A rickety chair, two hollow barrels, a plank, paper, pens, and infernally black ink, four leprously dingy white walls, no carpet, a cup of water, and a dry biscuit or two. Oh, I hear the leap of the Texan Camanche, as at this moment he goes crashing like a wild deer through the green underbrush; I hear his glorious whoop of savage and untamable health; and then I look in at Pierre. If physical, practical unreason make the savage, which is he? [*Pierre; or, The Ambiguities* (Evanston, Ill., and Chicago: Northwestern University Press and the Newberry Library, 1971), p. 302].

CHAPTER THREE

1. Louisa May Alcott, *Jo's Boys* (1886; rpt. New York: Puffin Books, 1983), pp. 42–43.

2. Alcott, *Jo's Boys*, pp. 45, 54–55.

3. Alcott, *The Journals of Louisa May Alcott*, ed. Joel Myerson, Daniel Shealy, and Madeleine B. Stern (Boston: Little, Brown, 1989), p. 183; see also p. 171. Alcott journal entries from this volume will hereafter be identified by the abbreviation *J* and followed by page numbers in the text.

4. See chap. 2, n. 17.

5. Alcott, *Little Men* (1871; rpt. New York: Grosset and Dunlap Illustrated Junior Library), pp. 211–12. With its scenes of tongue snipping and the tying-up of children, *Little Men* is a book of special interest to connoisseurs of nineteenth-century disciplinary practices. On Alcott's own career as a spanker, see *Journals*, p. 243: "New Year's day is made memorable by my solemnly *spanking* my child [Lulu, daughter of her dead sister May]. . . . the effect, as I expected, a failure. Love is better, but also endless patience."

6. Alcott, *Little Men*, p. 210.

7. Alcott, *Jo's Boys*, p. 121.

8. For a fuller narrative of Alcott's early life, see Martha Saxton, *Louisa May* (Boston: Houghton Mifflin, 1977) and chaps. 5 and 6 of Madelon Bedell, *The Alcotts: Biography of a Family* (New York: Clarkson N. Potter, 1980).

9. Alcott, *Jo's Boys*, p. 47. Compare Alcott's famous statement upon returning to the sensation fiction genre with *A Modern Mephistopheles* in 1877: "Enjoyed doing it, being tired of providing moral pap for the young" (*Journals*, p. 204).

10. See Saxton, *Louisa May*, p. 216; and *Journals*, p. 71.

11. For an especially important instance, see Alcott's accounts of the effect of Theodore Parker's sermon "Laborious Young Women" in curing her deep despair of 1858 in *Journals*, pp. 90–91, and in the novel *Work* (1873), where Parker appears as Reverend Power.

12. See *Journals,* pp. 64–69, 72, 73–74, and 76.

13. For this episode see *Journals,* pp. 108–12. The perennial enthusiast Elizabeth Palmer Peabody, once Bronson Alcott's assistant in his Tremont Street school, wanted Louisa May Alcott to take pupils for nothing to try out the then newly imported German plan for the kindergarten: an arrangement of idealism for me, exploitation for you that Alcott knew all too well.

14. William Dean Howells, *Literary Friends and Acquaintance,* ed. David F. Hiatt and Edwin H. Cady (1900; rpt. Bloomington: Indiana University Press, 1968), p. 71; see also pp. 15–16.

15. See Alcott, *The Selected Letters of Louisa May Alcott,* ed. Myerson, Shealy, and Stern (Boston: Little, Brown, 1987), p. 26, for Alcott's early, unsuccessful approach to Bonner; and *Journals,* p. 164, for his approach to her in 1868. For Bonner's support of other women writers see chap. 2, n. 13, and Susan Coultrap-McQuin's study of E. D. E. N. Southworth in her *Doing Literary Business* (Chapel Hill: University of North Carolina Press, 1990), pp. 49–78.

16. The most useful sources on story-paper and dime novel publishing are Albert Johannsen, *The House of Beadle and Adams and Its Dime and Nickel Novels: The Story of a Vanished Literature,* 3 vols. (Norman: University of Oklahoma Press, 1950–62), and Michael Denning, *Mechanic Accents: Dime Novels and Working-Class Culture in America* (London: Verso, 1987). The circulation figure for the *New York Ledger* comes from Kelley, *Private Woman, Public Stage,* p. 4; the slogan from *The Flag of Our Union* is found on the back page of the 1854 and 1855 editions.

17. My examples are taken from *The Flag of Our Union* 3 (Apr. 1848); 9 (Sept. 1854); and 15 (Jan. 1860).

18. For a heroically ingenious assemblage of evidence linking such fiction to an emerging working-class audience, see Denning, *Mechanic Accents,* pp. 27–46; Denning's account, however, is necessarily more persuasive in its inclusions than in its exclusions. For countervailing evidence of a native-born farmer readership for such work, see for instance Hamlin Garland, *A Son of the Middle Border* (1917; rpt. Lincoln: University of Nebraska Press, 1979), p. 120, and Joseph Kirkland, *Zury: The Meanest Man in Spring County* (Boston: Houghton, Mifflin, 1887), pp. 35, 533. My thanks to James Avery for the last example.

19. Howells, *Literary Friends and Acquaintance,* p. 15.

20. Ibid., p. 36.

21. For further evidence see *Journals,* pp. 99, 120–21, and *Letters,* pp. 91, 94, 103, which make clear, amid a certain amount of snarling, that Alcott wanted her most ambitious book, *Moods,* to be published by Fields and that she regarded Fields's acceptances as establishing her "best" writing when she was planning a first volume of stories.

22. Johannsen offers fascinating biographies of the Beadle and Adams

writers in *The House of Beadle,* vol. 2, which is where I take my information on E. S. Ellis's pen names (pp. 94–97).

23. On the form of authorship projected by dime novels and story
papers see Denning, *Mechanic Accents,* pp. 20–24. Denning is the source
of my information on Bertha M. Clay and William Wallace Cook. On
Edward L. Wheeler, see Johannsen, *The House of Beadle,* 2:293–96. For
the work habits of Badger and Ingraham (among many others), see ibid.,
2:25, 156; on Sinclair, see Christopher Wilson, *The Labor of Words: Literary Professionalism in the Progressive Era,* (Athens: University of Georgia
Press, 1985), pp. 120–21.

24. Cited in Stern's introduction to Alcott, *Behind a Mask: The Unknown
Thrillers of Louisa May Alcott* (New York: Bantam Books, 1975), p. xxvi.

25. *Letters,* p. 79.

26. See Stern, introduction to Alcott, *Behind a Mask,* and Judith Fetterley's important pieces "Impersonating 'Little Women': The Radicalism
of Alcott's *Behind a Mask,*" *Women's Studies* 10 (1983):1–14 and "*Little
Women:* Alcott's Civil War," *Feminist Studies* 5 (Summer 1979):369–83.

27. The standard history of this development is Wishy, *The Child and
the Republic.*

28. My phrasing here is consciously close to the words of Pierre Bourdieu cited in the epigraph to this chapter. Bourdieu's concept of the
literary field as a historically particular structure at once of cultural dissemination and valorization and of authorial self-conception has helped
my thinking throughout this chapter. See Bourdieu, "Flaubert's Point of
View," *Critical Inquiry* 14 (Spring 1988):539–62 and "The Field of Cultural Production; or, The Economic World Reversed," *Poetics* 12 (1983):
311–56.

29. Stern, introduction to Alcott, *Behind a Mask,* p. xxx.

30. Alcott is almost never self-altering in her letters, but there is something decidedly cringing—and most uneasily so—in her surviving letters
to Annie Fields, her second cousin (see *Letters,* p. 84). One of these makes
clear that Annie Fields both got Alcott's elegy for Thoreau into the *Atlantic*
and sent her "kindly criticism" of it; it seems obvious that she enjoyed
visiting her superiority upon her socially downscale relation. Alcott writes
as an uneasy outsider of the Fields salon later celebrated by Howells, Jewett, Henry James, and Willa Cather (about which more in chapter 5): "I
visited about at J. T. Fields the great publishers where I saw Mrs Stowe,
Fanny Kemble, Holmes, Longfellow, & all the fine folks besides living in
style in a very smart house with very clever people who have filled it with
books, pictures, statues & beautiful things picked up in their travels"
(*Letters,* p. 73). Alcott suffered perhaps the severest high-cultural condescension at this time from the twenty-one-year-old Henry James, who
reviewed her first novel disparagingly and "gave me advice, as if he had
been eighty and I a girl" (Leon Edel, *Henry James: The Untried Years* [Phil-

adelphia: J. B. Lippincott, 1953], p. 213). One wonders whether Henry James Sr.'s malapropism for Alcott's first novel does not betray condescension and unkindness as well: the book was named *Moods;* he called it *Dumps* (see Saxton, *Louisa May,* p. 311).

31. See Tillie Olsen's introduction Rebecca Harding to Davis's "Life In the Iron Mills" (New York: Feminist Press, 1972), pp. 69–174. This record of Davis's sense of degradation as she "fell" from the *Atlantic* and the order of serious artists into thriller writing, popular magazines, and the life of "a professional workhorse in the field of letters" (p. 135) makes vividly clear the status considerations that attached to high and low publication at the time of Alcott's debut.

32. *Letters,* p. 144.

33. Alcott, *Litle Women,* (New York: Bantam Classic, 1983), p. 391; all subsequent quotations are from this volume and are cited by page number within the text.

34. Warner, *The Wide, Wide World,* 2:201.

35. The collusion of "free" experience in the supporting of authority is extremely clear in *Little Men,* where Jo's charges are allowed a weekly pillow fight in exchange for their pledge of orderly behavior the rest of the week.

36. See Wishy, *The Child and the Republic,* pp. 81–104, and Daniel T. Rodgers, *The Work Ethic in Industrial America, 1850–1920* (Chicago: University of Chicago Press, 1978), pp. 125–52.

37. Henry James, *Letters,* ed. Edel, 4 vols. (Cambridge, Mass.: Harvard University Press, 1974), 1:262.

38. See Alcott, *Journals,* pp. 192, 201, and *Letters,* p. 123. May's reasons for expatriation—"she cannot find the help she needs here, and is happy and busy in her own world over there"—closely echo James's. Louisa May Alcott bankrolled her sister's more high-flown career, and so entered into the ambiguous patron position James sketches in *Roderick Hudson.* "The money I invest in her pays the sort of interest I like," Alcott wrote of May; "I am proud to have her show what she can do, and have her depend upon no one but me" (*J,* 201).

39. Alcott, *Jo's Boys,* pp. 8–9. Amy, Laurie, and Meg have moved out to the suburban Plumfield to avoid creeping urbanization and industrialization: "when the rapid growth of the city shut in the old house, spoilt Meg's nest, and dared to put a soap-factory under Mr Laurence's indignant nose, our friends emigrated to Plumfield, and the great changes began" (ibid., p. 8)

40. For a more extensive discussion of the child-woman/mentor couple in sentimental fiction, see Alfred Habegger, "Precocious Incest: First Novels by Louisa May Alcott and Henry James," *Massachusetts Review* 26 (Summer 1985):233–62, reprinted in Habegger's *Henry James and the "Woman Business"* (Cambridge: Cambridge University Press, 1989). This

book offers evidence of James's early involvement with the domestic writing from which criticism has detached him.

41. See Denning, *Mechanic Accents,* and Dee Garrison, *Apostles of Culture: The Public Librarian and American Society, 1876–1920* (New York: Free Press, 1979), pp. 67–88. For another account of Alcott's participation in middle-class reform efforts centered on reading habits and reading tastes, see Steven Mailloux, "The Rhetorical Use and Abuse of Fiction: Eating Books in Late Nineteenth-Century America," *boundary 2* 17 (1990):133–57. Alcott's self-distancing from the emerging working class is well discussed in Jean Fagan Yellin, "From *Success* to *Experience:* Louisa May Alcott's *Work,*" *Massachusetts Review* 21 (Fall 1980):527–39, esp. pp. 536–37.

42. Quoted in Saxton, *Louisa May,* p. 347.

43. Dorothy Richardson, *The Long Day* (New York: Century, 1905), pp. 85–86.

44. Ibid., p. 302. Reforming the working class by administering high literature to it in adult life starts too late, Richardson writes: "college-settlement folk . . . forget that Shakspere, Ruskin, and all the rest of the really true and great literary crew, are infinite bores to every-day people" (p. 300).

45. The phrase is Henry James's, from his 1875 review of Alcott's *Eight Cousins,* in James, *Literary Criticism,* 2 vols. (New York: Library of America, 1984), 1:195.

CHAPTER FOUR

1. For a discussion of another illusion of current canon reformation—the assumption that there is a relatively direct relation between literary inclusion and social representation—see John Guillory's important essay, "Canonical and Non-Canonical: A Critique of the Current Debate," *ELH* 54 (1987):483–527. My views on other problems with this reformation are expressed in "After the Opening: Problems and Prospects for a Reformed American Literature," *Yale Journal of Criticism* 5 (Spring 1992): 59–71.

2. Virginia Woolf, *A Room of One's Own* (New York: Harcourt, Brace, and World, 1929), p. 43

3. Ibid., p. 50.

4. This issue is not yet the subject of a dense history of consideration, but important earlier discussions exist. See, in addition to *A Room of One's Own,* Linda Nochlin, "Why Have There Been No Great Women Artists?" in *Art and Sexual Politics,* ed. Thomas B. Hess and Elizabeth C. Baker (New York: Collier Books, 1973), pp. 1–39; Roszika Parker and Griselda Pollock, *Old Mistresses: Women, Art and Ideology* (London: Routledge and Kegan Paul, 1981); and Janet Wolff, *The Social Production of Art* (New York: St. Martins Press, 1981), pp. 26–48.

5. Woolf, *A Room of One's Own*, pp. 48–50.

6. Ibid., p. 62.

7. Eudora Welty, *One Writer's Beginnings* (Cambridge, Mass.: Harvard University Press, 1984), pp. 29, 80, 81.

8. Richard Wright, *Black Boy* (1945; New York: Harper and Row, 1966), p. 133; see also pp. 135–44.

9. Ibid., pp. 150–51. For a concise history of Wright's career read as a history of literary disadvantage and advantage, see Kenneth Kinnamon, *The Emergence of Richard Wright* (Urbana: University of Illinois Press, 1972), pp. 3–74.

10. Stowe, "How Shall I Learn to Write?" *Hearth and Home*, 16 Jan. 1869, p. 56.

11. Edward Eggleston, *The Hoosier Schoolmaster* (1871; rpt. New York: Hart Publishing Co., 1976), p. 6; Thomas Nelson Page, *In Ole Virginia* (New York: Charles Scribner's Sons, 1887), unnumbered front page. Compare the notice on dialects at the start of *The Adventures of Huckleberry Finn*, the best-known example of this prefatory move.

12. See Ann Douglas Wood's bracingly opinionated "The Literature of Impoverishment: The Women Local Colorists in America, 1865–1914," *Women's Studies* 1 (1972):3–40.

13. The 1896 edition of Sarah Orne Jewett, *Deephaven* (Boston: Houghton, Mifflin) lists itself as the twenty-third edition. On Mary Noailles Murfree's circulation figures, see Nathalia Wright's introduction to Murfree's *In the Tennessee Mountains* (Knoxville: University of Tennessee Press, 1970), p. xiii. Harte's contract with the *Atlantic Monthly* is detailed in Howells, *Literary Friends and Acquaintance*, p. 252. On Sherwood Bonner, see H. H. McAlexander, *The Prodigal Daughter: A Biography of Sherwood Bonner* (Baton Rouge: Louisiana State University Press, 1981), esp. pp. 150–65.

14. Of the many histories of the incursion of translocal social structures on previously more isolated local-cultural economies, the most influential has been Robert H. Wiebe's story of the erosion of "island communities" in *The Search for Order, 1877–1920* (New York: Hill and Wang, 1977). The association of regionalism with the decline of local communities, a long-standing critical commonplace, is voiced especially eloquently in Warner Berthoff, "The Art of Jewett's *Pointed Firs*," *New England Quarterly* 32 (1959):49–53.

15. See Stowe, *Oldtown Folks* (1869; rpt. New York: Library of America, 1982), p. 885, and Wright's introduction to Murfree, *In the Tennessee Mountains*, p. xi.

16. For important arguments to this effect, see Steven Hahn and Jonathan Prude, eds., *The Countryside in the Age of Capitalist Transformation: Essays in the Social History of Rural America* (Chapel Hill: University of

North Carolina Press, 1985), especially the essays by Hahn and John Scott Strickland; and Hal S. Barron, *Those Who Stayed Behind: Rural Society in Nineteenth-Century New England* (New York: Cambridge University Press, 1984). For a related critique of the homogenizing local-to-federal historiography associated with the regional form, see Louis A. Renza, *"A White Heron" and the Question of Minor Literature* (Madison: University of Wisconsin Press, 1984), pp. 43–56.

17. See especially James Clifford, *The Predicament of Culture: Twentieth-Century Ethnography, Literature, and Art* (Cambridge, Mass.: Harvard University Press, 1988), pp. 215–51.

18. On the institutionalization of a self-conscious high culture in the United States, see Lawrence Levine, *Highbrow/Lowbrow: The Emergence of Cultural Hierarchy* (Cambridge, Mass.: Harvard University Press, 1988), and Paul DiMaggio's essays "Cultural Entrepreneurship in Nineteenth-Century Boston: The Creation of an Organizational Base for High Culture in America" and "Cultural Entrepreneurship in Nineteenth-Century Boston, Part Two: The Classification and Framing of American Art," *Media, Culture, and Society* 4 (1982):33–50, 303–22. I discuss the correlative establishment of a high-literary culture in *The School of Hawthorne*, esp. chaps. 3 and 4.

19. There is no comprehensive history of this development. For important partial accounts the following are especially helpful: Ronald Story, *The Forging of an Aristocracy: Harvard and the Boston Upper Class, 1800–1870* (Middletown, Conn.: Wesleyan University Press, 1980); E. Digby Baltzell, *The Protestant Establishment: Aristocracy and Caste in America* (1964; rpt. New York: Vintage Books, 1966), pp. 109–42; Wiebe, *Search for Order,* pp. 111–32; John Sproat, *"The Best Men": Liberal Reformers in the Gilded Age* (New York: Oxford University Press, 1968); and Burton Bledstein, *The Culture of Professionalism: The Middle Class and the Development of Higher Education in America* (New York: W. W. Norton, 1976). The Story quotation comes from *Forging of an Aristocracy,* p. 165.

20. For disaggregations of the social support for high culture in the Gilded Age, see Levine, *Highbrow/Lowbrow,* p. 227, and DiMaggio, "Cultural Entrepreneurship, Part Two," p. 308. See also Roger Stein, "Artifact as Ideology: The Aesthetic Movement and Its American Cultural Context," in *In Pursuit of Beauty: Americans and the Aesthetic Movement,* ed. Doreen Bolger Burke et al. (New York: Metropolitan Museum of Art, Rizzoli Books, 1986), pp. 22–51. Jane Addams recounts her self-depleting devotion to what she calls "the feverish search after culture" in the magnificent chapter "The Snare of Preparation," in *Twenty Years at Hull-House* (1910; rpt. New York: New American Library, 1961), pp. 60–74. On the nineteenth-century library as scene of genteel social engineering, see Garrison, *Apostles of Culture,* pp. 35–50. For a parallel theory of the art mu-

seum as instrument of reacculturation, see Joseph Choate's speech at the dedication of the Metropolitan Museum of Art's building in Central Park in 1880, cited in Levine, *Highbrow/Lowbrow,* p. 201.

21. J. B. Harrison, "Three Typical Workingmen," *Atlantic Monthly* 42 (Dec. 1878), p. 725.

22. The social history of American vacationing is a great book that remains to be written. This paragraph draws on two useful contributions to that history: Baltzell, *Protestant Establishment,* pp. 116–21, and Vincent J. Scully, Jr., *The Shingle Style and the Stick Style,* rev. ed. (New Haven, Conn.: Yale University Press, 1971), pp. 24–33 (and see all of the plates). Other brief but useful contributions to the nineteenth-century phase of this subject include Foster R. Dulles, *A History of Recreation,* 2nd ed. (New York: Appleton-Century-Crofts, 1965), pp. 148–53, and Rodgers, *Work Ethic,* pp. 95–96, 105–7.

23. See Thorstein Veblen, *The Theory of the Leisure Class* (1899; rpt. New York: New American Library, 1953), p. 47, as well as the whole chapter "Conspicuous Leisure," pp. 41–60. Veblen's theory of how leisure activities or "life-style" choices function symbolically to enact social status is revived and elaborated in Pierre Bourdieu's *Distinction: A Social Critique of the Judgment of Taste,* trans. Richard Nice (Cambridge, Mass.: Harvard University Press, 1984). In Bourdieu's terms the postbellum leisure class vacation would be an example of "the latest difference" (p. 247), the most recently acquired group exemption from material necessity, which functions with special salience in establishing distinction. Rodgers supplies the information about white-collar vacations in *Work Ethic,* p. 106.

24. On cultural competence as sign of privileged access to leisure, see the devastating chapter "The Higher Learning as an Expression of the Pecuniary Culture" in Veblen, *Theory of the Leisure Class,* and Bourdieu, *Distinction:* "If, among all these fields of possibles, none is more obviously predisposed to express social differences than the world of luxury goods, and, more particularly, cultural goods, this is because the relationship of distinction is objectively inscribed within it, and is reactivated, intentionally or not, in each act of consumption, through the instruments of economic and cultural appropriation which it requires" (p. 226).

25. Kenneth R. Andrews, *Nook Farm: Mark Twain's Hartford Circle* (Cambridge, Mass.: Harvard University Press, 1950), pp. 96–97; Mark Twain, *The Innocents Abroad* (1869; rpt. New York: New American Library, 1966), p. 22.

26. Warner writes in part 6 of *The Adirondacks Verified:* "The instinct of barbarism that leads people periodically to throw aside the habits of civilization and seek the freedom and discomfort of the woods is explicable enough. But it is not so easy to understand why this passion should be strongest in those who are most refined and most trained in social and

intellectual fastidiousness. Philistinism and shoddy do not like the woods" (*Atlantic Monthly* 41 (June 1878): 755–56). "A Cook's Tourist in Spain" ran in the *Atlantic Monthly* 54 (July 1884):33–51. Warner's *Their Pilgrimage* was serialized in several installments in *Harper's Monthly* 72 (1885–86).

27. "Dancin' Party" and the other works cited ran in the *Atlantic Monthly* 41 and 42 (1878); "Lonesome Cove" and the rest ran in *Harper's Monthly* 72 (1885); "A Humble Romance" and the rest in *Harper's Monthly* 69 (1884); and "The Revolt of 'Mother'" et al. in *Harper's Monthly* 81 (1890). Such conjunctions can be found for virtually all regional works: Woolson's "Rodman the Keeper" ran with James's *The American*, Wilkins Freeman's exquisite "A Poetess" with "Texan Types and Contrasts" and "Social Life in Oxford," and so on.

28. See *Harper's Monthly* 45 (July and Aug. 1872):161–68, 321–41.

29. See *Harper's Monthly* 81 (Nov. 1890):813–29.

30. The Boston population figure is cited in DiMaggio, "Cultural Entrepreneurship," p. 30. For extensive discussions of the anti-immigrant bias of the late nineteenth-century American elite, see Baltzell, *Protestant Establishment*, pp. 109–42, and Sproat, *"The Best Men,"* pp. 250–57. John Higham's *Strangers in the Land: Patterns of American Nativism 1860–1925,* 2nd. ed. (New Brunswick, N. J.: Rutgers University Press, 1988) is the standard history of the American response to immigration.

31. For a full account of these developments, see Baltzell, *Protestant Establishment*, pp. 114–42.

32. Ibid., pp. 118–19.

33. Levine cites this amazing fact in *Highbrow/Lowbrow*, p. 220. Levine writes eloquently about high culture as a mechanism deployed "to identify, distinguish, and order this new universe of strangers" (pp. 177): see particularly the chapter "Order, Hierarchy and Culture."

34. Ibid., p. 119.

35. See Horace Scudder, "American Classics in School," *Atlantic Monthly* 60 (July 1887), and my *School of Hawthorne*, pp. 59–61. The Scudder polemic ran in the same volume with Charles Waddell Chesnutt's dialect tale "Po' Sandy" and James's *The Aspern Papers*.

36. Veblen comments on correct speech's function as a class marker: "Elegant diction, whether in writing or speaking, is an effective means of reputability. . . . Great purity of speech is presumptive evidence of several successive lives spent in other than vulgarly useful occupations" (*Theory of the Leisure Class*, p. 257). Story's *Forging of an Aristocracy* (pp. 112–13, 120–21) notes the demarcation of a high-status style of speaking in the earlier nineteenth century at Harvard, a premier site of elite class formation. He also notes that at that earlier time the effort of the genteel was to differentiate themselves from countryfolk or the "rural element"—a

group that had ceased to be a threatening adjacency, and so that could become an object of nostalgic appreciation, in late nineteenth-century regional fiction.

37. My polyglot patchwork is taken from George Washington Cable's *The Grandissimes*, Wilkins Freeman's "An Honest Soul," Eggleston's *Hoosier Schoolmaster*, Page's "Marse Chan," Bonner's "Hieronymus Pop and the Baby," and Murfree's *The Prophet of the Great Smoky Mountains*, though a hundred other sources would do as well. Such quotation reveals how much, in dialect fiction, the apparently faithful record of different local speechways actually involves standard deformations of standard written English: the heavy use of the apostrophe, the picturesque misspelling of common pronouns and conjunctions, and so on.

38. The Anglo-Saxonism of the regional Other is sometimes an explicit part of its appeal: in Rose Terry Cooke's "Hopson's Choice," the folksy Hopsons live in a pastoral or nonindustrial New England valley first settled by "Andrew Hopson, yeoman, from Kent, Old England" (*Harper's Monthly* 69 [Sept. 1884]:607). Appalachia has always been mythically associated with a preserved remnant of pure English origins. A subject for further study is why American blacks should have become desirable objects of regionalist contemplation in the decade of steeply increased immigration from southern and eastern Europe—as if blacks became an honorary extension of "our" family in face of this more foreign threat.

39. On Harris's impeded speech, see Robert Hemenway's introduction to Joel Chandler Harris, *Uncle Remus: His Songs and His Sayings* (New York: Penguin Books, 1982), pp. 16–18.

40. I allude to Woolson's self-location in the title of her first volume, *Castle Nowhere: Lake-Country Sketches* (New York: Harper and Brothers, 1875).

41. For material on Constance Fenimore Woolson, see Joan Myers Weimer's introduction to her selection of Woolson stories, *Women Artists, Women Exiles: "Miss Grief" and Other Stories* (New Brunswick, N.J.: Rutgers University Press, 1988), and Rayburn S. Moore, *Constance Fenimore Woolson* (New York: Twayne, 1963).

42. See Garland, *Son of the Middle Border*, esp. pp. 318–76.

43. Garland, like many of his contemporaries in the 1880s, virtually equated *The Century* and *Harper's* with "literature" and (in the words of his memoir) "resolved upon being printed by the best periodicals." The extraordinary power of the literary establishment of this time to control the precinct of literary honor is revealed in Garland's self-abasing awe before the administrators of the "high": Howells's words of praise "were like gold medals" to Garland, and Gilder's praise "equivalent to a diploma" (*Son of the Middle Border*, pp. 376, 387, 412). Garland's love-hate relation to nineteenth-century high culture is well-discussed in Larzer Ziff, *The American 1890s* (New York: Viking Press, 1966), pp. 93–108.

CHAPTER FIVE

1. From the back cover of Sarah Way Sherman, *Sarah Orne Jewett, an American Persephone* (Hanover, N.H.: University Press of New England, 1989).

2. For treatments in this vein see Josephine Donovan, *New England Local Color Literature: A Woman's Tradition* (New York: Frederick Ungar, 1983), pp. 99–118; Marjorie Pryse, introduction to Jewett, *The Country of the Pointed Firs and Other Stories* (New York: W. W. Norton, 1981; subsequent quotations are from this edition and are cited by page number in the text); Elizabeth Ammons, "Going in Circles: The Female Geography of *The Country of the Pointed Firs*," *Studies in the Literary Imagination* 16 (Fall 1983): 83–92; Ammons, "Stowe's Dream of the Mother-Savior: *Uncle Tom's Cabin* and American Women Writers Before the 1920s," *New Essays on "Uncle Tom's Cabin*," ed. Eric J. Sundquist (Cambridge: Cambridge University Press, 1986), pp. 172–75; and Sherman, *Sarah Orne Jewett.*

3. The phrase is Donovan's, from the subtitle of *New England Local Color Literature.* How the prominent local color work by men is to be reconciled with the idea of this genre as a woman's tradition has yet to be explained.

4. Charles Miner Thompson, "The Art of Miss Jewett," *Atlantic Monthly* 94 (1904), reprinted in Richard Cary, ed., *Appreciation of Sarah Orne Jewett: Twenty-nine Interpretive Essays* (Waterville, Maine: Colby College Press, 1973), pp. 32–48. The passages quoted are from pages 35, 43, and 41. Jewett herself had proposed this historical occasion for her work in her preface to the 1893 edition of *Deephaven.*

5. See the chapter "Kate Lancaster's Plan" in *Deephaven* (Boston: J. R. Osgood, 1877), esp. pp. 11–15.

6. And not only urban: Jewett quite consciously chose to write of an outlying Maine distinct from the Maine she inhabited, which she felt to be insufficiently immune to the processes of contemporary development. In an 1877 letter she writes: "Berwick itself is growing and flourishing in a way that breaks my heart, but out from the village among the hills and near the sea there are still the quietest farms—where I see little change from one year to another—and the people would delight your heart" (Jewett, *Sarah Orne Jewett Letters,* ed. Cary [Waterville, Maine: Colby College Press, 1956], p. 33). To read Jewett's rare stories with an ethnic immigrant population—"Between Matins and Vespers" in *A Native of Winby and Other Tales* (1893), for instance—is to be struck by how other such characters are to her work's usual cast.

7. Donovan traces the prehistory of women's regional writing in *New England Local Color Literature,* pp. 11–38. On Jewett's introduction to Stowe and George Eliot by her mother and grandmother, see Sherman, *Sarah Orne Jewett,* p. 51.

8. See "Cape Cod, Nantucket, and the Vineyard," *Harper's Monthly,* 51 (1875): 63–65, and Celia Thaxter, *Among the Isles of Shoals* (1873; facsimile reprint Hyannis, Mass.: Wake-Brook, [n.d.]). Thaxter at last alludes to the "large house of entertainment" on the island she had made sound deserted in her last paragraph (p. 184) Other pertinent examples of the genre under discussion here are "Mount Desert," *Harper's Monthly,* 45 (1872):321–41; "Marblehead," *Harper's Monthly,* 49 (1874):181–202; another essay "The Isles of Shoals," by John Chadwick, *Harper's Monthly,* 49 (1874):663–76; and "Gloucester and Cape Ann," *Harper's Monthly,* 51 (1875):465–74. Thaxter's vacation-entwined artistic career—an intriguing variant on Jewett's—is considered in Stein, "Artifact as Ideology," and in Catherine Hoover Voorsanger's entry on Thaxter in "Dictionary of Architects, Artisans, Artists, and Manufacturers," both in *In Pursuit of Beauty,* pp. 31–32, 471–72. My understanding of Thaxter and Jewett's aestheticizations of former commercial sites has been helped by Alison Hickey's "Tamed and Untamed Nature: Jewett's *Country By-Ways* and the Writing of Postbellum Maine," typescript.

9. See Scully, *The Shingle Style and the Stick Style,* pp. 29–30. The Aldrich and Spofford articles ran in *Harper's Monthly* in 1874 and 1875, respectively; both of these authors became Jewett's friends.

10. Howells is cited in Henry Nash Smith, *Mark Twain: The Development of a Writer* (1962; rpt. New York: Atheneum, 1972), p. 62. "Angel-cake" was Walter Hines Page's phrase for the work favored by Horace Scudder, his predecessor at the *Atlantic* and Jewett's early mentor. See John Milton Cooper, *Walter Hines Page: The Southerner as American* (Chapel Hill: University of North Carolina Press, 1977), p. 130.

11. The point might be made here—against Jane Tompkins's implication that women writers as a group were demoted to subliterary status by a cadre of well-placed editors—that this hierarchization was produced through a social reformulation of culture in general in America, not by a mere clique, and that its workings favored some women writers (Jewett included) as it disparaged others. Here as usual the homogenizing categorization "women's writing" disguises the immensely different historical fortunes that different classes of writers have suffered and enjoyed. See Tompkins, *Sensational Designs,* pp. 3–37.

12. Quoted in Ellen B. Ballou, *The Building of the House: Houghton Mifflin's Formative Years* (Boston: Houghton Mifflin, 1970), pp. 444–45. As Ballou indicates, Scudder wrote a similar letter to Henry James.

13. On James T. Fields and the establishment of literary high culture, see W. S. Tryon, *Parnassus Corner: A Life of James T. Fields* (Boston: Houghton, Mifflin, 1963), and my *School of Hawthorne,* pp. 48–66. The Fields salon is vividly memorialized in Henry James, "Mr. and Mrs. James T. Fields" (1915), reprinted in James, *Literary Criticism,* 1:160–76; Willa Cather, "148 Charles Street," *Not Under Forty* (New York: Alfred A. Knopf,

1936), pp. 52–75; and Howells, *Literary Friends and Acquaintance,* pp. 33–41. See also Alcott's description in a somewhat different tone, cited above in chap. 3, n. 30. On the Sarah Orne Jewett-Annie Fields relation, see Sherman, *Sarah Orne Jewett,* esp. pp. 69–84; Lillian Faderman, *Surpassing the Love of Men: Romantic Friendship between Women from the Renaissance to the Present* (New York: William Morrow, 1981), pp. 197–203; and Judith Roman, "A Close Look at the Jewett-Fields Relationship," in *Critical Essays on Sarah Orne Jewett,* ed. Gwen L. Nagel (Boston: G. K. Hall, 1984), pp. 119–34. Donovan stresses Annie Fields's role as a contact point for women regionalists in *New England Local Color Literature,* pp. 38–49.

14. James, "Mr. and Mrs. James T. Fields," p. 176. To continue the enumeration, Jewett also yachted with the family of Henry Lee Higginson, premier Boston stockbroker and founder-patron of the echt-high cultural Boston Symphony Orchestra, off Cape Ann; she also, an editor assures us, "relished most the invigorating cruises along the Maine coast in the Forbes's majestic sailing yacht *Merlin*" (*Sarah Orne Jewett Letters,* pp. 33, n. 1; 66, n. 2). The railroad builder John M. Forbes owned the vacation island Naushon, off Martha's Vineyard.

15. Thompson reminds us that many members of the Boston Brahmin class of the mid- and late nineteenth century had their origins in coastal towns like Portland, Portsmouth, and Newburyport, so that Jewett took belated part in a larger class movement (see Thompson, "The Art of Miss Jewett," p. 35). The fullest detailing of the class dimensions of Jewett's life, including her long association with a socially eminent Boston coterie, is found in John Eldridge Frost, *Sarah Orne Jewett* (Kittery Point, Maine: The Gundalow Club, 1960); see pp. 38–39, 59, 66, 117–22.

16. Jewett, *Letters of Sarah Orne Jewett,* ed. Annie Fields (Boston: Houghton Mifflin, 1911), p. 54.

17. On Jewett's friendships see especially Sherman, *Sarah Orne Jewett,* pp. 69–84, and Frost, *Sarah Orne Jewett,* pp. 117–22. The subject of how late nineteenth-century high culture supplied a ground of artistic community for women—largely unconsidered by Lawrence Levine and Paul DiMaggio—is discussed in Stein, "Artifact as Ideology."

18. Cather, "148 Charles Street," p. 66.

19. Ibid., pp. 64–65.

20. *Letters of Sarah Orne Jewett,* pp. 14–15. On the sacralization of art in nineteenth-century high culture, see Levine, *Highbrow/Lowbrow,* especially pp. 132–34; DiMaggio, "Cultural Entrepreneurship," pp. 36–38; and—for literary examples quite close to the ones cited from Jewett—my *School of Hawthorne,* pp. 73–75. It is notable that in the letter printed after the one in which she testifies to her "perfect reverence" for Arnold, Jewett writes: "I have been to church myself for a wonder, since from one reason or another I have not been preached at for some months!" (*Letters of Sarah*

Orne Jewett, p. 54)—suggesting that the worship she brings to works of art has been freed from its earlier institutional locations.

21. I describe this transformation and its cultural background at length in "Henry James: Tradition and the Work of Writing," *The School of Hawthorne,* pp. 104–20.

22. Cather, "Miss Jewett," *Not Under Forty,* pp. 76–77; "148 Charles Street," p. 63.

23. So James speaks of "a display as of votive objects" in "the waterside museum" and Cather of a "sanctuary" ("Mr and Mrs. James T. Fields," pp. 165–66; "148 Charles Street," p. 61).

24. Sherman argues very resourcefully for a revived pagan classicism in Jewett, but readers of Harold Frederic's *Damnation of Theron Ware* (1896) will remember that in the 1880s and 1890s "paganism" belongs to the postreligious arsenal of aestheticist replacement religions.

25. For birthrate and emigration statistics for a real New England community comparable to Deephaven or Dunnet Landing (Chelsea, Vermont), see Barron, *Those Who Stayed Behind,* pp. 12–26.

26. James, "The Art of Fiction," *Literary Criticism,* p. 62.

27. Cather, "Miss Jewett," p. 81.

28. Horace Scudder, "Miss Jewett," *Atlantic Monthly,* 73 (Jan. 1894), reprinted in *Appreciation of Sarah Orne Jewett,* p. 18; James, "Mr. and Mrs. James T. Fields," p. 174; Cather, "Miss Jewett," p. 89; Sherman, *Sarah Orne Jewett,* p. ix.

29. *Letters of Sarah Orne Jewett,* p. 125; *Sarah Orne Jewett Letters,* p. 11; *Letters of Sarah Orne Jewett,* p. 81. In his otherwise rather tortuous attempt to evolve a general and seemingly transhistorical category of "minor literature" from a single story by Jewett, Louis Renza recognizes Jewett's as work consciously "*becoming* minor in relation to the major possibilities proffered it by the language and codes subtending its production" and notes the link between Jewett's self-appointed literary minority and her choice of form: "For a regionalist writer to write 'the things' she knew best was to court the literary limitations of her topos" (Renza, *Minor Literature,* pp. 37, 44).

30. James, "The Future of the Novel," *Literary Criticism,* 1:105; "The Lesson of Balzac," *Literary Criticism,* 2:116, 118; *Hawthorne* (1879), *Literary Criticism,* 1:361; "Mr and Mrs. James T. Fields," p. 174.

31. Cather, "Miss Jewett," p. 89; *Letters of Sarah Orne Jewett,* pp. 82, 195.

32. James, *Letters,* 1:252; Edel and Lyall H. Powers, eds., *The Complete Notebooks of Henry James* (New York: Oxford University Press, 1987), p. 233.

33. The documents most revealing of the conscious self-extensions James and Howells aimed for around 1880 are Howells's 1881 letter outlining *A Modern Instance* (see *Selected Letters of W. D. Howells,* ed. George Arms, et al., 6 vols. [Boston: Twayne Publishers, 1979–83], 2:277), and

James's 1878 reply to a critic of his slighter earlier works: "I have a constant impulse to try experiments of form, in which I wish not to run the risk of wasting or gratuitously using big situations. But to these I am coming now" (James, *Letters*, 2:193). See also my *School of Hawthorne*, pp. 90–94, 109–18.

34. Cather, "Miss Jewett," p. 89. On the major-minor question in regard to the length of *The Country of the Pointed Firs*, see also Renza, *Minor Literature*, pp. 177–78.

35. *Letters of Sarah Orne Jewett*, p. 47

36. See Kelley, *Private Woman, Public Stage*, pp. x–xi, 127–28, 145–46; Fern, *Ruth Hall*, p. 175; Catherine E. Beecher and Harriet Beecher Stowe, *The American Woman's Home*, (New York: J.B. Ford, 1869), p. 19; and Wilson, *Crusader in Crinoline*, p. 271.

37. *Letters of Sarah Orne Jewett*, pp. 247–50.

38. For the origins of Jewett's "best self," see Matthew Arnold, "Doing As One Likes," *Culture and Anarchy* (1869). The most comprehensive treatment of Arnold's American life is still John Henry Raleigh's *Matthew Arnold and America* (Berkeley: University of California Press, 1957). On elite fears of the new media at the turn of the century, see (among hundreds of other sources) the Bartley Hubbard chapters in Howells's *A Modern Instance*, or William James's remark: "Now illiteracy has an enormous literary organization" (quoted in F. O. Matthiessen, *The James Family* [New York: Alfred A. Knopf, 1947], p. 647). My "cheap" quotations come from Henry James, "The Lesson of Balzac," pp. 121, 133–34; Levine, *Highbrow/Lowbrow*, p. 134; Story, *Forging of an Aristocracy*, p. 179; and Cather, "148 Charles Street" and "Miss Jewett," pp. 63, 84, 93, 94.

39. The phrase is from Joan Myers Weimer's introduction to *Women Artists, Women Exiles*, pp. ix–x.

40. The case for the diminution of Jewett and her regionalist contemporaries from the more socially assertive authorship of Stowe's generation is made in an essay virtually ignored in recent criticism of this genre: Ann Douglas Wood's "The Literature of Impoverishment."

41. On Cather and Jewett, see Sharon O'Brien, *Willa Cather: The Emerging Voice* (New York: Oxford University Press, 1987), esp. pp. 334–72. On Wharton and nineteenth-century regionalism, see Wharton's memoir, *A Backward Glance* (New York: D. Appleton-Century, 1934), pp. 293–94, and Candace Waid, *Edith Wharton's Letters from the Underworld* (Chapel Hill: University of North Carolina Press, 1991), pp. 87–125.

CHAPTER SIX

1. Chesnutt to George Washington Cable, 11 Apr. 1895, and to Walter Hines Page, 14 Aug. 1898, quoted in Helen C. Chesnutt, *Charles W. Chesnutt* (Chapel Hill: University of North Carolina Press, 1952), pp. 73, 98. The idiom here reveals Chesnutt's high-cultural literary affiliations: com-

pare Henry James's "quite unabashed design of becoming as 'literary' as may be" or Howells's recollection of having "had his being . . . wholly in literature." See also my *School of Hawthorne*, p. 64. A note on citations from Chesnutt's letters: as Frances Richardson Keller explains in her more recent biography, *An American Crusade: The Life of Charles Waddell Chesnutt* (Salt Lake City: Brigham Young University Press, 1978), pp. 287–88, there are some discrepancies between Chesnutt's letters and the reproduction of those letters by Helen Chesnutt. On the other hand, Helen Chesnutt reproduces the letters much more fully than Keller, and provides their only substantial publication to date. I have checked the Helen Chesnutt transcriptions against the Chesnutt letters held in the Fisk University Library Special Collections and silently emended detected errors; I cite the Helen Chesnutt volume to indicate where a fuller transcription of quoted letters can be found.

2. For a fuller account of Chesnutt's early life, see Helen Chesnutt, *Charles W. Chesnutt*, pp. 3–33, and Keller, *American Crusade*, pp. 19–85.

3. Booker T. Washington, *Up from Slavery* (1901; rpt. New York: Viking Penguin, 1986), p. 29.

4. For general histories of black education in Reconstruction and after, see Robert C. Morris, *Reading, 'Riting, and Reconstruction: The Education of Freedmen in the South, 1861–1870* (Chicago: University of Chicago Press, 1981), and James D. Anderson, *The Education of Blacks in the South, 1860–1935* (Chapel Hill: University of North Carolina Press, 1988), which has a superb bibliography. On the Howard School at Fayetteville, named after General O. O. Howard, leader of the Freedman's Bureau, see Earle H. West, "The Harris Brothers: Black Northern Teachers in the Reconstruction South," *Journal of Negro Education* 48 (1979): 126–38. In *The Negro in North Carolina, 1876–1894* (Chapel Hill: University of North Carolina Press, 1964), pp. 142–43, Frenise A. Logan records evidence that the Howard Graded School was the most highly respected in the state. The literary record of country schoolteaching includes Washington, *Up from Slavery*, pp. 75–76; the memoir "On the Meaning of Progress" in W. E. B. Du Bois's *The Souls of Black Folk* (1903); and the final chapters of Frances E. W. Harper's *Iola Leroy; or, The Shadows Uplifted* (1892) and Chesnutt's *The House behind the Cedars* (1900). The founding of the normal school at Fayetteville is described in West, "The Harris Brothers," and Logan, *The Negroes in North Carolina*, pp. 143–45.

5. I take this figure on literacy in 1880 from Anderson, *The Education of Blacks*, p. 31. Logan gives a black illiteracy rate of seventy-five percent for North Carolina in 1880 (Logan, *The Negro in North Carolina*, p. 140).

6. From Chesnutt's unpublished journal (hereafter cited as Journal) in the Charles Waddell Chesnutt Collection in the Fisk University Library Special Collections. My edition of this journal is forthcoming from Duke University Press. This entry is from 13 August 1875.

7. West, "The Harris Brothers," p. 136. Helen Chesnutt records that Chesnutt's duties in the normal school were to teach "reading, writing, spelling, composition, and related subjects" (*Charles W. Chesnutt,* p. 15). He was, in other words, the principal agent of Harris's program of re-languaging.

8. Journal, 13–14 July 1875.

9. Journal, June 1879.

10. The classic discussions of this phenomenon are Wiebe, *The Search for Order,* pp. 111–32, and Bledstein, *The Culture of Professionalism.* I explore the extension of professionalism in this sense into American literary authorship in *The School of Hawthorne,* chap. 6. The full social history of the formation of a black professional class has yet to be written. For helpful preliminary discussions of the nineteenth-century phase of this history, see G. Franklin Edwards, *The Negro Professional Class* (Glencoe, Ill.: Free Press, 1959), pp. 17–26, and Logan, *The Negro in North Carolina,* pp. 105–16. Logan records that in 1890 2,063 North Carolina blacks, or less than one half of one percent of the black population, held professional careers—1,940 of them, or all but 123, as teachers and clergymen.

11. Du Bois, *The Souls of Black Folk* (1903; rpt. New York: Fawcett, 1961), p. 85.

12. Anderson, *Education of Blacks,* p. 49; on the theory and practice of the Hampton curriculum, see pp. 33–78.

13. Washington, *Up from Slavery,* pp. 80, 118.

14. Ibid., pp. 123, 122. The first of these passages—which sounds like nothing so much as a description of an intellectual—particularly incensed Du Bois.

15. These charges against Washington are at least as old as Du Bois's *The Souls of Black Folk;* see especially the chapters "Of Our Spiritual Strivings" and "Of the Training of Black Men." Anderson, a powerful restater of this case, gives the most historically detailed account of the correlations between school curriculum and level of job training in Hampton-model schools; see Anderson, *The Education of Blacks,* for example pp. 52–60, 144–47, 222–230.

16. Quoted in Anderson, *The Education of Blacks,* p. 49.

17. Washington, *Up from Slavery,* pp. 87–88.

18. See Anderson, *The Education of Blacks,* pp. 29–30.

19. Du Bois, *The Souls of Black Folk,* p. 87.

20. Washington, *Up from Slavery,* p. 263. On Washington's antiliterary bias, see also William L. Andrews, "The Representation of Slavery and the Rise of Afro-American Literary Realism, 1865–1920," in Deborah E. McDowell and Arnold Rampersad, eds., *Slavery and the Literary Imagination* (Baltimore: The Johns Hopkins University Press, 1989), pp. 70–74.

21. Washington, *Up from Slavery,* p. 220.

22. This example is cited in Anderson, *The Education of Blacks,* pp. 222–23.

23. Du Bois, *The Souls of Black Folk,* p. 87. But Du Bois only restates the sense of literature as refuge from stigmatization and social loneliness already fully expressed in Chesnutt's 1882 journal: "What a blessing is literature, and how grateful we should be to the publishers who have placed its treasures within reach of the poorest. . . . Shut up in my study, without the companionship of one congenial mind, I can enjoy the society of the greatest wits and scholars of England" (Journal, ca. Feb. 1882).

24. See West, "The Harris Brothers," p. 133.

25. Chesnutt to Washington, 11 Aug. and 27 June 1903, in Helen Chesnutt, *Charles W. Chesnutt,* pp. 193, 195; Chesnutt's relations with Washington are discussed on pp. 191–207 and in Keller, *American Crusade,* pp. 207–26. Helen Chesnutt's biography is the richest source of information on Chesnutt's lifestyle and class affiliations; for particularly revealing examples, see pp. 61–67, 74–75, 183–88.

26. Du Bois, *The Souls of Black Folk,* p. 78.

27. Journal, 26 Mar. 1881.

28. Journal, 16 Mar. 1880.

29. Journal, 29 May 1880.

30. Chesnutt, *The Conjure Woman* (1899; rpt. Ann Arbor: University of Michigan Press, 1969), pp. 1–3; all subsequent quotations are followed by page numbers in parentheses.

31. "Po' Sandy's" emphasis on self-location as a fundamental human need is echoed in the testimony Jacqueline Jones cites of a slave who felt she had to get away from her plantation and move around after emancipation in order to "*joy my freedom!*" as if the enjoyment of self-directed motion and the enjoyment of freedom were one and the same. See Jacqueline Jones, *Labor of Love, Labor of Sorrow: Black Women, Work, and the Family from Slavery to the Present* (1985; rpt. New York: Vintage Books, 1986), p. 51.

32. The *Oxford English Dictionary* (1933 ed.) defines "predial" as "arising from or consequent upon the occupation of farms or lands," "attached to farms or to the land."

33. For a suggestive historical account using South Carolina materials, see John Scott Strickland, "Traditional Culture and Moral Economy: Social and Economic Change in the South Carolina Low Country, 1865–1910," in *The Countryside in the Age of Capitalist Transformation,* pp. 141–78. See also Jones, *Labor of Love, Labor of Sorrow,* pp. 44–68.

34. For a historical account of the New South development of North Carolina—in 1860 the poorest Southern state but in 1900 the industrial leader of the South—see Dwight B. Billings, Jr., *Planters and the Making of a "New South": Class, Politics, and Development in North Carolina, 1865–1900* (Chapel Hill: University of North Carolina Press, 1979).

35. Chesnutt's letters make clear that he cared about where he was published in just such terms: "I would prefer that your house bring out the book; the author having first been recognized by you (so far as any high class publication is concerned,)" he wrote Houghton, Mifflin in 1891; in 1897 he reiterated of his stories: "their chance . . . will be very much enhanced if they are brought out by a concern of Houghton, Mifflin and Company's standing. It is not difficult to find publishers of some kind, on some terms—but there are publishers and publishers" (Helen Chesnutt, *Charles W. Chesnutt*, pp. 69, 86).

36. The phrase comes from James's notebook sketch for *The Ambassadors* in *The Complete Notebooks of Henry James*, p. 142.

37. James, "Alphonse Daudet," *Literary Criticism*, 2:242. For James's most eloquent account of the vicarious theory of reading, see his late essay, "The Future of the Novel."

38. Chesnutt to Cable, 5 June 1890, Helen Chesnutt, *Charles W. Chesnutt*, p. 57. Compare the stronger statement in a letter to Walter Hines Page of 22 March 1899: "The dialect story is one of the sort of Southern stories that make me feel it my duty to write a different sort" (p. 107).

39. Chesnutt to Albion Tourgée, 26 Sept. 1889, quoted in William L. Andrews, *The Literary Career of Charles W. Chesnutt* (Baton Rouge: Louisiana State University Press, 1980), p. 21.

40. Chesnutt, *The House behind the Cedars* (Boston: Houghton, Mifflin, 1900), p. 163. The bookcase scene in chapter 18 of this book suggestively conjoins access to literature with the birth of professionalistic aspiration.

41. See Chesnutt to Houghton, Mifflin, 8 Sept. 1891, for Chesnutt's proposal to Houghton, Mifflin; and Chesnutt to Cable, 11 Apr. 1895, for his link of *Rena Walden* with a self-consciously chosen "*debut*"; both in Helen Chesnutt, *Charles W. Chesnutt*, pp. 68–69, 73. Andrews summarizes the early history of *Rena Walden* in *Literary Career*, pp. 23–30.

42. Quoted in Andrews, *Literary Career*, p. 27. The phrases, including the emphasis, are Richard Watson Gilder's, who found no such lack of interest in Thomas Nelson Page's tales of black nostalgia for slavery days.

43. Walter Hines Page to Chesnutt, 15 Dec. 1897 and 30 Mar. 1898, in Helen Chesnutt, *Charles W. Chesnutt*, pp. 87, 91–92; the fullest account of this episode is on pp. 80–103.

44. The six 1898 conjure stories are "Mars Jeems's Nightmare," "The Gray Wolf's Ha'nt," "Sis' Becky's Pickaninny," and "Hot-Foot Hannibal," which were included in *The Conjure Woman*, and "A Victim of Heredity" and "Tobe's Tribulations," which Page left out. See Helen Chesnutt, *Charles W. Chesnutt*, p. 94. The two unadopted tales as well as the earlier "Dave's Neckliss" and three other Julius stories—"A Deep Sleeper," "The Dumb Witness," and "The Marked Tree"—are reprinted in Sylvia Lyons Render, ed., *The Short Fiction of Charles W. Chesnutt* (Washington, D. C.: Howard University Press, 1974).

45. See Andrews, *Literary Career,* pp. 121–36, for the outlines of this phase of Chesnutt's career. For Chesnutt's determination that he could afford this career change, see Helen Chesnutt, *Charles W. Chesnutt,* p. 73, 118.

46. Quoted in Andrews, *Literary Career,* p. 127. Chesnutt had said of this book: "upon its reception will depend in some measure whether I shall write, for the present, any more 'Afro-American' novels" (Helen Chesnutt, *Charles W. Chesnutt,* p. 176).

INDEX

Adams, Henry, 157
Addams, Jane, 124
Ainslee's Magazine, 2
Alcott, Abigail May, 73
Alcott, Bronson, 15, 73, 75
Alcott, Louisa May, 69–106; *Jo's
Boys,* 69–70, 71–72, 74, 98;
Little Men, 71, 89, 104; *Little
Women,* 69, 70, 71–72, 85–
106
Alcott, May, 97–98, 224 n. 38
Aldrich, Thomas Bailey, 139, 151
Ammons, Elizabeth, 144
Armstrong, General Samuel Chap-
man, 184, 185
Arnold, Matthew, 155–57, 170,
171, 175
Atlantic Monthly, 76–77, 79–82,
83, 84, 87–88, 97, 122, 124,
150, 152–53, 204, 207–9

Badger, Joseph E., Jr., 83
Baltzell, E. Digby, 134–35
Banner, Lois, 50
Barnard, A. M. *See* Alcott, Louisa
May
Barnum, Phineas T., 56, 58–59,
61, 62, 123
Baym, Nina, 46
Beadle, Erastus, 68, 78, 83
Beadle and Adams, 77–78
Beardsley, Aubrey, 3
Beecher, Catherine E., 19, 43
Berenson, Bernard, 11, 98
Bonner, Robert, 56, 77, 78
Bonner, Sherwood (pseud. of
Katherine Sherwood Bonner
MacDowell), 119, 122

Bourdieu, Pierre, 69, 223 n. 28,
228 nn. 23, 24
Braeme, Charlotte M., 105
Brown, Gillian, 50
Brownell, William C., 164
Buntline, Ned (pseud. of E. Z. C.
Judson), 82, 84, 88
Bushnell, Horace, *Christian Nur-
ture,* 18–19, 21, 47

Cable, George Washington, 116,
121–22, 138, 196, 200, 206
Cahan, Abraham, 117–18
Cather, Willa, 153–54, 156, 158,
163, 165, 169–71, 172, 173,
175
*Century Illustrated Monthly Maga-
zine,* 122, 124, 140, 208
Chap-Book, 3, 6, 7
Chesnutt, Charles Waddell, 117,
177–210; *The Conjure Woman,*
196–206, 208–9; "Dave's
Neckliss," 207; *The House be-
hind the Cedars,* 207–9; *The
Marrow of Tradition,* 209–10
Chicago Daily News, 2
Chicago Herald, 1
Child, Lydia Maria, 22, 45
Chopin, Kate, 3
Clay, Bertha M., 82–83, 84, 86
Cobb, Lyman, 20, 21–22, 29,
40–41
Cobb, Sylvanus, Jr., 78, 82, 86
Cook, William Wallace, 83
Cooke, Rose Terry, 79, 117,
170
Corporal punishment, 13–47
Cummins, Maria, 52

241